W9-BXD-860

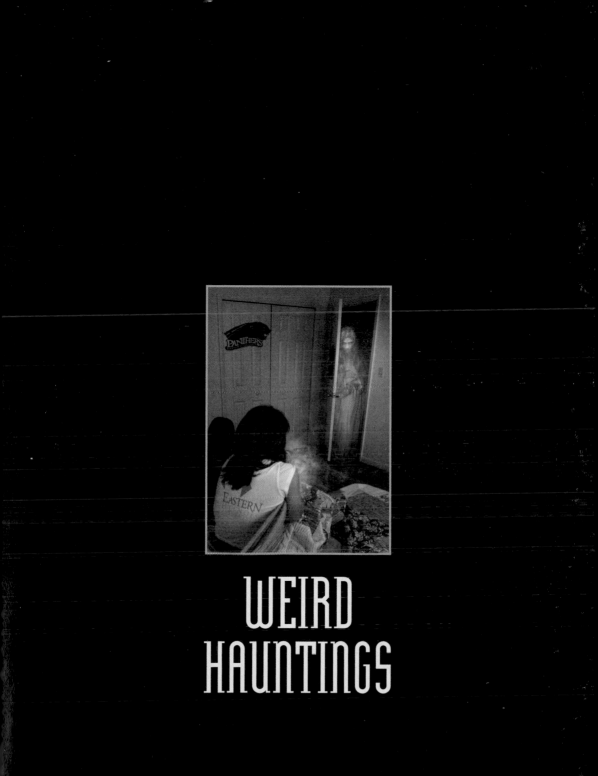

WEIRD
HAUNTINGS

Sterling Publishing Co., Inc.
New York

MARK MORAN AND MARK SCEURMAN,
authors of

present

WEIRD
HAUNTINGS
TRUE TALES OF GHOSTLY PLACES

Compiled by
JOANNE AUSTIN
Illustrated by RYAN DOAN

WEIRD HAUNTINGS

Published by Sterling Publishing Co., Inc.
387 Park Avenue South, New York, NY 10016
© 2006 Mark Sceurman and Mark Moran
Distributed in Canada by Sterling Publishing
c/o Canadian Manda Group, 165 Dufferin Street
Toronto, Ontario, Canada M6K 3H6
Distributed in Great Britain by Chrysalis Books Group PLC
The Chrysalis Building, Bramley Road, London W10 6SP, England
Distributed in Australia by Capricorn Link (Australia) Pty. Ltd.
P. O. Box 704, Windsor, NSW 2756, Australia

10 9 8 7 6 5 4 3 2 1

Manufactured in the United States of America

Photography and illustration credits are found on page 317 and
318 and constitute an extension of this copyright page.

Sterling ISBN 13: 978-1-4027-4226-2
Sterling ISBN 10: 1-4027-4226-6

For information about custom editions, special sales, premium
and corporate purchases, please contact Sterling Special Sales
Department at 800-805-5489 or specialsales@sterlingpub.com.

Design: Richard J. Berenson
        Berenson Design & Books, LLC, New York, NY

Weird Hauntings is intended as entertainment.
The reader should be advised that many of the
sites described in *Weird Hauntings* are located
on private property and should not be visited,
or you may face prosecution for trespassing.

To my dad for once being able to do a
running flip over thirteen people,
and to my mom for possibly being the
milkman's child. You are the first
and best sources from which my own
weirdness springs.

—Joanne Austin

CONTENTS

INTRODUCTION

One need not be a chamber to be haunted,
One need not be a house;
The brain has corridors surpassing
Material place.

From *Haunted,* by Emily Dickinson

THERE IS A GHOSTLY RENAISSANCE happening in the United States. Believing in ghosts is no longer considered "out there." Instead, it's now hip to see dead people.

All you have to do is look at the explosion of ghosts whispering in the entertainment industry. Movies about hauntings have always had a place in Hollywood, but never so many as now. And television has picked up the haunted ball. The home of the occasional haunting over time, it's now flooded with shows, both fictional and reality-based, devoted to ghosts and the people who investigate or communicate with them.

The spirit world has even manifested itself in commercials. One recent ad features a house severely infested with poltergeists. The female homeowner calls in paranormal investigators to get rid of them, and when they suggest that the family leave, she balks. She's consumed with a lust for her high-end bathroom faucets that the scariest ghost can't conquer.

Added to this spectral media feast are thousands of books, DVDs, and Web sites on the subject. You can even buy everything from haunted dolls to haunted fishing tackle on eBay. Ghost business is booming.

And if you think there's more to that banging sound in your basement than bad plumbing, you should know that membership in paranormal investigation groups is up. Record numbers of people are hunting, photographing, and recording the voices of what might be ghosts. Assistance from one of these groups is just a phone call away.

Fact is, whether or not you believe in ghosts, they are everywhere, if not in spectral form. And that brings us to *Weird Hauntings*.

To unearth stories from around the country for you, we tapped many of the authors who have written for our best-selling *Weird U.S.* series. We've also found some new authors who have hauntingly original perspectives on spirits. All are committed to the task of scaring you, and they do it in various spooky styles. Some authors invite you to witness the ghostly manifestations in their

homes, but others escort you to ghosts in different places, like the side of a road, the middle of the woods, a sterile hotel room, a neglected graveyard, or a crowded bar. Ghosts can manifest themselves anywhere.

The stories you'll read here differ slightly from those found in the *Weird U.S.* series. In *Weird Hauntings,* you will find that most stories are backed up with history and first-person accounts. You'll even find location information for many places, so you can check them out yourself. The stories are, as best we can determine, true—at least to the people who have experienced them.

Our goal is to at least make you jump a little when the doorbell rings, if not completely disturb you to the point of sleeplessness. The stories are a good mix of unrelenting violent tales and quieter psychological scares. Even the most battle-scarred horror fans should find something scary here. So read on, and know that you've been warned.

–Joanne Austin

WHEN I WAS STILL AT THE AGE where I needed to be tucked in, that precious period of life when the imagination is the most impressionable, my dad had a little prank he would like to pull. He would lovingly pull the covers up over my body and tell me how the monsters I was fretting about were not real. But then, as he slipped out, he would look back with puzzled concern.

"What, Dad?" I would say as I scanned the room for what caught his worried eye.

"Oh, nothing, Ryan. I just thought I saw something under your bed . . ."

With that, he would shrug and slip out the door.

My mother was complicit with this behavior, an accomplice to the mischief that I would grow to be ever thankful for. Often it was she who tucked me in. She wouldn't pretend to see something in my room as she left. She would simply shut the door behind her softly as I watched the love and peace on her face. As the last thread of light faded to nothing, I would hear the scratching begin under my bed. Imagination? No. It got louder and louder till my very bed shook. I didn't know at that moment that it was my father hiding under my bed, daring me to peer underneath.

Looking back at those formative years, I am ever thankful. My parents made me confront the common fears most people have with the things that go bump in the night. I learned at a tender age not to fear the unknown but to embrace it. That is what you will experience in *Weird Hauntings,* as you read various tales of horror all claiming to be true. Do we have absolute evidence that proves each story is the real deal? No. But does it even matter? Perhaps there are people like my father at the source of these hauntings. Or perhaps they are truly anecdotes of paranormal activity. As long as the stories raise your goose bumps, it doesn't make a difference. You can find these real locations yourself and figuratively "look under the bed" if you dare. So read and enjoy these various tales. As my prankster father would say, "Good fright and pleasant screams."

—Ryan Doan

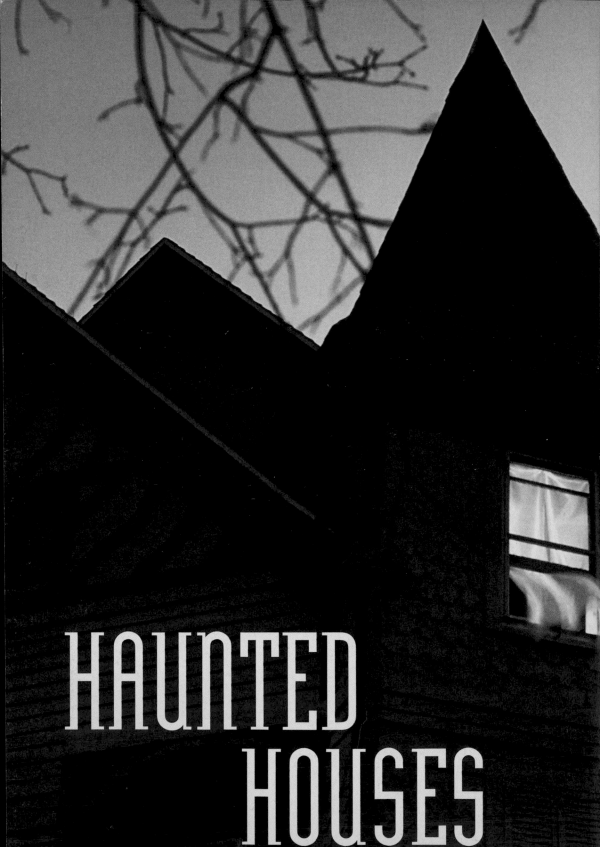

THE HAUNTED HOUSE STORIES in this chapter are a mixed bunch—some spine-tingling, some merely curious. But that's the norm when it comes to ghost stories. Even if they don't scare the daylights out of us, they rarely fail to intrigue. That's because no matter how far-reaching our knowledge of science and technology, we find the pull of the supernatural hard to resist. Our love of the eerie is universal and timeless, with accounts of hauntings appearing in some of the earliest writings known to man, be they from ancient Egypt or Greece or Rome. Even now almost every city or town has at least one house that's spoken of as haunted—the host to ghosts or a mysterious force.

One reason stories of haunted houses are so alluring is that few are tidily resolved. Was the person really seeing a ghost or only imagining it? Were the noises in the night caused by a restless spirit or do they have a perfectly logical explanation?

The stories recounted in these pages are no different. In one, two youngsters visiting their grandparents in rural Florida get more than they bargained for when they explore a mysterious vacant house nearby. In another, a single father in Missouri moves into a large old house with his three children and ends up having to flee, terrified, into the night. In a small town in Alabama, a newly arrived preacher and his wife accept the offer of a member of the congregation to live in a long-empty house—and soon come to regret it. On a different tack, a New Jersey couple comes to accept the spirits who share their home, considering them more of a curiosity than a threat.

As varied as these first-person stories may be, some have a number of surprising similarities. However seriously you take them, you'll find the ways people deal with a house full of ghosts (or even one!) as interesting as the ghosts themselves.

THE RENTAL IN THE SOURLANDS

by D. S. Gibson

AS SOMEONE WHO'S LIVED for thirty-two years in the Sourland Mountains of Somerset County, New Jersey, I've had more than one bizarre encounter in these desolate, mysterious hills. In this story, I will relate the most terrifying incident.

In 1980, I was twenty and anxious to move out of my parents' house. After my buddy Peter and I decided to look for a place, we consulted a local real estate agent. The woman assured us she had just the place for us and it was only a short ride away. In her car, we drove up into the Skillman section of the Sourland range, and we soon realized the apartment was much farther out than we'd hoped. Finally we stopped at an old farm on Spring Hill Road.

"That's it," said the real estate agent, pointing to what was obviously a converted two-story utility shed on a small incline behind the main farmhouse. The first thing I noticed was a 1959 hearse parked in front of the shed.

"Looks kind of creepy," said Peter. "And what about that hearse?" The agent told us that it belonged to one of the renters who lived above the vacant apartment.

After a few minutes, the landlord bounded off the farmhouse's back porch and approached us. He was a particularly big man, and the look in his eyes could only be described as scary. As he brusquely laid down the law on what was and wasn't allowed on the premises, I couldn't help but think that this guy would have made an excellent Luca Brasi in the movie *The Godfather*.

The apartment he showed us consisted of nothing more than an eat-in kitchen, a tiny living room, a bathroom, and a single bedroom. Peter and I had wanted our own rooms, but at $275 a month the less-than-ideal space was hard to pass up. Ignoring the bad vibes, we said we'd take it. Little did we know that we were in for four nerve-wracking months, the effects of which would linger long after we moved out.

A BAFFLING BREAK-IN

We signed the lease on Thursday afternoon and started to move in later in the day, and most of my stuff was in the apartment by Friday afternoon. Peter and I agreed we'd move the rest of his things in on Sunday, since he was leaving for Pennsylvania to stay with his girlfriend for the weekend. After Peter left, I

15

settled down to unpack. Shortly after dark, I began to get the eerie feeling that I wasn't alone. Not helping were some very strange sounds that seemed to be coming from behind the walls and beneath the floor. I walked around listening, looking out windows, and wondering if we had mice.

A bit spooked, I decided to lock everything up and go stay at my parents' house that night. It was a dark and lonely ride on the back roads that led down the mountain into Neshanic Station.

In the morning, my father (concerned, and rightly so) asked if he could come with me to see the place. So we jumped in the car and drove up the mountain. When we got there, I was puzzled to find that even though I could unlock the door, it wouldn't open. My dad and I both pushed hard, and slowly it moved. "There's something against the other side," he said. We were able to force it open enough to allow us to squeeze into the living room.

To our surprise, the obstacle against the door was the sofa bed. More astonishing was that it had been opened—and my only houseplant sat right in the middle of the bed, looking as if it had been carefully placed there; not even a speck of dirt had been spilled. If that weren't strange enough, the sofa bed was the only piece of furniture sitting right side up. The kitchen table, television stand, dresser—all just where I had placed them—were now upside down!

"You've been robbed," Dad said, motioning toward the clothes and kitchen utensils strewn about. Frantically I looked for my most treasured belongings. Nothing was missing except for one thing. Peter and I kept a large frog in a jar of formaldehyde, intended as a quirky conversation piece. And while the jar of formaldehyde was still there, the frog wasn't. Dad and I searched high and low for it, but the frog was nowhere to be found.

My father and I also discovered that the windows, which were quite high off the ground, were still locked. We couldn't figure out how in the world intruders could have blocked the door and left, leaving everything bolted from inside. But for some reason, our puzzlement didn't keep me from changing all the locks that day.

I called Peter and told him what had happened. He was as baffled as I was, especially after talking with the tenants upstairs and the landlord. No one had seen or heard a thing. On Sunday, Peter returned and we spent the rest of the day moving the last of his stuff in, both of us trying hard not to feel spooked about what had taken place.

That night, my girlfriend, Sue, and her friend Debbie drove up with me to see the place. Both were shocked to see how remote the area was. We pulled into the driveway and were approaching the back of the building when I noticed both girls were shifting nervously in their seats.

"Sue, this place has bad karma," said Debbie. Sue didn't like the look of the place either. She said she thought I should move out as soon as possible, and both girls couldn't wait to leave. All I could draw out of them was that the place wasn't "right." I think that I knew this secretly, too, but I wasn't about to give up my first apartment that easily. Now I know I should have listened.

A Turn for the Worse

What followed was close to four months of the worst luck I've ever had. Within weeks, my car died. Then my replacement car gave up the ghost, too. Peter and I both lost our jobs. We both suffered from constant colds, allergies, and ill health in general. The strange noises continued all the while, accompanied by weird dreams and the unnerving feeling that we were being watched. Near the end of the summer, I awoke one night to find the floor fan shooting out orange and blue sparks. Other appliances went haywire as well.

After eight weeks in the apartment, Peter and I made a grisly discovery. When preparing dinner one night, we needed a pot stored under the sink. Reaching underneath, I pulled it out and was about to put it on the counter when I saw something horrific inside: the missing frog. Worse yet was what was done to it. The frog's mouth had been forced open and a pencil had been shoved down its throat, exiting its rear. It was, in a word, skewered. I was certain I had looked under the sink the day my dad and I discovered the frog missing, and over the previous weeks I'd rummaged around under the sink for one thing or another countless times.

Horrified, I was ready to move out, but Peter talked me into sticking it out by reminding me of how cheap it was. Interestingly, I saw less and less of him as he conveniently spent more time at his girlfriend's house. I so disliked staying at the apartment alone that on many nights I slept at my parents' house.

One weekend when Peter was away, Sue and I decided to watch *Saturday*

17

Night Live. It was a humid, still night with no breeze, so we left the front door open as we sat on the sofa and watched TV. The door was right next to the television, giving us a clear view of both. Suddenly, the door slammed shut with such force that it shook the walls. Sue and I both jumped a mile. In a panic, she demanded that we leave immediately. There was no argument from me. "I want you out of here," she yelled, "because I don't want to come here anymore!" I promised to talk to Peter about moving as soon as he returned.

When Peter failed to show up on Sunday, I stayed away from the place until late Monday afternoon—only to find that Peter still wasn't there. So I decided to make some dinner as I waited for him.

Afternoon sunlight warmed the kitchen as I scavenged to see what I could prepare. I filled a pot with water and put it on the stove to boil, then turned to grab a package of rice off the counter. When I turned back to the stove, the pot of water was gone, though the burner was still lit. The hair on the back of my neck sprang up, and I was afraid to turn around. All of a sudden the sunny room felt as cold as a tomb.

For what seemed like an eternity, I just stood there listening, only to be met with total silence. I knew that I couldn't stand there forever—and besides, the front door was behind me, and that was the only way out. I spun around. The pot of water sat in the middle of the kitchen floor, five feet away from me. Once again, nothing was spilled, as if it had been gently placed there.

That was it. I picked up the pot, put it in the sink, turned off the stove, and headed out of the apartment as fast as I could. I told Peter the next day that I was moving. He was annoyed, but I couldn't have cared less. By the way, Peter didn't stay there much longer either; by the end of the month he had packed his stuff and moved out.

Someone once asked me if I thought that a particular place can be "bad." Considering my four months of contending with forces unknown, I told him that I would have to say, "Yes. Definitely."

SOME THINGS ARE BEST LEFT ALONE
by Charlie Carlson

"THERE WAS THIS CREEPY old house near where my grandparents lived, in a rural part of Alachua County, Florida," recalled Jennifer, an elementary school teacher who is still a little nervous about her eerie experience as a kid. "My grandparents lived on a dirt road about ten miles outside of Gainesville. Across from this big cow pasture was another property where an old two-story farmhouse stood. It was dilapidated, unpainted, and had been vacant forever. I don't know who owned it or why nobody lived in it, but there was a story about how a man had committed suicide there after killing his whole family with a butcher knife. My grandmother said it was just a yarn and that the house was vacant when my grandfather bought the five acres next to it many years before."

Jennifer and her brother often visited their grandparents during the summer months and would hang out with their two cousins, who lived a short drive down the road. It was a night in the summer of '76 that she first noticed something strange about the old empty house. "From the upstairs bedroom of my grandparents' house, where I slept, I had a clear view of the deserted farmhouse across the pasture, and it looked like a dark silhouette in the moonlight." On this particular night, Jennifer summoned her brother to take a look because there seemed to be a light in the upstairs windows of the house. They both squinted, trying to make sure it wasn't just the moonlight reflecting off the windowpanes. "It definitely wasn't a reflection," she said. "Plus, my brother knew that the panes in the upstairs windows had been broken out. That meant the light was coming from the inside—but no one lived there. Anyway, we paid it no mind and went on to bed."

The next morning, Jennifer and her brother asked their grandfather if they could explore the old house. Instead of granting permission, he sternly warned them to stay away. "Granddaddy seemed a bit upset that we even asked about the house," Jennifer recalled. "I asked my grandmother why he didn't want us to go, and she said my grandfather had a bad experience there and didn't like to talk about it. I never did find out what she meant, but it only added to the weirdness of the place."

Later that summer, Jennifer and her brother returned to spend another week with their grandparents. "It was just before school started, in early

19

August, and that old house was still on my mind. On the first night, my brother and I looked out the window and, like before, saw a light on upstairs. This time, for some crazy reason, we decided to go against Granddaddy's orders and go with my cousins to investigate."

COLD BREEZE IN AUGUST

The next day, Jennifer and her brother teamed up with their two cousins for a clandestine adventure. "We laid low until Granddaddy pulled out of the yard in his pickup to get some feed for his cows. Once he was out of sight, the four of us hiked across the pasture to the back of the old house. It was all overgrown with weeds, with three or four tall palmetto trees in the yard, and it looked like it had been standing vacant for a hundred years."

The four kids had planned to get a quick peek inside and leave. "The back door was barely hanging by rusty hinges and squeaked when we opened it. At the time, I was more afraid of seeing a snake or rat than a ghost. Anyway, we eased our way in, half expecting to see blood splatters or the butcher knife left over from the suicide and murder we'd heard about. I kept trying to remind myself of what Grandmother had told me: that it was just a far-fetched yarn."

Inside, the rooms were scattered with boards, broken pieces of wooden furniture, and musty remnants of clothing from an earlier time. From the windows, strands of shredded curtains hung like apparitions, adding to the spooky atmosphere. "Birds or bats had been roosting inside, because their mess was all over everything," remembered Jennifer with a slight shiver.

"It didn't take long for something really strange to happen," she continued. "I think we were in the front room or parlor or whatever, when all of a sudden this ice-cold wind rushed down the hall that ran through the house from front to back. It blew my hair back, and there wasn't even a breeze outside. It was a hot and humid Florida August, but inside the temperature was like forty-something degrees.

"One of my cousins wanted to go upstairs, so the rest of us followed. About halfway up the rickety steps, that mysterious cold wind started blowing again. This time it came down the stairs from the second-story hallway. We couldn't figure out how wind could blow through the house downstairs and then blow down from the second story. It was like someone had opened the door to a giant refrigerator. It suddenly stopped, but we could still feel the chill.

"All of a sudden there was a knocking sound inside the wall along the stairs. It was like something sealed up in the wall was trying to bust out. Then,

It just kept on while we stood there with our eyes bugging out. At that point, I was ready to leave, but my brother wanted to keep exploring that second floor."

For some reason, the upstairs was not willing to accept any intruders, especially four nosy kids who were disobeying their grandfather. "In hindsight," said Jennifer, "I think we should have listened to Granddaddy, because what we saw next has been in my mind ever since. The door at the head of the stairs slammed shut and locked itself just as we got there. Then a very bright, glaring light—I mean really intense—seeped out through the cracks around the doorframe as the door started knocking and banging, like you would knock on a door with your fist. I don't know what it was, but you could feel it was evil."

Jennifer described the sensation as an unnatural feeling that penetrated their souls. Needless to say, the four young intruders wasted no time exiting the old house. "It was like escaping from a refrigerator. I think we were lucky to get out of that place, and I shudder to think what could have happened if we'd stayed longer."

Jennifer never did learn what her grandfather had encountered in the old house, which has since been torn down. Nevertheless, she believes it had to do with what they had witnessed as kids, or perhaps something far more sinister. What she did learn is a valuable lesson: that some things are best left alone.

PEACEFUL COEXISTENCE

by Bob Kronemyer

HAVE YOU EVER WONDERED whether you could handle sharing a house with spirits of the dead? My wife, Jo, and I believe we can—and, in fact, have been doing so for just over a decade.

It was 1995 when I moved into my then fiancée's house—a custom-built split-level that had been built by Jo and her ex-husband on a wooded lot in rural New Jersey in 1971. All they knew of the history of the site was that the housing development was started by the township in 1952 and that Irish and German settlements were established in the area before the Revolutionary War. Living with us were Jo's son Scott and, in an apartment attached to the back of the house, her mother Josephine.

Over the next seven or eight years, all that struck me as strange were unexplained noises. After Josephine unfortunately suffered a stroke and had to be moved to a nursing home, I had begun using her apartment as an office. To communicate with anyone inside the main house who needed me, I put a baby monitor on my desk. As I worked into the wee hours, I would hear movements, banging, or other noises emanating from the monitor. Sometimes I got up and went into the house to see if Scott, who is disabled, was awake and moving about. Or perhaps the dog was responsible for the noise. But both Scott and our pet were always still asleep.

A ROOM OUT OF TIME

On a bright, sunny day in June 2003, I called an electrician friend and asked if he could stop by to make a repair. Little did I know he would be an eyewitness to something that would make the unexplained noises on the baby monitor seem like child's play. As we sat in the living room chatting during a lunch break, the sliding screen door to the back porch suddenly slid open all on its own. Incredulous but surprisingly unperturbed, we just looked at each other as I said, "Well, somebody just came in, or just went out." As if to prove we weren't dreaming, I measured the opening and found the door had moved eighteen inches in one motion. The next day, I spoke with a couple of builder friends, both of whom said it would be impossible for the wind to blow open a sliding screen door—especially to a foot and a half. And besides, there had been no wind that day.

22

An incident a month later made Jo and me realize how comfortable with—or perhaps the better phrase is unbothered by—spirits we were. We had dinner around 5:00 p.m., after which I went to the living room to watch the evening news; Jo and Scott were still finishing their meal. As I sat in front of the television, my peripheral vision picked up a figure emerging from the bathroom and moving toward the bedrooms. "Sweetheart," I called out to Jo, "someone just came out of the bathroom and went down the hallway." Her response was "Really?" As you can see, we aren't afraid of whatever it is we're experiencing. Don't ask me why, but I guess it's because we pick up that there's nothing to fear.

23

On a hot night that August, Jo was especially restless, sleeping for no more than an hour at a time. Finally, at 3:30 a.m., she decided to get up and go downstairs. After creeping out of the bedroom and closing the bedroom door, she turned to look into the spare room, which contains exercise equipment and lots of old photos of her family. To her utter amazement, what she saw was anything but the exercise room.

Before her was a room filled with antique furniture. She stared at it, rubbed her eyes, and tried to shake herself awake, but the phantom room was still there. Mesmerized, she said she looked at what she described as "something out of the 1800s" for a full fifteen minutes. She then walked into the bathroom.

When she came out, she looked into the exercise room again, to find it as it has always been. The room out of time was gone.

When Jo told me of the experience, I said I thought she might have been looking into a time portal. She responded that if she had seen any of her ancestors, she might have walked on in. "Please, not without me," I said. "How would I explain that to the police if you just disappeared?"

A CALL TO THE EXPERTS

One night shortly after the phantom room vision, I went online, typed in "Ghost Research," and was astonished by the number of links on the search engine's list. After narrowing the search to New Jersey, I found a local ghost research society and e-mailed a short account of what had happened to Jo. When they responded, it was to say they were willing to come and investigate. After Jo and I filled in and submitted a questionnaire, a three-person advance team came to our home to interview us in October. The investigators followed in November.

On the appointed day, Scott went to stay with his father and we took care to make sure the house was in its normal state. Once the investigators arrived and introduced themselves, the first thing they asked us to do was to turn off all the lights, the TV, and any other electric appliances. They then spent two hours taking pictures. Afterward, when the lights were back on and we stood in the living room talking, the team leader looked over my shoulder and said something that proved to Jo and me that we weren't imagining things: She had just seen a woman coming out of the bathroom and walking down the hallway. That she had no knowledge that I had seen the same thing confirmed that the spirits were real.

When the researchers went downstairs to the rec room, one of them hit a cold spot: The temperature in the room registered 70° F, but only 35° F in one area.

In her subsequent report, the leader wrote that the team had detected a strong presence in the house. According to her, the spirit isn't bound to the property or the land, but rather simply came or was brought here. The supposition was that the spirit likes our house and has no intention of leaving.

ACCEPTANCE

Since the investigation, Jo and I have had additional experiences. Once I was in the kitchen making lunch, when all of a sudden the cupboard door began banging by itself. I looked up and calmly said, "Do you mind? I'm making

25

lunch for Scott right now." The banging immediately stopped. I was intrigued. If "it" could hear me, then there had to be some way for us to communicate.

I have also seen an alarm clock move, Jo has seen a face on the wall, and both of us have heard footsteps going down the hallway and down the stairs.

Friends were witness to another incident: Jo's girlfriend and her husband came up for a weekend visit and we all went out to dinner. When we returned to the house, the coffee pot had turned on by itself, brewing coffee as if it knew where we'd been and that we would now want coffee and dessert.

That night, our visitors slept on an inflatable bed down in the rec room, as they had many times before. At about 3:00 a.m., the husband got up to use the bathroom. Then, instead of going back to the rec room, he lay down on a couch in the living room. His wife, who was waiting for his return, felt his side of the bed start to move like the motion of a waterbed. She heard a whoosh- ing sound next to her ear, and stayed awake the rest of the night, too paralyzed with fear to get out of bed, with the covers pulled up over her head. At 7:00 that morning, she came upstairs and informed us all that she would never again sleep downstairs in the rec room. This was of major interest to us, because it was the first time that a paranormal occurrence involved someone outside of the family—other, of course, than the ghost researcher.

We decided to have the researchers return for a follow-up investigation and to determine the identity of the spirit. Three researchers arrived in March 2004. The procedure was as before: Scott went to his dad's, everything electric was turned off, and Jo and I sat in the dark. The team spent two hours down in the rec room. Their batteries were being drained constantly. One of the researchers felt something move his hair in a gentle upward movement. A cold spot was picked up again. At one point, a woman on the team saw a little girl of ten or twelve peek around the doorway in the storage room.

The team moved upstairs into Scott's room, leaving behind a member who was still trying to get the batteries in her equipment to work. She called up to one of the guys to come down and help. "I can't come down now," the investi- gator yelled in reply. "I'm chasing something."

Jo and I looked at each other and asked, "Chasing what?"

The investigator's camera had captured a ball of light bouncing on Scott's bed, jumping up and down the way a little kid would. Both men in the room picked up the presence of a young boy. When Jo witnessed the scene on the playback of the video, she said that she'll never forget it for as long as she lives.

At the end of the investigation, Jo asked the research team leader what she

26

thought, and her response was, "You have a very interesting home."

When we received the formal report from the investigations, we found that it included numerous pictures, the video, and a recording of what is called an EVP (electronic voice phenomenon). The best we can make out of the words on the EVP is, "Where are the rest of the souls?"

Also during this time, I saw a dog of Jo's that had died three years before; since then, Jo has seen the dog as well. In May 2005, both she and I saw feathers floating down from the ceiling in the bedroom. I can't explain that one. Our current dog is sometimes seen barking at the wall. We see nothing there, but apparently he does.

According to the investigators, the actions of our unseen "guests" will reach no pinnacle. Whatever is going on will only intensify. We have no idea what is going to happen next, and at this point we are not afraid.

MISCHIEf IN ALABAMA
by Tim Stevens

MY FRIENDS BILL AND SHIRLEY are wonderful, devout folks who believe that most of life's mysteries have perfectly rational explanations. Even so, they found a mystery of their own that they were never able to solve.

The problem began when Bill and Shirley moved from Texas to Alabama, where Bill had taken a new preaching job. When they arrived in their new town, Piedmont, they gratefully accepted various temporary housing arrangements until they could find their own place. Finally, one church member offered to let them stay at her childhood home. It had been empty for years, she said, but was fully furnished. And everything was in working order except for the built-in microwave.

Bill and Shirley were extremely grateful. They'd brought a microwave with them, and they could put all their other belongings in storage for the time being.

Before moving in, they asked the owner about the house. She told them that her mother had passed away about eight years earlier and that her father had lived alone after she died. Trying to get on with his life, he would sometimes bring lady friends home—but each time he did, strange things would happen and the women would either leave suddenly or come up with reasons why they wouldn't be back. The man became despondent. Tragically, he was later found dead in his workshop, an apparent suicide. The daughter, plagued with marital problems at the time and uncertain of her future, decided it would be wise to hold on to the property.

SPOOK AFTER SPOOK

It didn't take long for strange things to occur in the house, which, after the suicide, had been uninhabited until Bill and Shirley moved in. The couple noticed that items they had moved out of one room would reappear in their original locations; it was as if the house's old knickknacks resisted change. One night as they sat in the den watching TV, they heard crashing noises in the hallway. Rushing to see what had happened, they found that all three of the pictures they had hung in the hallway had fallen to the floor—for no apparent reason.

On another night they were awakened by police entering their bedroom.

Shaken, Bill and Shirley asked what was wrong and were told that several 911 phone calls had been made from the house but that no one was on the line. The officers said that when they called the number back, there was no answer. Now bewildered and scared, the couple said that their phone hadn't rung at all.

Yet another frightening experience let the couple know for certain that they weren't in control of their surroundings. It happened one evening when Shirley went to a small room to look for something and called Bill in to help. After he entered the room, the door slammed shut. Stunned, they tried to open the door but couldn't—particularly odd, since the door had no lock and the knob appeared to be in working order. The door was simply being held shut, and Bill and Shirley were trapped in the room for hours. Luckily, a friend stopped by and entered the house to look for them. When the visitor heard the couple crying out, he went to the door and opened it with no trouble.

Even after this mystifying event, Bill and Shirley stayed on at the house for a while. They were happy when they finally found another place to live; but

before moving, they took a long trip to Texas to visit family. On their return, they smelled plastic burning as soon as they opened the door. They hurried to the kitchen, where the "out of order" microwave was running and some plastic inside it was melting. If they had arrived any later, the house could have burned to the ground.

Bill and Shirley were never able to figure out who—or what—was sharing their temporary home. While they were thankful to be given a place to stay, it's obvious they don't miss the place. Not one bit.

ONE CHILD'S STORY
by Lisa L.

WHEN I WAS A CHILD, I moved with my mother and stepfather from Wauke-gan, Illinois, to a small town in Missouri. From the time I first stepped into our new house, I felt uneasy. While not grand, the house was very big—an eight-bedroom former retirement home that came at a bargain price because it needed plenty of work. After my first walk through, I knew that neither of the two bedrooms at the end of the hall would be mine. They were ice cold in the middle of summer even though there was no air-conditioning.

On the first night, my bed wasn't set up, so I was to sleep in a recliner in the living room. As I lay there trying to drift off, something made me open my eyes. And there it was—a floating blue orb about the size of a tennis ball! Frozen, I watched it float in and out of the kitchen. Needless to say, I spent the rest of the night sleeping on the floor next to my mother's bed.

Afterward, I couldn't shake the bad feeling I had about the house. All of the bedroom doors had the locks on the outside, making me think the old people who once lived there had been kept locked in their rooms. And when I eventually found a room that didn't freak me out, it was next to the woods—and I spent night after night awake because of the weird noises just under my bedroom window.

Despite the eerie feeling of never being alone, I began to feel more relaxed until something truly strange happened. We all gathered around the radio one evening, listening to music as we talked and told jokes. Out of the blue, the radio went off, and we assumed it had become unplugged. It hadn't. Instead, the switch had been turned to the off position. I turned it back on. A few minutes later, the music stopped—again, because the radio had switched itself off. Did the spirits dislike the music?

As for those two rooms at the end of the hall, my parents eventually took one of them. Early one morning after we had left for school and work, my stepfather realized he had forgotten his wallet. Returning home to retrieve it, he opened the door to the room and immediately felt a cold rush of wind and something "pass right through him." He told his story to us only once, said that the experience made his hair stand on end, and that he would never speak a word of it again.

We soon moved to a different town, and today I travel past that old house about once a year. And though it has been remodeled and looks normal, it's still the same old haunted house to me.

THE MAN OF THE HOUSE

by Steven LaChance

DO YOU BELIEVE IN GHOSTS? I used to be like most people—a true skeptic, a real disbeliever. That was until a few years ago. Now I do believe, and I wish I didn't. Even now, I'm awakened in the night by the memory of the screaming man and the dark ghostly image that turned my world upside down.

It was May 2001, and as a single father with three children I desperately needed to find a place for my family to live. The lease on our apartment was up and we were about to find ourselves homeless. I had answered just about every Union, Missouri for-rent ad when I received a call from a woman telling me about a house she owned—a rather large old place, she said, that was in very good shape. She invited me to an open house that coming Sunday.

When Sunday rolled around and my daughter and I arrived at the house, we could barely believe our eyes. We gazed upward in the living room to see cherubs lining the top of the wallpaper. All of the original woodwork was intact, and a wooden partition separated the living room from the huge family room. Just as amazing, the smell of baking cookies had hit us as soon as we walked through the front door.

The house had two floors, three bedrooms, and a large family kitchen with a mudroom that led to the back door. Upstairs, a breezeway was accessible to both bedrooms, and the basement had been used as a fruit cellar. It was more house than we ever imagined for the price, and we immediately knew we had to have it. Anyone who has lived in an apartment with three children will understand how we felt.

There was a steady stream of potential renters at the open house, so we knew the competition would be tough. I asked the elderly landlady if I could fill out the rental application on the spot, and she immediately agreed. As I handed her my application, she asked, "Do you understand the responsibility that comes with living in an old house such as this?"

"Oh yes, I understand. It's beautiful," I quickly replied, never imagining what lay in store. "Well then, I'll get back to you," she said before walking off to attend to other visitors. I couldn't help but notice that there was something a little odd about the woman, and the way she showed people around wasn't typical of real estate agents. She showed the house as if it were a museum.

A week or so later, the landlady called to tell me she had selected me as

31

the renter. While I was thrilled, I was surprised to find her downright effusive. We agreed to meet the following day at a restaurant not far from my workplace to settle all of the paperwork and take care of the deposit and initial monthly payment. I was a little disappointed we wouldn't be meeting at the house because I couldn't wait to see it again—and, in fact, meeting in a restaurant seemed just as off-kilter as the landlady's sudden excitement.

Why worry about something so minor, I asked myself, when we'd lucked into such an incredible deal? I signed the papers just as planned the next day, and the children and I were all set to move in at the end of that week—Memorial Day weekend.

MOVING PICTURES, FALLING LEAVES

It seemed forever before moving day finally came; but once it did, we quickly got all of our belongings stored safely inside the old white house. I was hauling the last few items from the moving truck when a passing car slowed to a crawl. From the passenger side, a man leaned out the window and said, "Hope you get along okay here," before the car sped up and drove away.

"What do you think of that, Dad?" my daughter asked, slightly puzzled. "Friendly neighbors," I replied as I shut the sliding door of the truck.

The first night in the house passed uneventfully. Looking back, I wonder if that might have been because the house wanted to draw us in a little closer before beginning its series of assaults. However, I did notice something strange. Each of the interior doors had an old hook-and-eye latch, but not in the usual place. The latches were outside the doors, as if to keep something in.

A few days later, the first incident occurred. I was hanging a large picture of two angels in the living room after my daughter suggested it would complement the cherubs lining the ceiling. Finished, I turned to walk away. Then *crash!* The picture fell to the floor. I rehung it and turned away, only for it to fall again. After I hung it a third time and walked away, I felt a rush of air hit the back of my ankles.

"What the hell?" I thought. I turned to see the picture lying at my feet. More determined than ever, I hung the picture again, then shouted, "Stay there, dammit." I had to laugh because I was alone. Who did I think I was talking to? The kids were out playing on the front porch.

"Dad, come and see this," my daughter called from the front door.

When I stepped onto the porch, she said excitedly, "Sit down and watch this!"

"Watch what?"

Just as the words came out of my mouth, my daughter pointed to an old man walking down the sidewalk toward our house. When he reached our property line, he quickly crossed the street to the opposite sidewalk.

"They don't like walking in front of our house," said my daughter. "Isn't that weird?" And she was right. I sat on that porch for at least an hour, watching our neighbors cross the street. A couple of times I motioned as if to say hello, and they just dropped their heads and continued on their way. "Maybe they're uncomfortable with new neighbors," I thought, though in my heart I knew otherwise.

That Sunday, the kids returned from church excited because we had set aside the whole day to work in the yard—a big deal, since the only outdoor space they had ever been able to call theirs was the balcony outside our old apartment. We mowed the grass and cleaned the leaves from under the porch. We also needed to rake the lawn because the trees were shedding their leaves— even though it was spring, not fall. I made a mental note to mention this oddity to the landlady the next time I talked with her.

I asked my younger son to go inside and down to the basement to fetch the garden hose so we could clean the walkways and wash down the house's

33

weathered white boards. Only a minute or two passed before I heard screams, and I ran in frantically to find him. He was standing in the middle of the kitchen floor shaking, a puddle of urine at his feet.

"What's wrong? What happened?" I asked.

"Something chased me up the basement steps."

"What chased you?" I asked.

"I don't know, Daddy, but it was big."

My other two children and I checked the basement and found only the garden hose that my youngest had dropped in fear.

THE MAN IN THE MIST

Aside from this strange incident, we were incredibly happy those first few days in the house. My daughter was making plans for gardening and decorating, and my boys realized it would be easy to walk to their baseball games because the park was so close by. But this uneventful time wouldn't last for long.

It was the children's last week of classes, and that Monday we all arrived after school and work to find every light in the house switched on. My first impulse was to blame the children, who pleaded innocence. The same thing happened on Tuesday, Wednesday, and Thursday. On Friday, my daughter and I sent the boys to the car while we purposely toured the house looking for any forgotten lights. They were all off.

That night, we returned home to again find every light burning. I walked into the house feeling shaken. The only logical explanation for the lights being on was that someone was in our house. I searched the rooms in a panic, but found no one.

"Daddy, it's cold in here," my daughter called from the living room. What was she talking about? Sweat was pouring down my back. I stepped into the living room, and the temperature dropped what seemed a good thirty degrees. More ominously, I felt a presence. I didn't see anything, but what felt like an electrical current ran through my body and gave me goose bumps. I remember thinking, "What on earth was that?"

Now my daughter remarked, "Daddy, it's getting warm in here." And sure enough, the temperature was rising. That night my children slept with me, though I got hardly any sleep.

The following Sunday night, we were sitting in the family room talking. The kids had their backs to the kitchen—something I'm still thankful for, since what happened next haunts my dreams to this day.

I was getting ready to take a business trip the following morning to Indianapolis, and the children and I were watching TV and discussing the plans for their stay at Grandma's. I noticed it first out of the corner of my eye: something moving, then standing in the kitchen doorway. Not something, really—someone. I looked toward it again to see the dark figure of a man. Though he was human in shape, his body looked like a mass of churning black mist or smoke, and I heard heavy, labored breathing. I looked down, thinking my eyes were playing tricks on me.

After a moment passed, I looked up. He was still there, and began to move into the room. The churning black form stood in the doorway for what seemed an eternity but was actually only a few moments. He then melted into thin air.

I remember the thoughts that raced through my head; I have two choices. We could run out of the house screaming into the night or we could get up and quietly leave the house and figure all of this out.

My hands shook uncontrollably as I said to myself, That's what we'll do. We'll go quietly, orderly, as if nothing was wrong. I stood up shakily, and in my nicest, calmest daddy voice said, "Let's go get a soda and see Grandma." My youngest was instantly excited at the prospect of a soda before bed, but the two others looked at me as if I'd lost my mind. "Come on guys, it'll be fun."

Thankfully, my car keys were on the coffee table in front of us, and we moved in an orderly fashion out the front door. As I turned to lock it, the painful wail of a man welled up from inside, so loud that the neighborhood dogs began barking.

To hell with orderly, I thought. "Get in the car!" The drive to my parents' house is still a blur. I do remember that my younger son, who was trembling with fright, said, "Daddy, the basement monster is standing in the upstairs window." I looked back—and sure enough, the black form was watching us leave.

That night we stayed at my parents'. Early the next day, I gathered my things and left for my business trip. By the time I got back and picked up the kids, I had a whole week's worth of rationalizations for why we should return to the house. Where else were we to go? I had put everything I had saved and then some into the move. We returned that Friday, and to my relief the weekend passed without incident—not to mention very little sleep.

On Saturday, we explored the big shed at the back of the yard. In it we found personal belongings that clearly had belonged to several different people. This raised a question: Who had lived in the house before, and what might that explain?

THE TERRIBLE ENCOUNTER

My parents agreed that it would be a good idea for me to call the old landlady and ask her some straightforward questions about the house and its former occupants. Once I was able to reach her, I chose my words carefully and asked in my most polite voice whether any of the previous tenants had ever perhaps mentioned a ghost?

She answered, "Not that I can remember." She then said that there had been one strange tenant: a girl who claimed that her dead father came to visit her, but the old woman always thought she was crazy. The girl had left some of her stuff behind in the shed, but the landlady could never get her to come pick it up.

The other belongings were those of a man who had lived there and had left in the middle of the night, taking nothing. But, no, she had never heard of anyone talking about the house being haunted. I asked how long these people had lived there, and she replied, "Not much more than a year. Why do you ask?" The phone call wasn't much help. And it didn't calm my fears much, but what else could I do?

Sunday came and went with no trouble, and I was convincing myself that what we had gone through was just a one-time ordeal. But everything changed on Monday night. I was on the phone with my mom, and the kids were off playing in my bedroom. Suddenly, the doors inside the house rattled. I paused to listen, and they rattled again. I yelled at the kids to quit playing games and told my mom that everything was okay—just the kids playing tricks. At this point the doors rattled more loudly, but before I could scold again, my daughter's voice cut me off.

"Daddy, I'm in here reading and my brothers are asleep."

I will now try to recreate what happened as best I can. Some of it I remember clearly, but other parts are not clear to this day.

The temperature instantly dropped thirty degrees and I felt a terrible shiver run through my body. A horrible stench filled the air, and then the screaming started: softly at first, then growing louder. I shouted into the phone to my mother that she had to drive to our street and meet us at the top of the hill.

Now the whole house began to shake. From above I could hear something large coming down the stairs *(Boom. Boom! BOOM!)* . . . the screaming of a man, over and over . . . and my daughter screaming, "Daddy, what is happening?" One of my two bedroom doors led to the stairs, and I had to rescue my children!

The floor beneath me was shaking as I made my way to the opposite bedroom door. I felt something behind me but didn't want to turn around. When I made it to the door, it wouldn't open. Screaming myself by this time, I threw myself against the door, but it wouldn't budge. I tried again and again until it flew open. I told my older son to get his brother and run out the front door to the car, but my shocked daughter wouldn't move. A slap made her respond, and I grabbed her and headed for the door as I heard the other bedroom door open behind us. Whatever it was, it was coming for us. After we ran out onto the porch, I slammed the front door behind us.

As we jumped into the car, we could still hear the angry noises coming from the house. I sped away and parked at the top of the street, where I could look down into the house and wait for my parents. My children and I could see something through the windows: a blackness moving methodically through the house from room to room. It seemed to be searching—searching for us! That was our last night in the house, and my children never returned.

I went back a few times to collect our belongings, but never alone. Anyone who accompanied me would experience something strange—a scream, whispers, pounding from the floor above. One day while I was down in the dim basement, my brother snapped a picture of me. I can't say why, but perhaps after all I'd told him about the house and its spooky basement he just wanted to document my brief stay there—or maybe so that he could kid me about it for years to come.

38

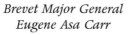

Brevet Major General Eugene Asa Carr

Nobody joked around, however, after we developed the photo and saw the cloudy image of a man standing behind me in a darkened corner of the cellar. Though shadowy, the figure was clear enough for us to make out some details. The man seemed to be from a different time, with old-fashioned clothes and a bow tie. His face was a very angry one.

About a month after we moved, my brother sent me an e-mail with a link to a Web site that he desperately wanted me to see. He said he had been doing some poking around online, looking into local history, when he found something that made his jaw drop. I went to the Web site he gave me, and the face of a man came onto my screen—the same face that showed up in the picture my brother had taken in the basement.

The man, Brevet Major General Eugene

Asa Carr, was apparently quite well known as a Civil War officer—a hero, in fact. He was also a very well-respected town citizen in his day and had once owned the house and surrounding land that my kids and I had fled from in the night. Still, there was nothing on the Internet that could explain why he might still be in the house or why he would want everyone else out of it.

EPILOGUE

About a year ago, an acquaintance of mine saw a police car race up to the old house one night, and then watched a family running out of the front door in their nightclothes. After that, the old lady turned the place into a dog kennel. I guess she ran out of people who could live in that old white house.

I still drive past it every once in a while when I get up enough nerve. As I look up at the upstairs window, I can still imagine "the man of the house" there—watching, waiting, angry. Sometimes the screams still wake me from my sleep. In my dreams I see a man standing in the basement, breathing. It's the breathing I'd hear when I was alone with him in a room. The breathing I'd hear that let me know he was there with me—heavy, labored breathing.

I remember what the old landlady said to me as I turned over the key after we moved out. The side of my arm was still bruised from throwing myself against that bedroom door that last night in the house. "Some people are meant to live in an old house like that," she told me, "and some people aren't. I never thought you were the old-house type." And I know now that she was right.

39

THE DARK WATCHER

by Charlie Carlson

"I CAN'T REMEMBER exactly how old I was when I began to feel something very strange in that house," said Amy as she began recalling her memories of weird experiences in the two-story stucco house where she grew up on the outskirts of Sanford, Florida. "I know it all began when I was very young. In the daytime, the rooms seemed friendly enough; but after dark, an unknown presence seemed to take over."

The house was built in the early 1920s and had large-paned windows. Downstairs was a formal living room with a large window facing east and French doors leading to a screened-in porch. Both the window and doors were hung with old-fashioned metal venetian blinds.

"Almost always when I was in that downstairs room after dark, I sensed something outside of the window, watching through the blinds, even though the blinds were nearly impossible to see through. Many times I could clearly make out the silhouette of a man standing at the window. He was usually smoking a cigarette, and as he raised and lowered it I could see the red glow of the burning end. At other times, I sensed the presence was on the porch, always watching."

Amy says the recurring experiences were terrifying for a young child. "My parents would constantly check to see if anything was outside, but they never found anyone. It got to the point where I hated to enter that room after dark. Sometimes the feeling of someone standing at the French doors was so strong I couldn't even force myself to look in that direction. I just knew in my mind that I would see something standing there.

"The large downstairs bathroom had the same eerie feeling of something outside, watching and waiting. There were times when I couldn't go into that bathroom because the feeling of foreboding was overwhelming. I knew that if I lifted the curtain and looked out, something would be looking back in at me."

Amy said she also had the same awful feeling about a room at the back of the house. "This room had a door that led to the outside, and there was something about the door that frightened me. To this day, I have nightmares about that door because I know something was on the outside waiting and watching. The strange thing is that adults couldn't seem to see whatever it was that occupied that house, yet children and teenagers always sensed it."

41

IN A CHILD'S EYES

Years later, Amy began to think the weird sensations might have been no more than a kid's imagination working overtime. But she thought otherwise once she learned that others had experienced similar sensations in the house.

"I lived in that house until I was sixteen years old, then I moved out and got an apartment in town. About ten years later, after our family had lived in the house for forty years, my mom finally sold it. She first offered it to me, of course, but I knew that I could never share that place with whatever was there. The new owners, with their two teenagers, moved in immediately and set up housekeeping. After living there only a few months, they moved out. They continued to own the house but rented it to a steady stream of people, none of whom stayed very long."

One day, Amy saw a FOR SALE sign in the yard of the old house. Curious, she called the real estate office to ask why the owners moved out of the place so quickly. She wasn't surprised when she heard the reason.

"It was because of the family's children," said Amy. "They refused to stay in the house." The real estate person had explained that the family's dog would sit at the bottom of the stairs, looking up and barking constantly, as if seeing an intruder on the landing. At night, the children would hear footsteps come up the staircase, then move to the wooden floor in the upstairs hallway. Anytime they went to investigate, there would be no one there.

As time went on, the footsteps continued to be heard and the dog kept barking at something unseen. One day, the dog finally rushed up the stairs, barking wildly, as if charging something. The children hurried to the staircase just in time to see the dog picked up and thrown, as if by invisible hands, over the upstairs banister to the first floor below.

For the frightened kids, enough was enough. They refused to stay in the house, and shortly afterward the family moved out.

The old house is now up for sale again, but what awaits the new buyer remains unknown. "I have no idea what's in that house, but it's unnatural. Also, whatever is watching and roaming at night seems to be detected only by children and animals. All I know is that I'd never want to live there again," Amy says.

FAMOUS CRIME, STUBBORN BLOODSTAIN

TRUMAN CAPOTE'S bestselling book *In Cold Blood* is a chronicle of the murders of the Clutter family by Dick Hickock and Perry Smith in 1959. This early example of what was called the New Journalism is hailed as an American classic, and a new generation became aware of the crime after the release of the 2005 film *Capote,* which takes the author's research and writing of the book as its central subject.

The horrifying event took place in a five-bedroom farmhouse outside of Holcomb, Kansas, when the two murderers shot Mr. and Mrs. Herb Clutter along with two of their children. Hickock and Smith were hanged six years later for their crime. Today the house is a private residence owned by another family. Visitors can view it from the nearest public road, but a NO TRESPASSING sign at the entrance to the driveway makes it clear that gawkers are unwelcome.

A legend persists that a bloodstain remains on the basement wall. No matter how many times the stain has been scrubbed or covered up by paint, it is said, it inevitably returns. Truth or fiction? Almost half a century after the much-publicized crime, we most likely will never know the answer.

THE HAUNTING OF SUMMERWIND
by Todd Roll

WISCONSIN'S most famous haunted house sat amid a stand of pine overlooking West Bay Lake, in the northern part of the state. This once proud mansion, called Summerwind, had fallen into disrepair as vandals, bats, and the harshness of the northern winter combined to reduce the shingled structure to a mere shell of its former self. Although it remained empty for a number of years, rumors spread that perhaps something—or someone—still lingered in its lonely halls.

Built in 1916 by Robert Patterson Lamont, who would eventually become Secretary of Commerce under President Herbert Hoover, the house was the family's summer retreat. The family still owned Summerwind when the first incident of paranormal activity occurred. Legend holds that Lamont confronted an intruder in the kitchen. Armed, Lamont shot the individual after he failed to respond when challenged. The two bullets passed through the figure and struck the door behind it. When the smoke cleared, the intruder had vanished but the bullet holes remained.

When I visited the mansion in 1987 as part of a small team of paranormal investigators, the door from the kitchen to the basement did indeed show two bullet holes. The door mysteriously disappeared some time between my first and second visits, and I've always wondered who took it and where it might be today.

SKELETONS IN THE CLOSET

Summerwind had many owners over the years, including Arnold Hinshaw, who bought it in the early 1970s. In the few years that Hinshaw, his wife,

Ginger, and their six children lived in the house, windows frequently refused to remain shut, voices heard in empty rooms grew silent when the rooms were entered, and electrical appliances malfunctioned yet mysteriously repaired themselves. The family was also visited on several occasions by an apparition of a lady in a white gown, whom they saw dancing in the living room, through the French doors of the dining room. Hinshaw's car burst into flames in the garage one day, and the source of the fire was never determined.

During a house renovation, Hinshaw discovered a crawl space behind a closet on the second floor. Looking inside it, he spied something suspicious. Too large to crawl in, he enlisted one of his children to investigate. The child came back terrified, saying he had seen a human skeleton. Hinshaw sent in a second child, who confirmed the story. For reasons unknown, the Hinshaws decided to leave the skeleton in place and never notified the authorities. What is known is that not long afterward, paranormal activity in the house increased. No doubt as a result, Hinshaw soon had a nervous breakdown and his wife attempted suicide.

Ginger Hinshaw's father, businessman Raymond Bober, believed the stately old house would make a perfect hotel and restaurant, and began planning the renovations. While taking measurements for the dining room, he noticed that the room seemed to expand and contract; measurements taken one day would change the next. It was also at this time that Bober learned from his daughter of the strange events she had experienced in the home. While historians differ on whether Bober actually ever bought the house, his plans never came to fruition.

Bober did, however, pen a book on Summerwind. Using the name Wolffgang von Bober, he wrote *The Carver Effect: A Paranormal Experience.* In his book, published in 1979, Bober claimed that the spirit of Jonathan Carver, an eighteenth-century British explorer, had revealed to him in a dream that the deed to the upper two thirds of Wisconsin was sealed up in the foundation of the house. The deed was supposedly given to Carver by the Sioux Indians. To hardly anyone's surprise, Bober's claims were later discredited. Some suspected that his aim was to cash in on the house's reputation by opening it for haunted house tours.

46

Capt. JONATHAN CARVER.
From the Original Picture in the Posfesion of J.C. Lettsom M.D.

ONE LAST SCARE

Abandoned, Summerwind stood empty for most of the 1980s and became a local magnet for people looking for a good scare. Tales continued of ghostly shapes seen in the hallways and mysterious lights in the windows. Vandals had their way with the house, breaking out windows and spray painting the walls. They also knocked holes in the foundation, looking for the lost deed that Bober claimed was hidden there.

It was during one of my visits to the mansion in the spring of 1987 that I had a paranormal experience. I was on the second floor taking measurements and photographs when I entered the bathroom off the master suite. Suddenly I had the sensation that something was in the room—not so much a presence as a feeling of dread. As I stepped back into the hallway, the feeling went away. Thinking that what I'd experienced was temporary, I again entered the bathroom. The feeling returned, and this time it was so overpowering that I felt nauseated. After I made a hasty retreat to the safety of the hall, the feeling faded.

During the course of my team's investigation, this overwhelming feeling of dread returned each time I entered the upstairs bathroom and left when I returned to the hall. In no other room of the home did I experience such a sensation, and in later visits I would have no trouble entering the room.

In June 1988, Summerwind met its end when it was struck by lightning during a violent thunderstorm and burned to the ground. Today only the foundation and chimneys remain. Recent visitors still speak of seeing lights hovering in the basement and having feelings of dread and foreboding. They also claim that animals avoid the place and plants won't grow on the grounds.

Was Summerwind ever haunted? We'll never really know, but the legend of "Wisconsin's most famous haunted house" lives on.

TERRIFYING
TRAVELS

You may bury my body, ooh down by the highway side.
So my old evil spirit can catch a Greyhound bus and ride.
–Robert Johnson, *Me and the Devil Blues*

S OME OF THE WEIRDEST hauntings occur during the most commonplace of activities—traveling from point A to point B. We do that every day, whether we're on a road, a bridge, in a train or bus. We're always traveling, and rarely thinking about it. Until our ordinary, boring little trip takes a strange—sometimes very strange—twist.

The stories in this chapter all have that strange twist. And if you're not chilled to the bone, you'll still probably want to buckle your seat belt.

Our haunted places range from the railroad tracks running alongside an old Vermont cotton mill to a California road where a motorcyclist lost his head. In Indiana, Louisiana, and Ohio, bridges have been the scene of some frightful—and in some cases, tragic—events. Byways in North Dakota, Wisconsin, and New York have their own embodiments of the ghostly bride who wanders about in her wedding dress, while soldiers in Civil War garb pop up in Kentucky and North Carolina.

In Missouri, the gravel trail called Zombie Road has inspired tales of so many spirits it seems they've gathered for some sort of otherworldly convention. Then there's the Bermuda Triangle of the U.S. highway system: the so-called Dead Zone, a fabled stretch of Interstate 4 outside of Daytona, Florida, that you may want to assiduously avoid.

Ready to hit the road?

THE MYSTERIES OF CREEK ROAD
by Greg Bishop

SITUATED A FEW SCENIC MILES above the Pacific shoreline, the town of Ojai is just far enough from the bustle of Los Angeles to make it seem like any other small Ojai Valley town. There are, however, enough Halloween-caliber stories here to keep any tour company busy throughout the year—and many of these tales are centered on or around Creek Road, which runs through Ojai and beyond. The best known concern a man who burned to death, a motorcyclist who met a shocking end, and a purported vampire.

THE BURN VICTIM

Possibly the most famous ghost in town is known as Charman, whose skin hangs in cooked strips from his skull and who reeks of burning flesh. No, this grotesque spirit wasn't the victim of some horrible backyard barbecue accident. So what happened? Accounts seem to differ on whether the man perished in a great brushfire in 1948, a downed plane, or a car crash. Stories about him have been told in the Ojai Valley since at least the 1950s.

The apparition has been sighted numerous times either near or on the Creek Road Bridge, a few miles south of town near Camp Comfort County Park. He's said to startle anyone who dares to walk the road at night, and reportedly tore the leather jacket off one terrified witness in the 1950s.

One story, probably one of hundreds told around late night campfires, says that Charman is the ghost of a man who was hiking back to his car with a can of gasoline late at night. Some of the gas spilled on his clothes, and for some reason he made the fateful decision to light up a cigarette, accidentally turning himself into a human torch. Most accounts, however, say he was a homesteader who was unable to save his family in a brushfire.

THE HEADLESS MOTORCYCLIST

Another popular tale concerns a ghost on wheels. In the 1950s, a motorcyclist who was trying to pass a truck on the narrow mountain turns of Creek Road was decapitated by a wayward steel beam that became dislodged from the truck bed. The incident happened so suddenly that the motorcycle sped on and passed the startled driver, who promptly had a heart attack and crashed in a ravine. The cyclist's ghost still rides at night, looking for his lost head.

In local lore, the unlucky biker and Charman are joined by a phantom hitchhiker and numerous anthropomorphic mists and shadows. One late-night motorist even claimed to have seen Bigfoot in the area where Creek Road exits highway 33. A simple nighttime drive on this twisting Creek Road, lined with gnarled oak trees, is enough to spontaneously generate spooky tales.

THE VAMPIRE

In light of all this, perhaps it is not so strange that the Ojai Valley is also home to a vampire legend. Sometime in the 1890s, so the story goes, a strange visitor arrived from Europe and promptly bought a ranch near—where else?—Creek Road. When cattle, and then people, started turning up drained of blood, settlers started to wonder about their new neighbor, who didn't seem to come calling in the daylight hours.

Armed with crosses, holy water, and a wooden stake, they crept up on the creature, who was lying in a stone sarcophagus under a tree. A huge black dog tried to stop them, but the holy water sent the beast howling away in pain. Opening the heavy stone lid, the posse quickly drove the stake home and sprinkled holy water in for good measure. "And the vampire has not troubled the residents of the peaceful Ojai Valley since," it is said. No one seems to know where the casket is, but aficionados of the supernatural keep looking for it.

> Creek Road is north of Los Angeles in Ojai, California, and is accessible by taking State Route 33/North Ventura Avenue to Hermosa Road, then southeast to (North) Creek Road. Camp Comfort County Park is located at 11969 North Creek Road, Ojai CA 93023.

INTERSTATE 4: WHAT LIES BENEATH?

by Charlie Carlson

DRIVING SOUTHWEST FROM DAYTONA on Interstate 4, Christine Torioni was shocked when her car blew its engine just past the bridge over the St. John's River. She coasted into the emergency lane and sat there wondering what to do. Adding to her distress was a very strange coincidence: Her car had previously blown its engine in the very same spot.

What Christine didn't know was that this part of Interstate 4 is known as the Dead Zone—a quarter-mile section that has been the scene of an exceedingly high number of traffic accidents, many of them fatal. Believers in the supernatural put the blame on what lies beneath the asphalt.

In 1886, Henry Sanford established a small colony in these parts for the purpose of selling real estate to German immigrants. Yellow fever soon raced through the settlement, claiming the lives of four members of one family. The victims—two children and their parents—were buried in the woods, well away from the colony. Here the dead rested in peace until 1960, when construction began on Interstate 4 and fill dirt was dumped onto the four graves to elevate the new highway. Ever since the interstate opened, motorists driving through the infamous stretch have reported static on their radios, cell phones that won't work, floating orbs, and apparitions seen by the roadside. It was in the middle of this mysterious spot that Christine's car broke down.

THE SILVER-AND-WHITE TRUCK

"After sitting in the car, I started walking," said Christine, a New York transplant unaware of the local legend of the Dead Zone. "It was hot as blazes, and the cars were whizzing by like crazy. I came to a short bridge that went over some railroad tracks. It had a short railing, and I'm so afraid of heights I was afraid to cross it with all the cars speeding by."

Christine made it to the center of the bridge and then froze, fearful of losing her balance and falling to the tracks below. "Then this big tractor-trailer truck pulled off the road ahead of me and I heard the truck driver calling my name—strange, because I have no idea how he knew it. He kept telling me to walk toward him and not to look down." Step by careful step, she made it to the truck, where the driver offered her a lift to the next exit.

"I climbed into the cab," remembered Christine. "It was like brand new

inside. I mean just spick-and-span. The only thing in it was a clipboard that, strangely enough, didn't have any papers." She said the trailer was silver-colored and the cab was pure white. The driver was neatly dressed and very clean-looking. "Actually, I really didn't think he looked like a trucker."

The trucker pulled off at the next exit and stopped in front of a gas station. "He asked if I needed any money for a phone call," Christine recalled. "I told him no, and then offered to buy him something cold to drink for his help. But he declined."

What happened next was beyond weird, said Christine. "I turned to go into the store and noticed I didn't hear the truck engine running. I turned to look and the truck was gone. There was a man sitting on a bench in front of the store, and I asked him if he had seen the truck that was just there. He gave me a puzzled look and said, 'I've been sitting here all morning and haven't seen any trucks pull in.'" Even though she didn't know it at the time, Christine had encountered the spirits of the Dead Zone.

Her experience, like those of others, is linked to previous events. The first traffic accident in this section of the interstate involved a silver-and-white refrigerated semi that jackknifed, killing the driver. It happened in the very spot where Christine's car broke down, not just once but twice.

Interstate 4 can be accessed via Interstate 275 in Tampa or Interstate 95 in Daytona Beach FL. The St. John's River Veterans Memorial Bridge is located in the vicinity of the 101 and 104 exits of Interstate 4.

REPORTS FROM THE DEAD ZONE . . .

WE'VE BEEN E-MAILED more than a few reports from men and women who have had a brush with mysterious goings-on while driving the fabled stretch.

"I always heard about this strange part of the highway but didn't believe it until I had two accidents in two different months right in the middle of the Dead Zone. I don't know if my accidents were caused by spirits or some other anomaly, but I do know that spot's too dangerous. I encourage everyone to read up on the Dead Zone and make up his or her own mind. I, for one, plan to steer clear of the place." —*Scotty*

"One explanation that hasn't been considered for 'dead spots' like the one on Interstate 4 is limestone deposits close to the surface. My grandfather, an engineer, tells me that limestone absorbs radio waves. I have found that many of the local spots where I lose my cell phone signal have large limestone deposits." —*Kyrie*

"The only car accident I ever had happened right where those graves are. What's really eerie is that my steering wheel locked for no good reason, causing me to crash into the guardrail and tearing up one whole side of my Buick. So I'm a true believer in the I-4 Dead Zone and warn others to take heed." —*J. Collins*

"I just read about the Interstate 4 Dead Zone. Being new to Florida, I had no idea about the graves. My daughter and I are sensitives, and we've wondered why we get very uncomfortable and almost frightened when we drive over that area—so much so that I avoid it at all costs, even if I have to drive 20 miles out of the way. Now I know why." —*Bambi*

"I visit Florida frequently, riding my motorcycle down from South Carolina. I guess you can say I'm 'sensitive' to paranormal things to a point. I usually can feel and sense a presence more often than actually seeing it. I've been on Interstate 4 many, many times and have felt something riding over that bridge and through the surrounding area." —*Dano*

"I read about that Dead Zone on Interstate 4 near the St. John's River. Believe it or not, the last two times I vacationed in Central Florida I had a car accident at that very spot. The area is now under construction but I don't think it will change things—there's just something very strange about that section." —*Johnnie L.*

"I believe there is something evil about that section of Interstate 4. I've been involved in three accidents there, once as a driver and twice as a passenger in another person's car. But get this: My neighbor's cousin was killed in a motorcycle crash at that same spot a few years ago. Yes indeed, something is paranormal about the zone. They can fix that bridge all they want, but the Dead Zone will still be there." —*Jan*

ZOMBIE ROAD

by Troy Taylor

TRAVELING WEST ALONG what used to be old Route 66, you soon leave the buildings and houses in the western suburbs of St. Louis behind as you enter a rugged, wild Missouri landscape of forests, rivers, and caves. It is here that mysteries lie.

If the stories told about one forgotten stretch of roadway are even partially true, then a place called Zombie Road may be one of the weirdest spots in the region. Zombie Road (a name by which it was known at least as far back as the 1950s) was once listed on maps as Lawler Ford Road. (Where the "Lawler" came from is lost to time, but a ford crossed the river here.) People were sometimes ferried across the river at this location, which no doubt explains why the road was placed here.

The road may have originally been an American Indian trail that was later converted into a roadway by European settlers. The railroad came through the area in 1853, and in 1868 the Glencoe Marble Company started to quarry the nearby limestone deposits in what is now the Rockwoods Reservation. A side track was laid from the deposits to the town of Glencoe, and Lawler Ford Road became a gravel and dirt road providing access to the railroad tracks and the Meramec River. It's likely that wagons were used to haul quarry stone up the road, and trucks later were used on the narrow road, which was paved at some point.

TALES TAKE SHAPE

The quarry operations were shut down and the road fell into disuse. Those who recall the road during that period say that the narrow, winding lane, which runs through roughly two miles of dense woods, was always enveloped in a strange silence and a half-light. Shadows were long, even on the brightest days, and it was impossible to see past the trees and brush to what was coming around the next curve. If you were driving and met another car, one car would have to back up to one of the few wide places on the road to allow the other car to pass.

Thanks to its seclusion and abandonment, in the 1950s Lawler Ford Road became known as a lovers' lane and a party spot for local teenagers. It still sees a traveler or two today, though most who come here are hardly looking for a party. Instead, they come for a taste of the unexplained.

Like many similar locations, Lawler Ford Road gained a reputation for being haunted. Numerous legends and stories exist, from the typical tales of murdered boyfriends and killers with hooks for hands to more specific tales of a local killer who was dubbed the Zombie. Supposedly living in a dilapidated shack by the river, he was said to attack young lovers who wanted someplace quiet and out of the way. As time passed, the stories of the madman were told and retold so often that the road's original name was largely forgotten, replaced by Zombie Road—the name it is known by today.

Even now, there is no shortage of stories about the road. Resident ghosts include a man killed by a train in the 1970s and a mysterious old woman who yells at passersby from a house at the end of the road. The tales of American Indian spirits and modern-day devil worshippers could fill a small book.

Is there any truth to the ghost stories—or at least a history that could explain how they got started? For the answer, read on.

American Indian Spirits. There is no record of the first inhabitants of the area, but they were probably the Indians who built the centuries-old Cahokia Mounds, located near present-day St. Louis. Many other tribes passed through the region as they were moved out of their original lands in the east, but they never stayed. If these indigenous people left an impression behind, it could be the reason why Indian spirits are still encountered here today.

Civil War Soldiers. During the Civil War, the city of St. Louis found itself in the predicament of being loyal to the Union in a state predominantly dedicated to the Confederate cause. For this reason, men in the Home Guard were picketed along the roads and trails leading into the city. Confederate spies, saboteurs, and agents used less trafficked paths to get in and out of the area, including the trail that would later be known as Lawler Ford Road. Troops from the Home Guard were stationed at the ford, and a number of men died here in short battles with them.

Could this violence explain some of the hauntings along Zombie Road? It's possible that the bloodshed that occurred here during the Civil War left its mark on the site, as it has on so many other locales.

The Railroads. The railroads figure large in stories of the road. Della Hamilton McCullough, the wife of a local tanner and shoemaker, was killed in 1876 after being struck down by a railroad car. It may be her death that started the Zombie Road legend of the ghost of the person who was run over by a train, since there's no record of fatal train accidents in modern times.

Today, the old line can still be seen at the end of the road, where it is believed the railroad ghost walks. Many accounts over the years have described a translucent figure in white who walks up the abandoned line. Those who've claimed to see it say the phantom glows with bluish-white light but always disappears if anyone tries to approach it.

Some of the other restless ghosts could be those of accident victims along the rail line. Sharp bends in the tracks at Glencoe were the site of frequent derailments—so many that eventually service was discontinued around the bend in the river.

MORE STORIES STILL

Many of the people I've talked with about the strange happenings on and around Zombie Road speak of unsettling feelings and the sensation of being watched. Some felt they were being followed on the trail, as though someone was trying to keep pace with them, although they saw no one. Also, it's not uncommon for visitors to report seeing the shapes or shadows of presences in the woods, some of which have been mistaken for actual people until the hiker confronts them and finds no one there.

Visitors to Zombie Road often end their journey at the Meramec River. Many claim to have had strange encounters near the old shacks and ramshackle houses along the beach area at the end of the trail. These date back to about 1900, when the area around Glencoe was a resort community. One of the long-standing legends is of the ghost of an old woman who screams at people from the doorway of one of the houses. But when sought out, the old woman is never there.

Could she and other apparitions sighted here be former residents of days gone by? Perhaps the haunting of the old roadway has nothing to do with violent events of the past but happiness instead. Some of Glencoe's former residents may have returned to their cottages after death because the resort homes were places where they knew peace and contentment in life.

I have to confess that when I first began researching the hauntings of Zombie Road, I thought they were little more than myths that arose from the vivid imaginations of generations of teenagers. I never expected to discover the dark history of violence and death in the region or anything that might substantiate the tales of ghosts and supernatural occurrences. It was easy to find people who believed in the legends of Zombie Road, but I never expected to be one of those who came to be convinced.

> Take Old State Road to Ridge Road. Lawler Ford Road (a.k.a. Zombie Road) will be on your left, just after a school. It might only be marked with a chain link fence. The road can also be accessed from the Al Foster Meramec Greenway Trail.

THE LEGEND OF MARY'S BRIDGE
by Tim Westcott

DOWN IN LOUISIANA, between the Cajun villages of St. Martinville and Broussard, lies a road with an ill-omened bridge. The name of the road is Rue Bayou Tortue (Turtle Bayou Road), but most locals know it by its nickname: Stone Road, for the teenagers who used to get stoned on drugs there. At the parish line, a small bridge crosses over eerie Bayou Tortue, where tall cypress trees draped with Spanish moss line the banks. Although alligators and water moccasins teem in the waters, most people are more concerned with the ghost of a Cajun girl named Mary.

A Horrible Death

Against the wishes of her parents, Mary was dating an *Americain*—the term used by the locals for a non-Cajun or Creole. A good Catholic girl, Mary refused to give in to her boyfriend's sexual advances. Just before midnight on the last day of her life, Mary and her boyfriend, who was dead drunk, were driving through the countryside when he shouted, "Give in, or I'll throw you in the bayou." Mary begged him to take her home, but the boy repeated his ugly threat.

When Mary tried to flee, the story goes, her boyfriend hit her in the back of her head with a whiskey bottle until she lost consciousness. He then dumped her in the bayou, where the gators would undoubtedly do the rest.

Despite the intense search that followed the sickening crime, Mary's body was never found. The boyfriend disappeared about a week later, but all of his belongings were left at his house. It is rumored that Mary's father damned the boy to the same fate as his only daughter, and it appears the hex must have worked.

61

To this day, they say if you go to the bridge at midnight, turn off your car, and then call out "Mary, Mary, Mary," your car won't start and you'll have to push it off the bridge before you can get it running. But that pales in comparison to another supposed occurrence: At midnight on the anniversary of her brutal death, you can see Mary frantically circling the bridge in a long, white dress—imprisoned there after her life was cut short by an evil boyfriend.

The exact location of Mary's Bridge is not specified, but you can find Rue Bayou Tortue by taking U.S. 90 west, turning right at St. Nazaire Road, left at La Flamme Road, and right onto Rue Bayou Tortue.

TRIP TO A CURSED TOWN
by Justin T.

I'M FROM EAU CLAIRE, Wisconsin, just a short drive down Route 85 from the tiny town of Caryville. Strange stories about Caryville have been circulating for as long as I can remember. Word was that the whole village was cursed and that a lot of people who had traveled through it had seen plenty of things they wish they hadn't. One night, some friends and I decided to hop in the car and go check out the town for ourselves.

From Schoolhouse to Boat Landing

Probably the most famous haunted site in Caryville is the abandoned school-house. Local lore says one of the students didn't want to go home when school was over one day because his drunken, violent father was physically abusing him at home. The boy hid in a closet until all of the other kids and the teacher locked the doors and windows and left. What he hadn't counted on was the lack of heat in the dark classroom in the dead of winter. Unwilling to leave, the boy just sat at his desk and froze to death.

The spirit of the doomed boy supposedly haunts the old schoolhouse, and if you go in and sit at his desk, they say you can supposedly feel his presence pass through you. When my friends and I got to the school, we were all determined to go inside—that is, until we actually saw it. The school looked so eerie that we changed our minds. Besides, we reasoned, we didn't even know which desk belonged to the ghost boy, so how would we know where to sit to test the story?

We sat there in the car and stared at the school in silence. Suddenly, one of my friends said, "Hey, look at that!" and pointed toward the school's dark-ened windows. I didn't see anything, so asked my friend what she'd seen. "It looked like eyes up there," she answered. "Two red ones, looking out at us. But then they just disappeared."

My friend was so freaked out that I believed her. Everyone in the car was uneasy, but we decided to get out because the next site on our tour was right across the street: the old Caryville church.

The church was the second one to stand at this location. The priest who built the first church, the story goes, went mad when plans were made to demolish it. In protest, he walked up to the belfry, locked the door, and hanged himself. These days people say that on certain nights you can see his lifeless body hanging there. To be honest, I really couldn't see much. But the silhouette of the tower in the moonlight was a spooky sight, and it wasn't hard to imagine the priest's black robes ruffling in the breeze.

The next haunted stop on our midnight drive sat on the banks of the Chippewa River—the Meridean boat landing, so named because a local girl named Mary Dean drowned there long ago. From here you can see an island where an insane asylum once stood. The asylum was run by a cruel doctor who bred vicious dogs to keep the inmates from escaping, and we'd heard stories that one of the beasts still haunts the area and chases people away—a large black mongrel with glowing red eyes, a hellhound the locals dubbed Blackie. The prospect of meeting up with Blackie, along with reports of the mysterious disappearances that the landing is known for, was enough to make us chicken out. So we hit the road once again.

CREEPY CEMETERY, PHANTOM TRUCK

Not far from the landing is a small graveyard officially named Sand Hill Cemetery but more often referred to as the Caryville Cemetery. When we arrived, we all got out of the car and began to walk among the tombstones. I'm not kidding when I say this is one creepy place! Woods and cornfields surround it, and graves of the wicked are said to be off in the woods away from the consecrated ground. But there was no way we were going to venture out there to see for ourselves, especially since legend says Blackie is sometimes spotted here too. Not only that, but people say you hear the sounds of children laughing and playing in the corn. The whole scene was just too weird for us, so we headed back to the car, where we felt a little safer.

The next stop was the bridge on 240th Avenue, past where routes 85 and H split. We'd heard that the ghost of a local teenage girl has haunted the site ever since her car plunged over the bridge one night when she was driving drunk. It is said that she frightens passing drivers, and that if you look over the bridge you can still see the headlights of her car shining beneath the dark waters.

Even though we'd pretty much wimped out at the previous stops on the tour, we felt brave enough to attempt this one because we could stay close to the car if we parked on the bridge. As we neared our destination, the friend who was driving noticed what appeared to be a large black pickup truck coming up very fast behind us. What alarmed him was that the truck didn't have any lights on. When the rest of us looked back, we could see the truck only because the moon was full that night. Our driver sped up, but the truck just

64

kept gaining on us as if it wanted to ram into our car. Then, all of a sudden, its lights came on and we were blinded.

Everyone let out a shriek. When our eyes adjusted a moment later, the truck was gone. It hadn't backed off, nor was there any place where it could have turned or pulled over. It had simply vanished.

That was it. The driver pulled the car over to gain his composure. We all sat there for a minute trying to calm down. My heart was beating so fast I thought it was going to burst up out of my chest. After about a minute, some-one said in a hushed, breathless voice, "Let's turn around. I want to go home." Our driver didn't wait for someone to second the motion. Our midnight tour through Caryville was over—and we were one very relieved bunch.

Caryville, in Dunn County, is located off Interstate 94.
The cemetery and schoolhouse have been subject to vandalism
and are under police surveillance.

WISCONSIN'S CHICKEN ALLEY

DUE EAST of Caryville across Wisconsin is the town of Shawano. If you're looking for phantom trees, disappearing street signs, disembodied lights, ghostly
voices, and chickens from the grave, then this is the place for you. Chad Lewis
and Terry Fisk, who run the Web site unexplainedresearch.com, describe it here.

"Chicken Alley is a short L-shaped road nestled in the quiet countryside just
outside Shawano. Though short, this picturesque county road has been the
scene of more than one bizarre occurrence. Witnesses traveling the route have
reported spotting several chickens running down the road. But they aren't just
any chickens––you can see right through them! Often these phantom chickens vanish into thin air.

"If you find yourself driving through this area, you might consider exiting
at the intersection of French Road and Chicken Alley. If you stand in the middle of the intersection, some say, ghostly voices will yell for you to get out of
the road. These voices are often interpreted as a warning signal with ominous
overtones. However, you may have difficulty finding the eerie intersection,
since many witnesses swear that the Chicken Alley street sign disappears or
isn't there at all.

"Should you muster the
courage to investigate, look
for a large disfigured tree
hunkered down by the side
of the road, which reportedly can be seen only on full-
moon nights. Many prior
witnesses are amazed to discover that this easily identi-
fiable tree isn't visible on
every trip.

"Before leaving Chicken
Alley, be sure to check your

car's rearview mirror. Some residents have reported seeing mysterious disembodied lights zooming in on their vehicles at great speeds, only to instantly
disappear. The lights take on several shapes, colors, and sizes, and have
approached from all directions. Can you spell YIKES?"

THE COTTON MILL GHOST

by Joseph A. Citro

A STORY FROM OVER ONE HUNDRED years ago supports the notion that ghosts stick around for a reason: to conclude unfinished business, to impart a final message, or to accomplish some necessary task. That story is set in Burlington, Vermont.

Early in the twentieth century, a specter called the Cotton Mill Ghost haunted the area around Lakeside Avenue in Burlington. What makes it differ from most other ghost stories is that literally hundreds of people saw the phantom. In fact, its many appearances made ghost hunting a popular pastime for Burlingtonians, and accounts from the time suggest that searchers were rarely disappointed.

The events, reported in a series of articles in the Burlington *Free Press* during 1900 and 1901, began when a 22-year-old French-Canadian laborer named Marie Blais (pronounced "Blay") moved into one of the factory tenements in Lakeside Park. She worked at the nearby Queen City Cotton Mill (still standing, and today housing a branch of General Dynamics Armament Systems, Inc.).

Early in the evening of June 28, 1900, Marie and two companions—her sister and a friend—were running back to work after a break. A fierce storm raged around them, and heavy winds lent force to the stabbing rain. As the girls raced toward the mill, the 6:40 train was heading up the railroad tracks from Rutland.

Two of the girls dashed safely across the tracks, but something happened to Marie. Maybe she tripped. Maybe her skirt caught on a railroad spike. Maybe the rain blinded her or the wind knocked her down. Or perhaps she was just too slow.

In any event, the engine struck Marie, sending her body seventy-five feet through the air and killing her instantly.

But the big news was yet to come.

CROWDS DESCEND

People soon began to report seeing Marie in the area where she died. Her ghostly form was spotted near the tracks, around the tenement houses, even in the cotton mill itself. Millworkers reported her transparent outline hovering near the looms at night. Others saw Marie, glassy-eyed and pale, wandering aimlessly in the workplace. That fall, frequent appearances of the ghost drew crowds of hopeful spectators to the cotton mill, where witnesses reported strange noises and other unsettling phenomena.

A year after Marie's death, she was still making her presence known. On May 8, 1901, the *Free Press* said her ghost had appeared again, near the lake. Crowds of ghost hunters quickly followed.

Scary details became associated with the story. For instance, people repeatedly heard a soul-shattering shriek near the spot where Marie had died. Phantom obstructions appeared on the tracks, then vanished when the train slowed or stopped. The engine's headlight mysteriously failed in the vicinity of the crash. Just as chilling, Marie would unfailingly appear to the same engineer, at the same spot, every time he drove the train north from Rutland. It is said that her ghost pursued the poor man so relentlessly that he eventually quit his job.

The story of Marie Blais's death and supernatural reappearance became so persuasive that crowds flocked to the spot night after night. But in time, Marie failed to meet them.

WHITHER MARIE?

One possible explanation for Marie's departure came in 1908, eight years after her death. That year, the railroad, fearing more train-pedestrian collisions, installed an elevated bridge at the spot where Marie had met her end. People could enter the factory by crossing an underpass, so no one ever had to set foot on a railroad track.

No one really knows, but perhaps in her wanderings Marie was trying to get the train to slow down as it passed the fatal spot. And because the bridge is still there today, Marie no longer needs to be.

> The building that once housed the Queen City Cotton Mill
> still stands on 128 Lakeside Avenue in Burlington, Vermont.
> The train tracks where Marie Blais was killed are close by.

APPARITION ON SNAKE ROAD
by Tara Fletcher

A FEW YEARS BACK, my young cousins told me about a haunted road in Sanger, California—a small rural town about twenty miles from where I lived. Its name, they said, was Channel Road, but the locals called it Snake Road because it has so many sharp twists and turns that follow the river running alongside.

They also told me the legend behind the road.

Late one night, a young woman was driving along with her two daughters. She failed to negotiate one of the sharp turns, and the car careened off the roadway into the river. The woman was thrown from the car and died instantly as her daughters sat trapped in the sinking vehicle. Unable to escape, they drowned. The car, with the bodies still inside, was found about a mile downstream. Ever since, many people say they've seen the woman walking the road and the riverbank looking for her children.

I was intrigued by my cousins' story, but also very skeptical. Nevertheless, after they begged to be driven down the road one night, my friend and I decided to indulge them. We found Channel Road on a map and set off for it at about 9:00 p.m. Though we followed the directions carefully, we were unable to locate the road. This part of Sanger, on the edge of town, was a mass of trees, weeds, overgrown bushes, and trash. In fact, the overgrowth was so thick it even enveloped the street signs, meaning we had no idea which street we were on.

Low on gas and frustrated over not being able to find the road after almost an hour, we decided to head home. But by this point, we were completely lost. I figured that since I lived south of Sanger, I'd take a road that headed in that direction. I happily turned south onto the first street I came to—though I might have thought twice if the street sign hadn't been obscured.

We were on the road for about two minutes when one of my cousins, who had fallen asleep in the back, suddenly woke up. She started whimpering that she was scared and wanted to go home. A few moments later, she began screaming for us to "get out of here fast!" I assured her that's exactly what we were trying to do. Hoping to calm her fears, I sped up until I was doing 65 mph on the dark country road.

Suddenly, I saw what I thought was a small patch of fog about fifty yards in front of us. My friend quickly said what she saw was an apparition.

69

Regardless of what it was, I slowed down to about 15 mph. As the car neared it, the "fog" began to evaporate—and by the time we reached it, it was gone.

A GHOSTLY WARNING

I was about to speed up again when I saw a faded sign reading, "Dangerous Curves Ahead." Had I not slowed down, I would have missed it.

I thought to myself, "Could this be Snake Road?" I quickly dismissed the notion because the road had been straight so far. A quarter mile farther up the road, we were surprised by a series of sharp, twisting turns, each only twenty or thirty yards from the last. The road twisted crazily for a nerve-wracking three miles until it straightened out again.

We drove another two miles or so until we saw the blinking red lights that signal a stop sign. As we slowed, I asked my friend to see if the street name was visible. I'll never forget what happened next. All the color drained from her face as she answered, "Yes. And it's Channel Road."

That fog, I thought, it must have been . . . I hit the gas and we took off as fast as we could.

No longer a skeptic, I truly believe the apparition we saw was that of the young woman. I also believe she wasn't there to scare us but to save our lives. If she hadn't appeared when she did, I would have been driving along at 65 mph, too fast to see the faded sign and hurtling toward the dangerous curves with no warning. We might have suffered the same fate as the woman and her daughters.

Shortly after our trip down Snake Road, my grandparents were looking to buy a house. They narrowed their search down to two, one of which was on Channel Road. One of the pictures the real estate agent showed them was a side view of a riverfront house. About five yards from the house was a sign with the words "Dangerous Curves Ahead." If my hair didn't stand on end, a cold chill certainly ran down my spine.

From Academy Avenue in Sanger, take Annadale Avenue until it becomes East Annadale Avenue. Look for South Channel Road (a.k.a. Snake Road) on your right. A tributary of the Kings River runs parallel to the road for awhile.

THE NOB HILL GHOST
by Mike Marinacci

IF YOU'RE WALKING along California Street in San Francisco's Nob Hill between Powell and Jones and a young, happy girl in a Victorian-era white gown walks by and smiles at you, smile back. Then watch her very closely. If you see traffic and pedestrians pass right through her body, and if she disappears suddenly and completely, you've seen the Nob Hill Ghost.

She's commonly believed to be Flora Sommerton, a young woman who disappeared on the eve of her social debut in 1876. Flora's parents were pressuring her to marry a wealthy young man whom she despised, so rather than bend to their wishes she took her Paris-made debutante gown and skipped town.

71

DEBUTANTE TO HOUSEKEEPER

News of her disappearance made headlines across the nation, and a $250,000 reward for her return stood for many years. In 1926, she was finally located—dead, in Butte, Montana, where she had been known as Mrs. Butler and worked as a housekeeper. According to police reports, her room was filled with newspaper accounts of her disappearance. She died wearing the same white dress that she'd last been seen in as Flora Sommerton 50 years earlier.

Ghost hunters say Flora still walks in that gown, not in the form of an aged, lonely woman but as a fresh-faced debutante, still trying to find the party that she missed over a century ago and recapture the life she once knew.

San Francisco's Nob Hill Ghost can be found on
California Street between Jones and Powell streets.

HAVE SWORD, WILL TRAVEL

by Lee Jorgensen

ONE NIGHT IN 1994, as I made my way back from a bar in Louisville, Kentucky, to the army base where I was stationed, I took a spectral soldier for a short ride.

At first, I didn't know he was a ghost. My headlights caught him standing by the side of the road, and I stopped a little ways past him before reversing my car and offering him a ride to the base–a good four or five miles off the highway.

As he got into the car, I saw that the uniform he was wearing was an old Civil War outfit, complete with sword. I just assumed he had taken part in one of the Civil War military reenactments sometimes held in the area, so his outfit didn't bother me. I didn't even think it odd that this was happening at three or four in the morning.

WHERE DID HE GO?

We drove no more than a mile or so and were about a hundred yards past an overpass when it happened. The soldier suddenly picked up his sword and asked me to stop. I asked him if he was sure, telling him it was too cold to walk the rest of the way to the base, which is where I assumed he wanted to go. Plus, I explained, if he was Regular Army he would have to be getting up in a few hours like the rest of us. He said "No, thank you" and told me he appreciated the ride.

Dressed in full Confederate garb and very polite besides, he opened the door and got out of the car. After he shut the door, I looked in the passenger-side mirror to see where he was walking–but he wasn't there. I looked on the other side of the car and again saw nothing. I put the car in reverse to use the backup lights, and still saw nothing. I turned the car around and tried to use my headlights, only to see, yet again, nothing. Short grass was all that covered the ground for as far as the eye could see, so no trees or buildings obstructed my view. Yet the soldier was gone.

I went home to my barracks and didn't think anything about it until the next day, when I told some friends what had happened. They said I must've been drunk, but I'd only had a few drinks earlier that night. I wasn't tired either, even though the drive from Louisville to the base took over an hour. I know what I saw, just as I know what I didn't see—the person who had been there seconds before.

I never thought seeing a ghost would be something I would experience, especially a spirit dating from the Civil War, but I'm certain that's what happened to me that night on a Kentucky road.

"DON'T MOCK THIS ROAD!"

ANOTHER SOLDIER once stationed in the South, who uses the e-mail moniker CoutuJA, describes his own encounter with what may have been the ghost of a Civil War soldier.

"Highway 24 runs through Jacksonville, North Carolina, and past Camp Lejeune, and this stretch is said to have been a Civil War trail used by the Union Army. It is also where the Union Army slaughtered a whole company of Confederate soldiers. Many locals believe it is haunted.

"While stationed at Camp Lejeune, I witnessed plenty of weirdness in my many late-night travels on this road. One time I was right in front of the base's front gates when my car's headlights dimmed and the sounds on the radio faded to nothing. At first I thought my car was breaking down, but then something much stranger happened: The gas pedal hit the floor all by itself and the car took off toward a tree. It was about to slam into the tree when it suddenly came to a dead stop. And over the radio I heard a faint voice saying, 'Damn the living who mock this road!'

"Was I hearing the voice of a long-dead Confederate soldier? I'll never know, but I'll also never forget what happened that night."

BRIDE Of THIRTEEN CURVES ROAD

by Chris Gethard

OVER SIXTY YEARS AGO, a terrifying car accident occurred on Cedarvale Road, in Onondaga, New York, just ten miles southwest of Syracuse. Since that fateful day, it has been said that the road, known better by its nickname Thirteen Curves Road, has been haunted by the souls of those who died there.

How the road came to be haunted depends on which of the many legends you believe. But all involve the untimely deaths of a young bride and groom.

The most popular legend says the doomed pair was negotiating the road on their wedding night. While coming around one of the curves of Cedarvale Road, the car veered out of control and into a nearby creek. The impact killed the newlyweds instantly. Since that day, travelers on the road have seen the ghostly image of a bride with glowing eyes. Sometimes she is covered in blood or carries a lantern. In some instances, she simply stands on the hills alongside or walks along its shoulder. At other times, the bride seems vindictive, leaping toward drivers and causing cars to crash.

74

Variations on the legend are almost endless. Among them are the following:

• The couple was riding in a horse-drawn carriage, not a car.

• Only the groom died in the accident, and the bride returns over and over again to search for her deceased lover.

• The accident occurred on a Friday the thirteenth, and the bride has returned on that date ever since.

• The bride appears only on Halloween night, around midnight.

Some who've encountered the phantasmal bride say that she has actually entered their cars. While driving along Thirteen Curves Road, drivers have been stunned to look in their rearview mirrors and see the ghostly lady, dressed in white and usually splattered with blood, sitting in the backseat. By the time they turn around, she has vanished.

MAKING THE PAPERS

It has long been a tradition for people in and around Syracuse to travel to the dark, twisting road on Halloween. Young and old alike have taken nighttime spins on the precarious curved thoroughfare over the years, and dozens have reported brushes with the ghostly bride.

A MIDWESTERN COUNTERPART

IN MOST WAYS, state Highway 66 in Stevens Point, Wisconsin, seems like any other road. Those who know its history, however, will tell you that a section of the highway is cursed by an angry ghost in a wedding dress.

Local lore holds that the road has long been haunted by the spirit of a young woman who was struck and killed by a car while crossing the road on her wedding day. Angered by the fate that befell her, she likes to toy with present-day drivers along the fateful stretch.

The most popular tale involves a police officer. While speeding down the road late one night, he was stunned to see a woman in a wedding dress standing in the middle of the road. She turned and faced him as he bore down on her, and he quickly slammed on the brakes. But it was too late. The officer crashed right into the young woman.

"Where did she come from?" he asked himself in panic. "What's a woman in a wedding dress doing out on the road in the dead of the night?" As the thoughts spun through his head, the horrified cop turned around to look out his rear window—only to come face to face with her ghost sitting in the backseat.

This seems to be one of the favorite tricks of the ghostly bride. Many people say she appears, sometimes with her groom, in the backseat of their cars as they make their way down Highway 66. Others who have seen her report that she simply walks along the side of the road at night.

Whether real or imagined, the lady in white has bequeathed a long-standing nickname to the section of asphalt she haunts: Bloody Bride Road.

Even newspapers have reported the tales of Thirteen Curves. In 2000, the Associated Press distributed a feature story on the ghostly encounters. Syracuse resident Angie Styb, who claims to have seen the bride, was quoted in the story as saying, "It was exciting, shocking, exhilarating—and a little frightening. I know it was real."

Legions of locals claim that Thirteen Curves Road is fraught with danger. For that reason, anyone driving along it should beware. The bloody bride who calls this place home apparently remains as unpredictable as ever.

Thirteen Curves Road, a.k.a. Cedarvale Road, is located to the west of Interstate 81 north, just before the Tanner Valley Golf Course in Syracuse, New York.

THE BRIDGE ON WHITE LADY LANE
by Mindy Reznik

IN PEMBINA COUNTY, North Dakota, the White Lady of local lore was a young farmer's daughter destined for sorrow. The story goes that after she bore a child out of wedlock, her fervidly religious parents forced her to marry against her will. The unhappy bride returned home after the wedding ceremony only to find that her baby had died in its crib.

Apparently, her distress over the baby's death and the thought of having to spend the rest of her life with a man she didn't love were too much for her. Still clad in her wedding gown, the young woman left home and walked to a lonely lane on the outskirts of town, where she hanged herself from a bridge. Today, many people claim that if you travel to the bridge at night, you can see the ghost of the grief-stricken girl hanging there in her white dress.

The bridge spans a small creek between the towns of Leroy and Walhalla, near the Minnesota and Manitoba borders. It is reached by a narrow, overgrown road off county Route 9 that leads through the Tetrault Woods. Known locally as White Lady Lane, the gravel road narrows until it's barely wide enough for a car. The woods surrounding the rickety bridge are dark and eerie. All in all, it's the kind of place that would scare you even if there weren't a ghost lying in wait.

AN OMINOUS FEELING

I'm a student at North Dakota State University in Fargo, and a trip up to the bridge has often been the evening activity of choice for my friends and me. While some of them swear they've seen the White Lady hanging from the bridge, I've yet to see her for myself. Still, I get a strange sensation every time I visit the bridge—an ominous, unsettling feeling that I've never experienced

A HAUNTED RAILROAD BRIDGE?

A SUPPOSEDLY HAUNTED bridge in the Midwest has no ghostly apparition—only the sounds of screams, as reported by Stephen Canner.

"When I was a kid, I lived right down the road from a haunted bridge in Avon, Indiana—a big arched railroad bridge made of concrete. Most of the stories involve the sound of someone screaming or crying as a train crossed over the bridge, and I've heard different explanations of the screams' source. One person said they come from a worker whose body was never removed after he fell to his death in the wet concrete during the bridge's construction. Another says the screams are those of a woman and her baby who had died there, screaming in agony as trains pass over them.

"My dad told me that when he was a teenager in the '50s, he climbed into one of the arches and saw a piece of a saw blade sticking out of the concrete, as if it had been dropped there by a worker when the bridge was being built. He went back later, and the blade was gone.

"I lived within earshot of the bridge for a couple of years and I can't say I ever heard any screaming. But the bridge is on an unlit back road and is positively spooky at night. I wonder if that could be the reason these stories even exist."

anywhere else. It's as if a melancholy presence were hovering nearby. It seems to be everywhere, yet it's nowhere to be seen. The sensation goes away as soon as I leave the spot.

I've heard that other visitors believe they've had closer encounters. They claim that the spirit of the White Lady has actually climbed into their cars or followed them as they left. They've also said that the feeling of being tailed ended as soon as they left White Lady Lane.

The old bridge in the woods always scares the daylights out of me, but my friends and I keep making the long drive north to see it. Someone, or something, keeps drawing us back. Perhaps one day we'll find out whether it's the White Lady herself who's beckoning.

White Lady Lane is difficult to find, but if you take Highway 32 about a mile and a half south of Walhalla, you will come to the entrance of Tetrault Woods State Forest.

AMY OF LICK ROAD

by James A. Willis

DESPITE its innocent-sounding name, Lick Road, in northwest Cincinnati, isn't a road you'd choose for a Sunday drive. It twists and turns its way through woods before dropping you down a steep hill, where it abruptly ends right at the border of Hamilton and Butler counties. Signs say the area beyond the dead end is a park, but it certainly doesn't look like a good place for a quiet nature stroll.

If it's intrigue you're after, however, step this way. Once you've shaken off the ominous vibes the area gives off and learned to ignore the occasional gunshot blasts from nearby target shooters, you might be able to uncover a secret or two about the legend that clings to Lick Road: that it's haunted. No one is sure what happened here, but it wasn't pretty. And it involved a woman named Amy.

Depending on the age of the person you ask, you'll get one of three stories explaining how the road came to be haunted. About the only thing the three most popular legends have in common is Amy's violent, untimely demise.

• On prom night, Amy and her boyfriend decided to park at the end of Lick Road for a little postprom romancing. The evening ended with Amy being raped and killed inside the car by her boyfriend.

• While Amy was out for a moonlit stroll one evening, she was attacked by an unknown assailant—though in some versions the assailant was her stepfather. Amy tried to escape by running into the woods at the end of Lick Road, but she barely made it to the woods' edge before she was caught and killed.

• Amy was killed by an unknown assailant on nearby West Kemper Road. The killer then dumped her body at the far end of Lick Road.

"HELP ME!"

Regardless of the competing versions, they all end with Amy's ghost haunting the end of Lick Road and the adjacent woods. Her modus operandi also varies. In one version, Amy's ghost simply floats through the woods and along the dead end of Lick Road, occasionally either crying out for help or simply screaming at the top of her lungs. A creepier version has her leaving messages on your car. It's said that if you park your car at the end of Lick Road, lock it, and walk away, the windshield will be fogged up when you return. Not only

DOES AMY HAVE COMPANY?

JOSHUA W. VAUGHN and a friend were determined to see for themselves whether Amy really traces "Help me!" on the fogged-up windows of cars parked on Lick Road. Three attempts failed, usually because they and other friends got too spooked by one thing or another. It was the fourth trip, an account of which follows, that was most noteworthy.

"This time, my friend and I took my girlfriend Laura in kind of an experiment. She claims to see spirits all the time, so we thought it would be interesting to see what she saw. Immediately after we parked, she started to stare at something outside of the car. She was silent for a long time, then asked if we could drive away immediately. We did, and when we got somewhere safe, I asked her what the problem was. She said, 'I saw a huge, black figure staring at you through the window on your side of the car.'

"I've also heard that other people have claimed to see a blank-eyed little girl standing at the side of their car, just staring at them. They say that blood covers the girl's dress.

"There is no doubt in my mind that something is out there, but I don't know how sinister it might be. I think Amy is a good spirit, but the one my girlfriend saw—perhaps that's some sort of demon trying to collect Amy's soul"

that, but the words "Help me!" will be written in the condensation . . . from the inside!

A story that popped up recently connects Amy with an old abandoned bridge in the woods off Lick Road. The story says that if you stand in the middle of the bridge and shout, "Amy, I have your baby!" her ghost will appear and chase after you. The reason why she does so is unclear, though some say Amy is angry at having died before she was able to have a child. They believe she may consider the shout to be mocking. Another theory says Amy's ghost comes after you because in life she secretly gave birth to an illegitimate child that she killed by throwing it off the bridge—and Amy's not the type to let other people know her secrets.

From Ohio Route 27, exit onto West Kemper Road.
Lick Road will be on your left.

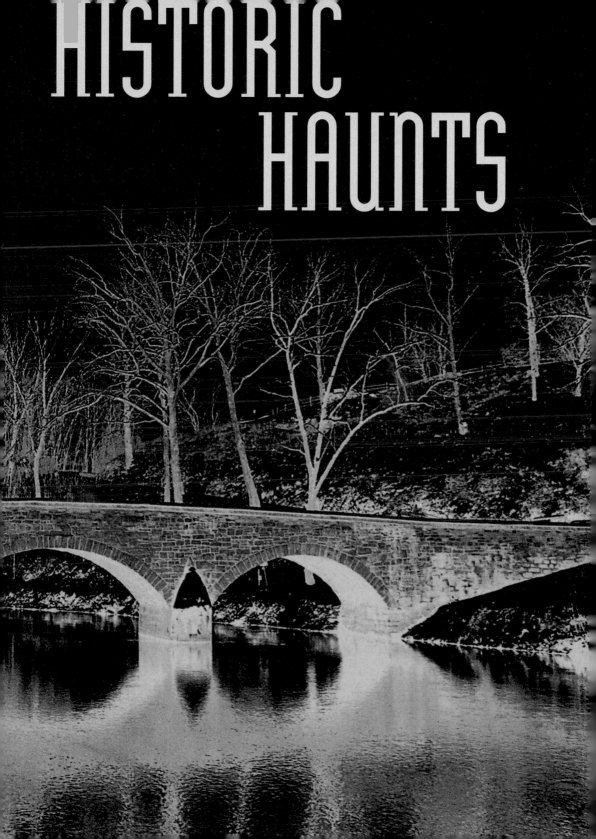

HISTORIC
HAUNTS

I F SOME OF THE HAUNTINGS in this chapter strike you as more noteworthy than those found elsewhere in this book, that's only because they occurred (or still occur) in famous places, including the battlefield at Gettysburg, Pennsylvania, and the Kennedy Space Center at Cape Canaveral, Florida. But for every such site there are at least two you've probably never heard of: a nineteenth-century New Orleans mansion, the ruins of a castle in upstate New York, a long-gone lifesaving station on Florida's east coast, a ramshackle old inn in Nutley, New Jersey.

Moreover, none of the spirits you'll meet here are those of the American statesmen or industrialists or prizewinning authors you remember from your history textbooks, nor are they the ghosts of legendary stars from the world of sports and entertainment. In this chapter, it's the places haunted by spirits that have some kind of historical significance, whether because the sites were in some way tied to a historic event or are simply representative enough of a former era to be accurately described as historic. Some of these sites can still be visited, while others are either off-limits or no longer standing.

And the ghosts themselves? Among the cast of characters are Civil War soldiers who may or may not still roam the fields on which they fought, slaves who suffered horribly at the hands of an imperious society figure in old New Orleans, a music-loving young girl in Memphis who made an ornate theater her home, and ghostly would-be shoppers who poke around the stalls of a famous Seattle market.

Who says that adding a few supernatural shenanigans to your knowledge of history isn't a good idea? And surely picking up a few real-world historical facts on the occasional page is a bonus.

NEW ORLEANS'S HAUNTED MANSION

by Troy Taylor

FOR GENERATIONS, the LaLaurie Mansion of New Orleans has been considered the most haunted house in the French Quarter. The stage was set for the ghostly tales that surround 1140 Royal Street in 1832, when Dr. Louis LaLaurie and his wife, Delphine, highly respected and renowned for their elegant soirées, moved into their newly built mansion. Madame LaLaurie was the most influential Creole woman in the city, and she pampered her guests with the best of everything. Friends would note her extraordinary kindness, but there was a dark side to this woman—a side that some merely suspected but others knew as fact.

Maintenance at the ornate LaLaurie residence was the job of dozens of slaves. Many guests remembered Delphine's sleek mulatto butler: a handsome man who wore expensive livery and never ventured far from her side. In stark contrast, the other slaves were thin and hollow-chested and moved about the house like shadows, never raising their eyes.

Stories began to circulate about Madame LaLaurie's cruel treatment of her staff. It was said that she kept her cook chained to the kitchen fireplace, and that many of the slaves fared much worse. Also, many of these poor unfortunates seemed to leave, never to be seen again.

One woman in the neighborhood witnessed the death of a young slave girl who jumped from the mansion's roof to escape Delphine's whip. The woman also claimed that she later saw the girl being buried in a shallow grave beneath the cypress trees in the garden. The authorities who investigated were appalled by the condition of the slaves, who were then impounded and sold at auction. To their misfortune, the slaves were sold to relatives of Madame LaLaurie, who in turn secretly bought them back. She explained to her friends that the death of the girl had been a horrible accident, but so many people remained skeptical that the LaLauries' social standing went into decline.

HOUSE OF HORRORS

It was a terrible fire in April 1834 that exposed the LaLauries for who they truly were. In the chaos, Delphine's only concern was for her valuables. When asked about her slaves, she snapped that her neighbors needn't interfere with family business. When neighbors and firefighters disregarded her and began to search for the slaves, they discovered a locked iron-hinged door leading to the attic. After Dr.

86

LaLaurie refused to open it, they broke down the door.

What greeted them was almost beyond human imagination. More than a dozen slaves, both male and female and all naked, were chained to the wall of the confined chamber. Others were strapped to makeshift operating tables or locked in dog cages. Human body parts were scattered about the room, and bloody organs were placed haphazardly in buckets. Bones and human teeth were stacked on shelves and next to a collection of whips and paddles.

According to newspaper and eyewitness accounts, the slaves had been tortured. Worse, torture had been administered in such a way as to make death occur slowly. Fleeing the scene in horror and disgust, the rescuers summoned doctors, who rushed to the slaves' aid.

News of the atrocities soon spread throughout New Orleans, and angry crowds gathered in front of the mansion. It was believed that Delphine alone was responsible for the horrors, with her husband turning a blind, if knowing, eye.

Those who had first broken into the attic made formal statements to the authorities about their discovery in the attic chamber. And a female slave testified that Madame LaLaurie would sometimes inflict torture on the captives while the couples' guests dined and danced below. But before any arrests could be made, Madame LaLaurie and her family escaped, never to be officially seen in New Orleans again. Nor was she ever tried for her crimes.

Her flight so enraged the crowd that they took out their anger on the house Madame LaLaurie had left behind. By the time authorities arrived to restore order, the contents were almost completely destroyed. The mansion was closed and sealed and remained silent, uninhabited, and abandoned. Or did it?

WAILING SPIRITS

The stories of hauntings at 1140 Royal Street began almost as soon as the LaLauries fled. The mansion, which remained vacant for a few years after its sacking by the mob, fell into a state of ruin. Many people claimed to hear screams of agony coming from the empty house at night and to observe apparitions of slaves walking on the balconies and grounds. Some stories claimed that vagrants who had entered the mansion seeking shelter were never heard from again.

The mansion was placed on the market by the LaLauries' agent in 1837. But the man who bought it lived there for only three months, plagued by strange noises, cries, and groans in the night. He tried leasing the rooms, but the tenants stayed for a few days at the most. The new owner finally gave up, and the mansion was abandoned.

After a turn as an integrated high school, then a school for black children, the mansion once again became a center for New Orleans society in 1882, when an English teacher turned it into a "conservatory of music and a fashionable dancing school." That ended after a local newspaper apparently claimed the teacher engaged in some improprieties with female students, and the school was closed.

The mansion was abandoned again until the late 1890s, when it was bought and converted into cheap housing for a new wave of Italian immigrants. For many of the tenants, not even the low rent was enough to keep them there—hardly surprising, given the strange occurrences. One man claimed to have been attacked by a naked black man in chains, who then suddenly vanished. Others claimed to have found butchered animals in the

87

A TEMPORARY LODGER?

IN THE LATE 1880S, rumors tied the eccentric son of a wealthy New Orleans family to the LaLaurie Mansion. Joseph Edouard Vigne supposedly lived secretly in the house for several years until his death in 1892. He was found dead on a tattered cot, apparently having lived in filth.

Hidden away in the surrounding rooms was a collection of antiques and treasure. A bag containing several hundred dollars was found near his body, and another search uncovered several thousand dollars hidden in his mattress. For some time after, rumors that the mansion held a concealed treasure circulated, but few people dared to go in search of it.

How much of the tale is true is lost to time. Still, was Vigne's ghostly voice one of the many that frightened later inhabitants of the cursed house?

---

mansion. Children were attacked by a phantom with a whip, and others saw strange figures wrapped in shrouds.

One night, a young mother was terrified to find a woman in elegant evening clothes bending over her sleeping infant. The mysterious woman vanished when approached. Aside from the ghost sightings, the sounds of screams, groans, and cries—said to have come from the locked and abandoned attic—regularly reverberated through the house at night. After word spread of the strange goings-on, the mansion was deserted once again.

A SUCCESSION OF OWNERS

The mansion later became a tavern, then a furniture store. The tavern owner, taking advantage of the building's history, named his establishment The Haunted Saloon. The owner even kept a record of any strange things encountered by patrons.

The furniture store didn't fare so well. The owner first suspected vandals when, on more than one occasion, he found all of his merchandise covered in a dark, foul-smelling liquid. He waited one night with a shotgun, hoping the vandals would return. When dawn came, the furniture had been ruined yet again, even though no one had entered the building. The owner soon closed down the store.

The mansion changed hands several times until 1969, when a retired New Orleans doctor bought it. He restored the house to its original opulent state, though with a common living room in the front and five luxury apartments in the rear. While he was able to attract new tenants, not all of them lived in the mansion without incident. In the early 1970s, a tenant named Mrs. Richards claimed to have witnessed a number of unexplained events in her apartment: water faucets turning on by themselves, doors opening and closing, and assorted minor annoyances. Other tenants spoke of a young girl's screams coming from the courtyard at night.

These stories lived on for years. Only after the mansion again became a private residence did the strange occurrences cease. Many in New Orleans believed the hauntings had simply faded away with time. That is possible, of course, but only if spirits born of a tragedy so horrifying could ever find their rest.

EPILOGUE

A number of years ago, the owners were remodeling the LaLaurie Mansion when they found skeletal remains in a large pit beneath the wooden floor of one of the back rooms. The haphazard positioning of the remains suggested that the bodies had been dumped unceremoniously into the pit.

Speculation is that this was Madame LaLaurie's own private graveyard—that she had removed sections of the floor and hastily buried the bodies to avoid detection. While the discovery of the remains answered one question, it unfortunately created another. Solving the mystery of the sudden disappearance of many of the LaLaurie slaves made some people wonder just how many other victims Madame LaLaurie had claimed—and to wonder how many of them might still be lingering behind.

> This building was converted to a private residence by the current owners, who ask that readers please respect their privacy.

A FAMOUS MARKET'S SPIRITS
by Jefferson Davis

SEATTLE'S WORLD-RENOWNED Pike Place Market grew from an act of outrage in 1907, when the price for a pound of onions went from ten cents to one dollar. On August 17, 1907, eight farmers parked their wagons at the corner of First and Pike streets and sold directly to their customers. While the market that took root expanded to several buildings, some of the traditional shops have occupied the same stalls for ninety-plus years.

If there ever was a place that reminds me of a doorway into an alternate universe, it's Pike Place Market. I always find a surprise just around the corner or down another narrow stairway. Sometimes I walk down stairs that end at solid walls. Other passages open into galleries. Many tourists assume the mar-

ket is limited to the main building, but it actually extends through many buildings on and around Pike Place Way.

AN ASSORTMENT OF GHOSTS

The throngs of shoppers and tourists who browse the countless stalls aren't the only presences in Pike Place Market. Three or four resident ghosts haunt the shops and corridors, if numerous shopkeepers and visitors are to be believed. Over the years, I took it upon myself to investigate, and in the process I heard stories of the following cast of characters.

The American Indian. This female ghost is the most well-known spirit at the market. She spends a lot of time in the "down under" shops below the ground floor of the Main Market building. Some people believe she is Princess Kickisomlo, the daughter of Chief Seattle. (The Suquamish princess died in 1896 at the age of 85 and was buried at nearby Lake View Cemetery.) Witnesses describe the ghost as elderly, with her gray hair tied up in long braids. One person reported that she glowed with a white light.

The merchants say the ghost has been seen everywhere—often only yesterday, and not just in the lower level. She's been spotted at the Sound View Café, in the Leland building, along Flower Row, and in the Craft Emporium in the Main Market building. In the past she was associated with the Old Friend Memorabilia Shop, the former Goodwill Store (now the Market's childcare facility), and the Shakespeare & Company bookstore (now Lionheart Books).

The Craft Emporium is also known as the Bead Shop. Several years ago the owner, Lynn Roberts, saw an elderly Indian woman looking at the collection of seed beads. When Roberts asked if she could help her, the woman disappeared.

The Little Boy. The Craft Emporium had a second ghost who spent time there—a small boy. One day he walked up to proprietor Roberts, tugged her sleeve to get her attention, and then suddenly disappeared. The next day, a radio turned on all by itself. Roberts unplugged it, but even without power it kept playing. Was the tyke easily aggravated? Possibly so, because he also had a tendency to throw beads at employees and customers.

When I visited the shop in 1998, I was told that a shaman had performed an exorcism there, and that most of the strange goings-on had stopped. Maybe the ghosts just moved on to another shop?

The Large Woman. Sightings of the ghost of an obese woman date to a time when an overweight female customer fell through a weak floor and onto a table or floor below. However, I haven't been able to find anyone who knows where—or even if—the incident actually happened.

The Tall African American. The ghost of a tall black man was said to have haunted the Vitium Capitale restaurant. This contention cannot be further investigated, however, because the Vitium Capitale is no longer at Pike Place Market. The mystery became even more elusive when no one I spoke with seemed to know which building or space the restaurant had occupied.

MORE STRANGE HAPPENINGS?

There are a few hauntings at Pike Place Market that aren't associated with a specific spirit. Here are two examples:

• At a candy store in the Main Market building, employees put the candy scoops away in a storage cupboard at the end of the day. In the morning, the scoops are back with the candy.

• At Left Bank Books, located in the Corner Market building, some employees have said that when they're alone in the store, they've heard footsteps in the empty aisles.

However many ghosts wander the shops and corridors and sidewalks of Pike Place Market—or ever floated through in the past—it somehow makes sense that this sprawling complex would become their residence of choice. It could be said that the life and colorful atmosphere that made the market famous make it that much more attractive to the spirits of the dead.

PIKE PLACE MARKET
1531 Western Avenue, Seattle WA 98101

THE WHITE LADY'S CASTLE
by Erik A.

IN ROCHESTER, NEW YORK, lie the ruins of what is called the White Lady's Castle. The castle was destroyed in a fire many years ago, and all that's left is a large stone wall and pillars facing Lake Ontario. Behind the wall and south of the lake are dense woods with several trails leading to swamps, all within Durand Eastman Park.

The story, as I understand it, begins about a hundred years ago when a very rich man moved to Rochester and built the castle for his wife. It was set back in the woods, and the grounds led back toward the lake and ended at a wall high above the rocky shoreline.

The couple had a daughter, and the family led a very happy life. One night, the daughter was left home alone with two Doberman guard dogs for protection. Thieves broke into the castle, killed the dogs, and discovered the daughter, who was hiding. They raped and killed her, then threw her lifeless body over the wall and onto the rocks below. It took days before her body was discovered.

In time, the girl's mother went insane from grief and jumped to her death at the very spot where her daughter's body was found. The loss of his family made the man go mad as well. He eventually set fire to the castle he had built for his wife.

It's said that if you go up to the woods behind the ruins late at night, you can hear the daughter's screams. Just as frightening, a large white glowing orb—thought by some to be the mother—floats through the woods. Two smaller red orbs, which might be the guard dogs, circle it. Usually, the orbs appear after the screams are heard.

This area is something of a lover's lane for teens, and it's reported that some of the young men who have parked here have seen a green fog appear around their cars, followed by the white and red orbs. One horrifying version of this scenario claimed that when the orbs disappeared, so did the young men—and that their bodies were always found in the nearby swamps.

Spirits of Antietam
by Troy Taylor

OF ALL OF THE CIVIL WAR SITES where the dead are said to walk, none are as haunted as the battlefields. It was on these fields where men fought, lived, died, suffered, screamed, and bled—and where, most likely, they left a little piece of themselves behind. On the battlefields are the spirits of the past.

On the far western edge of Maryland is the Antietam Battlefield, found just outside of the small town of Sharpsburg. Perhaps the best preserved of all of the sites the National Park Service administers as National Battlefields, it looks much as it did at the time of the battle in 1862. On a clear day, when a crisp wind is blowing across the grass, you can almost imagine yourself in another time. You feel that if you looked up, you might actually catch a glimpse of a weary soldier, trudging on toward either death or victory.

The Battle of Antietam took place on September 17, 1862. It would become known as the bloodiest single day of the entire war, with combined casualties of 23,100 wounded, missing, and dead. The battle itself was considered a draw, but the effect on both sides was staggering. The wounded were left behind at places like the Lutheran Church in Sharpsburg, a house west of the town of Mt. Airy, and at Grove Farm, which President Lincoln visited after the battle. It has been said that the floorboards in this house are still stained with the blood of those who fell, and that more than 140 years later these stains can't be sanded or scrubbed away.

Many other tales still linger about the battle, and some people believe that the soldiers—and the aftermath of the deeds committed here—may linger too.

"FAUGH-A-BALLAUGH!"
The battle at Antietam was centered in the middle of General Lee's line, at a sunken country road dividing the fields of two farmers. Lee ordered the center of the line to be held at all costs. On the day of the battle, the road served as a rifle pit for two Confederate brigades. Union troops approached within yards of the road before being fired on. The Union commander fell at once and his men wavered and then retreated, only to charge the Confederate line five more times.

The Federals repeatedly tried to overrun the sunken road, with unit after unit falling back under the rain of fire from the Confederate opposition.

Finally, they reached a vantage point where they could fire down on the road's defenders. The once seemingly impregnable position had become a death trap. In the last stages of battle, which Union soldiers would later describe as "like shooting animals in a pen," the road rapidly filled with bodies two and three deep. The road soon came to be known as Bloody Lane.

Perhaps the most heroic participants at Bloody Lane were the 69th New York Infantry, part of the famous Irish Brigade. The Union troops attacking the road had been in serious trouble until they caught sight of the emerald banner of the Irish Brigade on the horizon. The Irish announced their arrival with the sounds of drums and volleys of fire as they attacked the Confederate position. As they charged, the brigade screamed loudly and shouted the battle cry *faugh-a-ballaugh* (fah-ah-bah-LAH), Gaelic for "clear the way!"

The thunderous sound of weaponry filled the air as men fell on both sides. The brigade fought fiercely, but battle cries eventually became fainter. The Irish Brigade lost more than sixty percent of their men that day and wrote their name in the bloody pages of American history.

REPLAYING THE PAST?

In the decades since the end of the Civil War, enough strange things have taken place on or around the Antietam battlefield to make many believe that events of the past are still being replayed today. Some who visited have reported hearing phantom gunfire echoing along the sunken road and smelling smoke and gunpowder. Others claim to have seen the apparitions of men in both Confederate and Federal uniforms, often assumed to be reenactors of some event on the battlefield until they abruptly vanish.

Following are four of the places where strange incidents have been reported—three on the battlefield and one in Sharpsburg.

Bloody Lane. Several years ago, a group of boys from the McDonna School in Baltimore took a school trip to Antietam. After touring the battlefield and Bloody Lane, the boys were allowed to wander about and think about what they had learned. They were then asked to record their impressions for a history assignment. The most attention-getting comments were written

by several boys who walked down the road to the Observation Tower, located where the Irish Brigade charged the Confederate line.

The boys wrote of hearing strange noises coming from the field near the tower. Some described the noises as a chant, others as a song similar to the Christmas carol "Deck the Halls"—specifically, to the lyrics *fa-la-la-la-la.* Had they heard the sounds of the Irish Brigade "clearing the way"?

Another eerie occurrence was reported by battle reenactor Paul Boccadoro of Company G, 96th Pennsylvania Volunteers. One night, after an annual living-history event, Boccadoro and three other men broke off from the dozen or so members who had stopped to rest on the banks of sunken Bloody Lane and walked to the Observation Tower at the end. After a while, the captain sent two men to fetch them, and Boccadoro wrote of what happened next.

"No sooner had those two begun to walk toward us than one of the men who'd stayed on the banks started to hear the sounds of shoes with heelplates—horseshoelike plates we wear on our leather shoes—on the gravel and earth. They first heard two pair of heelplates, then four pair, then six, and so on. They could also hear equipment rustling around on bodies: knapsacks, canteens, and cartridge boxes.

"If anyone knows what it sounds like when men march on a dusty road with full gear on, it's reenactors. Just as the other men began to sit up and peer into the darkness down the road, the sounds faded away as quickly as they came. One man jumped up, went down the road, and looked over the fences and road banks, only to find weeds and small shrubs.

"After talking later that night, we figured that if this was some sort of 'ghost regiment,' it might have followed the two men who had begun to walk down the road to the tower to fetch us."

Phillip Pry House. This brick farmhouse, which overlooks the battlefield, was commandeered by the Union Army's General George McClellan to use as his headquarters during the battle. Shortly after the battle began, General Joseph Hooker was brought to the house for treat-

97

ment of the wounds he suffered. He was followed by General Israel B. Richardson, who died of painful abdominal wounds at the house more than six months after the battle had ended.

Today the house is owned by the National Park Service and isn't open to visitors—but that hasn't stopped it from spawning strange stories. In 1976, the house caught fire and about a third of it was gutted. It was during the restoration that many unexplained events were recorded.

One day, during a meeting of park personnel, the wife of one of the park rangers met a woman in old-fashioned clothes coming down the staircase. She asked her husband who the lady in the long dress was, but he had no idea what she was talking about.

A short time later, workers arrived at the house to see a woman standing in an upper window—in the room where General Richardson had died. They searched the house, and after going upstairs they realized the room where the woman had been standing had no floor! Could the apparition have been that of Richardson's wife, Frances, who cared for him on his deathbed?

It wouldn't be the last time the ghost was seen. On one occasion, a new

MANASSAS MIST

IN NEIGHBORING Virginia, the hallowed Civil War battlefield at Manassas also has been the scene of strange occurrences. Matt Voshell describes an eerie evening that he and his friends spent there.

"On Halloween Eve 2004, a few friends and I went to the Manassas Civil War battlefields. We walked around the main battlefields in the dark for an hour and saw nothing. A few people grew bored and left, leaving only six of us.

"We then ventured to the other side of one battlefield, which contained a few monuments and a cemetery. Immediately after we started to walk down a long and curvy paved road, a thick mist rolled in. It was so thick I couldn't see six inch-es in front of me. This was accompanied by what I'm sure was the sound of cannon fire and horses.

"A few friends had gone about two hundred feet ahead of the rest of us and into the cemetery. They ran back, claiming that they had heard the same thing and that someone had also ridden a horse right past them.

"We left immediately after that."

contracting crew had to be hired when the original crew working in the house caught a glimpse of the spectral figure and abandoned the project.

It is also reported that phantom footsteps have been heard going up and down the staircase. Might they have belonged to the worried generals, pacing up and down in anticipation of battle? Or perhaps to Fannie Richardson as she climbed the stairs to minister to her dying husband? No one knows for sure, but those who have heard the footsteps are convinced they're not just the sounds of the old house settling.

Burnside Bridge. People who have spent time at the battlefield area known as Burnside Bridge—especially park rangers and Civil War reenactors who have been there after dark—say that strange things happen in the vicinity of the bridge as well. Historians report that the fighting that took place here in 1862 left a number of fallen soldiers behind, and many of them were hastily buried in unknown locations near the bridge. Nighttime visitors to the bridge report seeing blue balls of light moving about in the darkness and the sound of a phantom drum beating out a cadence that gradually fades away.

St. Paul Episcopal Church. Near the center of Sharpsburg is another site connected to the battle: St. Paul Episcopal Church. It was used as a Confederate field hospital following the battle, though it was heavily damaged. Those who have lived close to it claim they've heard the screams of the dying and injured coming from inside the long-since restored church. They have also seen unexplained lights flickering from the church's tower.

99

The battlefield at Antietam is a place where thousands of soldiers fought, suffered, and perished, their lives ending long before they should have. If ghosts linger because they haven't finished the business of a life cut short, it is hardly surprising that Antietam has more than its share of spirits.

ANTIETAM BATTLEFIELD VISITOR CENTER
5831 Dunker Church Road, Sharpsburg MD 21782

THE HAUNTED LAUNCH PAD

by Charlie Carlson

ON JANUARY 27, 1967, America was shocked by the news that three astronauts had lost their lives in a tragic accident at Kennedy Space Center. It happened on Launch Pad 34 during a preparation test just two weeks before Lieutenant Colonel Virgil "Gus" Grissom, Lieutenant Colonel Edward White, and Lieutenant Commander Roger Chaffee were to blast off into space on Apollo mission AS-204. While they were secured inside the cabin of their command module, a short circuit in the wiring beneath Grissom's seat caused a spark, resulting in a fire. Because the cabin was filled with pure oxygen, the fire spread rapidly, engulfing the three astronauts. They never had a chance.

The old Apollo-Saturn launch complex was abandoned decades ago, but at one point became a stop on the Space Center visitors tour. However, according to an unofficial source at the visitors center, "It is no longer included on the tour due to strange occurrences."

Indeed, stories of agonizing screams and floating apparitions have circulated for years about the Apollo launch pad where the three astronauts died. A former NASA security guard recalled, "Everybody talked about it being haunted. I mean, after all, look at what happened there: three astronauts burned up. I used to patrol that area, and I'd always get an eerie feeling out there around them old buildings, especially at night. I've heard a few guys say they'd heard screams there, yet there would be no sign of anyone. Of course, nobody ever made an official report or they would've been called loony."

THE WANDERING PATCH

Kennedy Space Center, with its tight security, is not an easy place to conduct a paranormal investigation—unless, that is, the investigators are the Spookhunters, an Orlando-based paranormal investigative group founded by Owen Sliter. A mixture of skeptics and believers, the group seems to have no difficulty getting permission to snoop around even the most secure places, including government sites.

In 2004, Sliter and his team visited the abandoned launch complex at the Space Center for the purpose of examining paranormal activity. "Knowing the horror behind Launch Complex 34, you can't help but feel solace and respect for what happened there," says Sliter, a skeptical ghostbuster. "It was almost

dark when we got there and it was really freaky, but we were on a mission to find out if the three astronauts were haunting the old launch pad."

The Spookhunters use both conventional and nonconventional devices in their investigations. "With us, you may see anything from EMF [electromagnetic field] detectors to Ouija boards," Sliter explained. "At the Visitor Center's souvenir shop, I even purchased an authentic Apollo 1 shoulder patch. I figured if the launch pad was haunted and I left something connected to the tragedy, maybe the spirits would show themselves." He carefully placed the patch in the exact center of where the three astronauts had lost their lives.

"After leaving the patch, we went to search for an underground room in Section Four," said Sliter. "We had a little trouble finding it because it was incredibly dark. I went down into the darkness of the room but found nothing. We then checked the old control rooms in Section Two. I wasn't scared of ghosts, but this area was really creepy. One room connected to another room that connected to another, and so on, like a dark maze. There was a long, dark tunnel that ran under the launch pad. We had no idea of what was lurking in there, but we could hear croaking frogs, because it was flooded with water.

"We finally made our way back to the surface. And despite that eerie feeling, we didn't find any ghosts. We were about to pack up when I remembered the patch."

Sliter then described what happened next. "We went back to retrieve the patch, which took a while because it wasn't where I had placed it. Strangely, the patch was about thirty feet southwest of where I had left it."

Sliter admitted he couldn't explain how the patch had mysteriously moved a full ten yards. Others theorized that the spirits were unhappy with the intrusion and caused the patch to move. Could it have been a subtle message from the ghosts of the three astronauts? Whatever the case, the old Apollo launch complex is the only part of the Kennedy Space Center that has ever been connected to anything even remotely supernatural.

KENNEDY SPACE CENTER
NASA Parkway (East State Road 405), Cape Canaveral FL 32920

THE GHOST WITH THE MISSING SHOE
by K. Martin

IT WAS A DREARY, overcast November school day in Nutley, New Jersey, when my friends and I decided to cut school and devote the day to our favorite pastime: hanging out in Yanticaw Park, smoking cigarettes. But we soon got bored. I mean, how many cigarettes can you smoke?

We looked across the park and noticed a bunch of construction workers packing it up for the day. They were working on the old Military Hall, an inn that dates back to the 1700s.

I passed Military Hall every day as I went to and from school. It was decorated on three sides with portraits of British soldiers preparing themselves for battle, but it was hardly something pretty to look at. The shingles on its roof were either scruffy or missing, and warped wooden gutters made the place seem as old as time itself. Broken panes of glass in the windows on the second floor resembled the teeth of a prehistoric monster, ready to rip apart anything in its path (in my teenage imagination, at least). The place, in short, was an eyesore.

It looked as though the construction workers were about to demolish it and make way for some new something-or-other. Being young and adventurous, we headed toward the abandoned building with our schoolbooks in our arms and exploration on our minds. If only we'd known what was in store!

AN OUT-OF-THE-BLUE REQUEST
After the construction workers left, we approached the front door. Pushing hard, we managed to rip off the hasp and padlock and gain entrance. We found ourselves in the main bar area, in darkness because the windows had been boarded up. Though we could barely see the bar, we could tell it was still intact, down to the old whiskey bottles lining the shelves. Rows of tables and chairs remained where patrons of the inn once sat, and a dilapidated player piano sat in the corner.

I can still smell the musty aroma that filled the air that day. Shadows darted back and forth in the rays of light that seeped through the boarded-up windows. The sunrays looked almost alive, like they were performing some kind of ritual dance. Just standing there sent shivers down my spine.

Someone suggested we explore the cellar, or maybe the upstairs. As far as

103

I was concerned, the cellar was out of the question, and I had a feeling that the others felt the same. So we made our way to the long, cathedral-type stairs. Glancing up, we saw that half of them were missing. We'd need a ladder if we wanted to get to the second floor and, like it or not, we had to check to see if there was one in the cellar.

The door to the cellar had an old lock that was easy to break off, unlike the hasp on the front door. The adrenaline flowed as we slowly pushed it open. I could have almost heard the heart of the guy next to me beating if my own hadn't been pounding so loudly. The door creaked and moaned as if its hinges hadn't moved in a century. Once the door was fully open, a damp musty odor rose up. We must have found a wine or root cellar, I thought.

Flicking our Bics, we stepped deeper into the darkness. As I had guessed, we were in a wine cellar. Seeing all the dust-covered bottles wasn't exactly a thrill for a bunch of young boys, so we climbed the stairs back up to the first floor.

That's when we heard it: a movement of some kind. We made it into the bar area in time to see a shoe tumbling down the stairs from the second floor to the first-floor landing. We walked over to look at what turned out to be a woman's leather shoe—small, tattered, and topped with a tarnished gold buckle.

Then came the voice. "Could someone help me find my shoe?" a woman called down to us from somewhere on the second floor.

We turned and looked at each other, our feet frozen to the floor. We knew nobody could have made it up to the second floor. And since we'd just broken in, it wasn't likely that someone else was in the inn with us. It didn't take a genius to figure out that something strange was going on.

The voice rang down the stairs again, only this time it was deeper and less like a woman's. "Please, could you get my shoe?" it growled.

105

OUR HASTY RETREAT

Looking up to the second floor, we could see the black shadow of a figure. That was all we needed to hightail it out of there, kicking up a trail of dust behind us. And I'm certain I heard "her" laughing as we ran away. I don't think I've ever felt that scared in my life, and just writing about the encounter is making the hair on the back of my neck stand on end.

I remember that day very clearly, down to leaving my books behind on the bar. Oh well, they're long gone, just as Military Hall is. The spot where it stood on Williams Street is now a municipal parking lot.

Maybe on some moonlit November night on Williams Street, you might cross paths with the ghost with the missing shoe. If you're brave enough, you could do me a favor and ask her if she still has my books!

STRANGE NIGHTS AT FORT MIFFLIN

by Rodney Anonymous

ON A COLD and windy April night in Philadelphia, my nephew Jeff and I were chased out of Casemate Number 5 at historic Fort Mifflin by weird sounds and strange occurrences.

But before I begin my story, a little history is in order.

In September 1777, British soldiers marched from Maryland to Pennsylvania and defeated George Washington's Continental Army at the Battle of Brandywine. After the British took control of Philadelphia, the only thing stopping them from crushing the Continental forces was a strained supply line—to wit, the Delaware. Because the occupiers would have to capture Fort Mifflin before they could bring provisions upriver from Chester, Washington devised a plan that would buy him enough time to get the bulk of his army to Valley Forge for training. He sent three hundred men to hold the fort, and despite a fierce attack from the British, they managed to hold out for three weeks, enabling Washington and his troops to reach Valley Forge. There—despite the toll taken by disease during a harsh winter—the troops would change from a loose-jointed army to a fighting force that would prevail over the British in the end. Hence the nickname earned by Fort Mifflin: "The Fort That Saved America."

MEET THE GHOSTS

Considering Fort Mifflin's turbulent past, it's not surprising that some people consider the place to be haunted. While ten or eleven spirits have supposedly been encountered, Billy Howe and Elizabeth Pratt are the most well known.

Billy Howe was a deserter from the Civil War. When a detachment from the fort was sent to retrieve him, Billy shot and killed an officer while being captured. Returned to the fort, Billy was held in Casemate Number 5, one of a series of dungeonlike structures dug below the fort's eastern perimeter. He was later tried, convicted of murder, and sentenced to death.

His hanging turned into a giant party. Legend has it that Billy, still angry about the giggling women in the raucous crowd, remains at the fort's Casemate Number 5, where he sometimes attempts to strangle any female visitor who dares to intrude.

Elizabeth Pratt, who allegedly haunts the officers' quarters where she is said to have committed suicide, is known as the Screaming Lady. On several occasions, the police have been called to Fort Mifflin to investigate what sounds like a woman's screams. It's also rumored that a police report notes that the officers once pursued the figure of a female onto the ramparts, only to see her vanish.

MY FIRST VISIT

In my spare time, I'm a reporter for the Paul Kircher Show on WWDB in Philadelphia. In March 2003, Paul called to say he wanted to do a piece that involved my spending the night in a supposedly haunted location. Sure, I thought to myself. Why not? We settled on Fort Mifflin. After a few phone calls, Paul got permission for me to spend the night there.

I was positive that the evening would pass by uneventfully. I made a preliminary visit to the fort to interview some of the people who worked there. When the time came to stay overnight, I decided to take my 19-year-old nephew Jeff with me—because if there's one thing I've learned from watching countless horror movies, it's that teenagers attract ghosts.

Accompanied by Paul, ghost-magnet Jeff and I arrived at the fort in the late afternoon on a perfect April day. We spent a couple of hours exploring, then started making preparations for the night.

To ensure maximum ghost-spotting potential, we all thought Jeff and I should spend the night in Billy Howe's supposed stomping ground, Casemate Number 5. So as the sun was setting, we dragged two large wooden pallets that would serve as beds down to the casemate and then built a roaring fire in the casemate's fireplace.

My first inkling that things might go a little less smoothly than I'd anticipated came shortly after we finished getting everything ready. Wayne, the on-site groundskeeper, was giving us a tour of the other casemates when the four of us entered Casemate Number 1. Wayne was well into a lecture on the history of the cryptlike casemates when the door to the casemate suddenly began to rattle loudly. The rattling continued for a full minute. When it stopped, Wayne said, "Wow, it's never done that before."

We composed ourselves and returned to the warm glow of the fire in Casemate Number 5, where Wayne and Paul stayed until about 11:30 before leaving Jeff and me on our lonesome.

Jeff and I sat and chatted a while when an uneasy feeling settled on the room and we fell silent. For the next hour or so, we barely spoke, our attention constantly drawn to the casemate's door.

Around 1:00, we were so nervous I decided we should exit the casemates

107

for a little while and roam the fort "interviewing" the ghosts. Our MO would be to walk into the various buildings with a tape recorder, ask questions, and then wait for a response. I didn't plan on listening to the tapes until after I had returned home.

After conducting the "interviews," we returned to Casemate Number 5. Right away, we got the same creepy feeling we'd had earlier, so we abandoned the idea of sleeping in the casemate altogether.

There were two reasons we made this decision. First, Paul had started calling me on my cell phone to relay an assortment of fun facts he'd picked up on the Internet about the fort's supposed ghosts. Second, we started hearing loud noises. We took our sleeping bags out of Casemate Number 5 and set them out on the fort's northern rampart facing the reassuring lights of Philadelphia. Then we began to hear strange banging sounds coming from different directions, followed by a loud thud that sounded like a bass drum coming from almost exactly below us.

I called Paul and told him that we'd be very appreciative if he'd get down to the fort ASAP so he could join in the fun. A certain degree of panic surfaced when I realized my cell phone was about to lose power, even though I'd charged it the night before. All of a sudden we wanted out of there.

Paul finally agreed to stick it out with us until the sun came up. About forty minutes later, he pulled into the parking lot and Jeff and I let him in.

Shortly after he arrived, the three of us set up my tape recorder on the windowsill in a room rumored to be haunted by Elizabeth Pratt (a.k.a. the Screaming Lady). We did it because Wayne had told us that someone had once left a recorder running there and had gotten a pop that sounded like a gunshot.

We spent the rest of the night talking in the vending-machine room.

When it came time to leave, Paul, Jeff, and I returned to the room to retrieve the tape player. It was exactly where we had left it and was still running, only now it was upside down. Searching for a logical explanation, I figured that because I was so tired, I must have placed it that way, but Paul and Jeff swear that I placed it on the windowsill right side up.

Naturally, I was curious to hear if anything was on the tape. After returning home, I turned on the recorder. The tape was blank. In fact, all of the tapes I made at the fort the previous night were blank. The trusty tape recorder that had usually served me so well had stopped working.

LIKELY EXPLANATIONS

While I enjoy a good mystery, what I enjoy even more is a mystery explained. So a few months later, Paul, Jeff, and I again arranged to stay the night at Fort Mifflin. But this time we were joined by Bob and Eric from PhACT—the Philadelphia Alliance of Critical Thinkers.

Within a few hours of arriving, Bob and Eric had resolved why the battery in my cell phone had died. In the underground casemate, the phone was constantly searching for a signal, which rapidly drained the battery. They also explained why Jeff and I had been so uneasy in Casemate Number 5. That roaring fire we built was sucking all of the oxygen out of the poorly ventilated casemate, and our survival instincts kicked in and told us to get out.

Scoring bonus points, they came up with a possible explanation for Elizabeth Pratt's "screams." Under the right atmospheric conditions, the roar of cars drag racing nearby echoes through the fort and can sound like human cries.

Emboldened by these findings, I retired to Casemate Number 5 and drifted off to sleep. Of course, I would have slept a lot more soundly if Bob and Eric could have explained how my tape recorder flipped over.

FORT MIFFLIN
Fort Mifflin Road, Philadelphia PA 19153

THE GHOSTS OF DONNER STATE PARK
by Janice Oberding

Indeed if I do not experience something far worse than I have yet done, I shall say the trouble is all in getting started.—Tamsen Donner, June 1846

TAMSEN DONNER could not have foreseen the horror that awaited her high in the Sierras when she penned those words to a friend. She was among the 87 people who left Independence, Missouri, in the spring of 1846 headed west to California and a better life. They might well have arrived safe and sound, their names unknown to history, if not for a fateful decision that led to tragedy.

Experienced travelers warned them not to take the advice found in a certain book, but the Donner Party leaders' minds were made up. They would follow the new route suggested by Lansford Hastings, author of *The Emigrants' Guide to Oregon and California;* it would, according to Hastings, shave off several days' travel time. Anxious to reach California, they led the party onto the Hastings Cut-off that wound its way across the treacherous Wasatch Mountains of Utah. It was a costly mistake. Instead of saving time, the route slowed their travel and caused them to lose both livestock and food.

It was late October, and a storm was brewing off the coast of California as the Donner Party headed west toward the Sierras. By the time they reached present-day Verdi, California, snowflakes were flying. A broken wagon axle slowed down George Donner; and as the snow continued to fall, he and his family were forced to stop and camp in a hastily thrown-together shelter at Alder Creek.

At Donner's urging, the rest of the party moved onward. Six miles west, they too were stopped by the heavy snowfall. They huddled in crudely built shelters and planned to wait out the snow. But with each passing day, the snow piled higher. They were trapped; they could not retreat and they could not move forward. They would wait here near the water's edge at Truckee Lake until a rescue party arrived.

Weeks passed and the food supplies dwindled. Hunting was all but impossible in the ten-foot snowdrifts, and the travelers had already butchered the livestock. Tempers were short as food was rationed and fought over. In desperation, the men and women boiled shoes and laces to make a soup of sorts. Then came the day when there was nothing left to eat. From this day on, some

members of the Donner Party would resort to cannibalizing those who had succumbed to the harsh conditions.

A PARK VISITOR'S STORY

Each year, thousands of motorists drive past Donner State Park unaware of the horrendous events that took place there in the winter of 1847. Others come to the park because of their fascination with the Donner story. They camp, hike, picnic, and just enjoy the outdoors; a few have had a brush with the supernatural. Such is the case with a computer technician, Don Nelspeth (name changed to protect his privacy), who shared the following story with me during a recent conference.

"The first time I ever camped at Donner State Park, I was about ten years old. Every summer after that, my family would drive up from the Bay Area to spend a few days in what my dad called 'peace and quiet in the wilderness.'

"But it isn't really. The park is so close to Interstate 80 that you can hear

cars and trucks speeding past at all hours of the day and night. I remember my dad used to walk us around and point out where the Donner Party's shelters had stood, the big rock with the plaque that bore all their names, and where the remains are supposedly buried.

"These childhood memories came rushing back to me when I learned that the company picnic campout was to be held at Donner State Park, and I was thrilled. It had been years since I'd been up to the park; this would be like going home, in a way. My wife, who isn't an outdoors person, didn't share my enthusiasm.

"'What a creepy place,' she said, shuddering.

"'You'll change your mind once we get there,' I assured her.

"My wife and two daughters and I arrived the day before the scheduled campout day so we could enjoy some family time. As we pulled into the park, I was happy to see that things hadn't really changed all that much; there were more cars on the interstate and a designated walking trail and picnic areas had been added, but Donner Park remained the same. Nostalgia took hold of me as I pulled my wife and daughters to the monument and explained the Donners' plight. The girls yawned and my wife nodded sullenly. 'Can you imagine being up here with snow as tall as this monument, and no food to eat?' I asked, trying to generate some enthusiasm for the weekend ahead. 113

"My youngest answered, 'But I saw a Burger King down the street!'

"'That was long before fast food,' I explained.

"When she asked if there were any dinosaurs here, I decided she was still too young to appreciate the story.

"My older daughter shivered and asked, 'What about ghosts?'

"'No such thing,' my wife assured her.

"There was no point in telling them about Tamsen Donner's glowing ghost that people say roams this park at night, I thought. My parents and I had always laughed at the story, and we even made up a song about it: *I see Tamsen's ghost up in the tree, I hope she gets you instead of me!*

"I doubted my wife and daughters would see any humor in the ghost or the song. We pitched our tent in a clearing near tall pines and watched birds flit about. The sound of water rushing over boulders was soothing, but we could still hear the whir of cars rushing along the interstate.

"Darkness fell early; it always does in the mountains. Traditionalists, we hoisted our hotdogs on sticks over the fire till they were crisp and blackened. After dinner, we bundled up and sat around the glowing campfire.

"My older daughter complained, 'This place is crawling with bugs' as she swatted at the air. 'Looks like those Donners could have eaten them,' she smirked.

"'Except that it was winter,' I explained. 'And bugs aren't generally out, and . . .' I stopped in mid sentence. Directly across the park was something that looked like the glowing figure of a woman; it hovered slightly above the ground and vanished.

"'What is it?' my wife asked.

"'I lost my train of thought,' I lied.

The Wisp in the Tent

Now Don related the part of the story that gave me cold chills—and still does.

"Wrapped up in their sleeping bags that night, my family fell asleep quickly. But I couldn't. I got up, sat outside the tent, and spent the next few hours trying to convince myself that what I had seen earlier was nothing but a reflection from a passing car. Maybe it would come back and I would know for sure.

"It didn't return until the next night. We were all sleeping soundly when I was suddenly awakened by something that felt cold and wet on my face. Startled, I sat up; that's when I saw her. She was yellowish and almost seemed to be see-through. She hovered a few inches off the ground and looked around the tent curiously. I have never been as cold as I was in the icy air that emanated from her. I was scared, all right. But I didn't want to raise the alarm and frighten anyone else. Assuring myself that this wasn't a dream, I watched as she slowly floated up to the top of the tent and evaporated right through it.

"'Tamsen Donner's ghost. I've just seen Tamsen Donner's ghost. The stories are true,' I whispered to myself.

"I know what I saw was real. It wasn't lights somehow being reflected through the park. I clearly saw its facial features, and it was a woman's ghost. I'm not sure what she was looking for, but I am convinced I saw Tamsen Donner's ghost that night."

DONNER MEMORIAL STATE PARK
12593 Donner Pass Road, Truckee CA 96161

MUSIC-LOVING MARY
by castleburk22

THE ORPHEUM THEATRE, in the center of downtown Memphis, is one of those old, elaborate theaters that looks as though it could've been an opera house. Nowadays they use the place for entertainment of many types, from concerts to movies. In fact, the theater rose from the ashes of a 1923 fire and changed with the times to become what's been called "the South's finest theater."

The Orpheum has still another claim to fame: It's haunted by a little girl named Mary. I've heard that she even has a favorite seat there!

Over the years, Memphis residents heard different versions of how Mary came to reside at the theater. The first says that she was killed by a horse and carriage while crossing the street to buy a ticket and see a show. The second says that she fell from the upper balcony to her death. Nobody really knows who she is or where she came from—they just know that she's supposed to have been wandering around the theater for a long, long time.

The Ghost According to Vince

I'm acquainted with a very old gentleman by the name of Vince, who used to work as the organist whenever the Orpheum held showings of classic silent films during the summer. Vince swore up and down to me that he could make Mary "come out."

He explained that she was very shy and reclusive, and that whenever the showings were over and the crowds were gone, he would hang around and play tunes on the organ. As the organ music floated through the theater, Mary would magically appear in the balcony. Vince said that this happened on more than one occasion, and that he even figured out which tunes were Mary's favorites.

CLOSED DUE TO GHOST
by Charlie Carlson

IN THE 1870S, Florida's east coast was a 350-mile stretch of isolated beach that offered little refuge to shipwreck survivors. The federal government established a series of lifesaving stations along the coast in 1875, an initiative that eventually led to the formation of the U.S. Coast Guard. Of the ten lifesaving stations along the Florida coast, only one remains: the Hutchinson Island station, which survives as a historical site.

Over the years, the original stations were deactivated for various reasons. One of them, located 29 miles south of St. Lucie and maintained by a Captain Dodd and a small crew, was shut down because of supernatural occurrences—or so reported a Boston *Globe* article dated November 16, 1897.

The paper reported that in 1895 a ship was wrecked during a hurricane, and the only survivor was a pretty eighteen-year-old girl. She was rescued and brought safely to shore by William Smith and Henry Johnson, two surfmen assigned to Captain Dodd's lifesaving station.

Both men promptly fell in love with the girl, and in 1896 she married William Smith. Not surprisingly, the marriage didn't sit well with Henry Johnson, who apparently became angry at both Smith and his new bride.

Shortly after the marriage, the young Mrs. Smith was reported missing. A search was launched, and a week later her body was found drowned in the waters behind the station. It was noted that Henry Johnson became especially moody after the body was discovered. Locals said he was out of his mind and showed signs of suicidal behavior, although no evidence connected him to the girl's death.

A WEEPING SPIRIT

In September 1897, reports began cropping up about a ghost seen walking on the beach near the station. At that point, Captain Dodd announced that Henry Johnson had committed suicide after confessing to having drowned Mrs. Smith.

After Johnson's death, more and more people reported seeing a spirit walking in the vicinity of the station. Captain Dodd admitted that he had twice witnessed what he thought was the ghost of a woman on the beach, reporting the sightings only after finding out that others had seen the same thing.

The ghost appeared, said Dodd, "to be the indistinct form of a woman floating through the air, a few feet above the earth, clasping her hands and weeping." Sometimes the ghost would come up to the station, and on other occasions a series of wild and unearthly screams was heard at midnight.

The haunting, reported the newspaper, became so "disrupting of the life-saving station's purpose that there was cause to close it."

Though the lifesaving station no longer exists, aficionados of the eerie can get a sense of what it was like by visiting a museum on nearby Hutchinson Island: Gilbert's Bar House of Refuge. The museum features exhibits of old life-saving equipment, a history of the lifesaving service, and various marine arti-facts. No ghost walks its rooms, as far as anyone knows, so perhaps the weep-ing spirit of the young woman found her peace.

THE GHOSTS OF GETTYSBURG
by Paul J. Forti

WHEN I WAS A BOY, I remember reading about the Battle of Gettysburg, the most famous battle of the Civil War. During the battle, some 45,000 soldiers on both sides were either killed or wounded. The fighting was intense and terrifying, and many soldiers died of their wounds because of the shortage of medical assistance.

When the battle ended, it left behind a ghastly and ghoulish scene. The smell of death was everywhere, and it was several weeks before all of the dead soldiers were buried.

More than 1,200 Confederate soldiers were interred where they fell, in makeshift graves on the main battlefield. The Union soldiers were buried in an extension to the local cemetery, which became the National Cemetery at Gettysburg.

118   I first visited Gettysburg in May 2000, and I was overwhelmed by the place. I was most impressed with the cemetery. While I didn't believe in ghosts, I had an eerie feeling as I walked over ground holding hundreds of soldiers who died in defense of that in which they believed. As I finished the tour, I heard about a ghost walk that was provided to visitors, and I decided to take it the next night.

FROM SKEPTICISM TO BELIEF

The tour started at 8:30 p.m. and was led by a guide dressed in Civil War attire. We visited a number of supposedly haunted sites in the town of Gettysburg and the surrounding battlefields, and it was almost 10:00 when we arrived at the last stop—the National Cemetery.

The tour guide told us there had been many ghost sightings here. He was a good storyteller, and I thought this was part of his act: a way of creating a little excitement for the group. The night was moonless, cool, and quiet. Many people on the tour were asking questions about ghosts, and the tour guide seemed to be embellishing stories he had heard. While I thought he was doing a good job, as a nonbeliever in ghosts I thought much of what he said was mere hype.

So I decided to test the tour guide. I asked him if it was possible to get a photo of an orb on a digital camera. (In the paranormal realm, the word "orb" usually refers to floating, glowing spheres of unexplained origin.) He answered yes, and that he had taken many orb photos with his digital camera.

I decided to try to photograph an orb myself, even though I honestly didn't believe it would happen. I took my digital camera out of its case, turned it on, and tried to find something that I could focus on; it was very difficult to see any headstones or markers. I decided not to use the flash, pointed the camera in the direction of the cemetery, and just hoped for the best.

Not even five seconds had passed before the image appeared on the viewfinder. A woman on the tour was looking at the viewing screen with me, and as the image appeared she screamed, "Oh my God, there's an orb!"

I looked at the screen and saw a series of what looked like small flashlights glowing in the dark. I was thinking, "How could a photo taken in total darkness, where there was no light or reflective material, show any form of light?" Unable to explain it to myself, I turned to the tour guide and asked for his opinion. He looked at the image and said, "Yep, you have a great photo of an orb."

I wasn't convinced that my "orb" photo proved anything, so I returned to the edge of the cemetery alone at 10:00 the next night, where I unsuccessfully tried to reproduce the previous night's results. But as I looked into the distance, I saw an indisputable sight: a soldier dressed in what appeared to be a Union uniform and marching around a group of graves. I noted that there were no lights or reflections that might cause an optical illusion. I called out to the soldier, but he walked into the darkness. I didn't know what to think.

The next morning I went to the National Park Service headquarters and asked whether any Civil War reenactors had been walking around after dark. A park ranger told me that no one was allowed in the cemetery after dark, nor had there been any rangers on the property at 10:00 the night before. It was at that point that I became convinced that there really are ghosts at Gettysburg.

Over the years, my visits to Gettysburg have made me more of a believer in ghosts. I feel that the more that people believe in the presence of spirits, the greater the chance they will see them. At the same time, I feel that the spirits at Gettysburg are just looking for a little respect. Could it be possible that they present themselves to certain visitors as a way of saying thank you for believing in them?

GETTYSBURG NATIONAL MILITARY PARK

97 Taneytown Road, Gettysburg PA 17325

THE GHOST THAT MOVED

by Joseph A. Citro

TO THE TRAVELER heading north on Vermont Route 7, the Shelburne Museum, between the highway and Lake Champlain, looks for all the world like a small fenced-in village. Twenty-five of its thirty-nine buildings were moved to the museum grounds because of their historic significance. Visitors find houses, barns, a meetinghouse, a one-room schoolhouse, a lighthouse, a jail, a general store, a covered bridge, and even a 220-foot steamboat. While the structures contain exhibits, they are also exhibits in themselves.

And one of them is hauntingly unique.

The Dutton House, relocated to Shelburne from Cavendish, Vermont, was the first structure in the museum's architectural collection. Constructed in 1782 by Salmon Dutton, the house began life as a typical colonial saltbox. But over the years, Dutton descendants expanded it with continual additions. At different times, it was used as a family residence and a place of business including a tavern, an inn, and offices.

During most of the first half of the twentieth century, the Dutton House sat deserted. Uninhabited for four decades, the old, scary-looking place gained a reputation for being haunted; everyone around knew to avoid it because

120

there were ghosts inside. Perhaps Salmon Dutton himself walked the empty rooms and collapsing stairways. Or perhaps it was his wife Sarah, a family member, or one of the many people who stayed–or died–at the inn.

Scads of scary stories were told about the derelict saltbox. When I was a boy, my father told me of the time he and two of his friends ventured there in the mid-1930s, stoked up by fright and curiosity. While he and another boy peered through the slats of boarded windows, the third searched for a way to enter.

Suddenly my father was startled by a scream. The third boy ran from behind the house and dashed across the street. From the safety of the other side, he cried for the others to hurry. "We gotta get out of here!" he yelled over and over, his face wild and his eyes glassy with tears.

In all the years between the incident and my father's death in 1970, my father's friend would never reveal what had frightened him so badly.

By the 1940s, the empty house, now a local eyesore, was in danger of being torn down to make way for a widened road. But the Shelburne Museum rescued it. In 1950 they carefully took it down piece by piece and reassembled it on the museum grounds.

The odd thing is, the Dutton House ghost moved with it. A growing number of inexplicable experiences prove that the Shelburne Museum exhibits a true oddity among its historic structures: a real haunted house.

THE SPECTER(S) UPSTAIRS

I first learned the ghost had been transported with the house from a retired woman who volunteered as a guide at the museum. "They don't much like us to talk about it," she told me. "But anyone working in the house knows about it. Even some of the visitors have had experiences."

In October 2004, I spoke with one of the museum security guards, Burt Levitt, who told me that he'd routinely entered the Dutton House at night. Alone. On certain occasions, he said, he could feel the house charged with a discernible mood. Sometimes he felt very comfortable, and at other times extremely tense, as if he had walked into a room where an argument was in progress. These visits were after hours, of course, when the museum was closed and no one else was allowed in the building.

Mr. Levitt habitually checked the whole house to be sure no one was hiding anywhere. But before he locked up and left, he'd stop by the door and listen. He would often hear the fall of footsteps upstairs–footsteps in a room he knew to be empty. When he went back up to double-check, he would sometimes discover that the antique adult-size cradles on display—which look very much like coffins—were rocking all by themselves.

Other security guards reported hearing children's laughter in the upstairs rooms. One saw an unearthly face hovering outside an upstairs window.

In general, the ghost—whoever it may be—seems to favor the upstairs, where people have seen flashing lights or felt cold breezes blowing through the rooms on hot summer nights. One of the ghosts occasionally takes a rest, it seems. And when he (or she) does, it is on a specific upstairs bed. Employees repeatedly find that bed disturbed in the morning, as if someone had been lying on it. Sometimes an impression is clearly visible, while at other times the bedclothes are in disarray.

On rare occasions, full-form phantoms have been seen in the Dutton House. Though these apparitions cast no light on the identity of the house's spectral occupants, they do suggest that they number more than one.

In early 2005, two security guards heard feet pounding across the upstairs floorboards (the guards now travel in pairs when visiting the Dutton House). One guard remained by the door as the other raced upstairs, certain he was about to trap an intruder. What he found was a terrified little girl at the foot of one of the beds. As he turned away to call his partner, the girl vanished.

One day an elderly volunteer tour guide, who I'll call Gladys Whipple to protect her privacy, was working in an upstairs room. Though she hadn't seen or heard anyone come in, she suddenly felt as if she were not alone. As she furtively glanced up, her eyes met those of an unsavory looking man standing in a corner. There was something very wrong about this out-of-place stranger. The clothing. The scowl.

When the specter began to growl at her, Gladys left. As she hurried down the stairs, the apparition followed, pursuing her out the door and into the yard.

Not surprisingly, Gladys says she'll never enter the Dutton House again. In fact, over the years many museum employees and volunteers have preferred not to work in this building alone, though it can be argued that no one is ever alone in the the Dutton House.

SHELBURNE MUSEUM
U.S. Route 7, Shelburne VT 05482

THE SPRAGUE MANSION

by Jeff Belanger

"TELL MY STORY . . ."

Ghostly legends surrounded the Sprague Mansion long before a home-made Ouija board spelled out those eleven letters inside the home back in 1968; but since that fateful spirit-communication session, talk of ghosts in Cranston, Rhode Island, has been omnipresent.

The Sprague family came to Cranston around 1712. They built a financial empire and rose to social and political prominence. By the Civil War, the Spragues were the wealthiest family in America, but within two decades, their fortune would be lost. Today, all that remains of their kingdom is their stately mansion, their story, and—if we're to believe the many eyewitnesses, paranormal investigators, and passersby—their ghosts are still around, too.

The Sprague Mansion was built around 1790, and it was the heart of the Sprague's growing textile empire. Brothers Amasa and William III took over the family business when their father, William II, died a peculiar death that involved choking on a bone while eating his breakfast in 1836.

123

Both Sprague brothers were elected to the state legislature, but Amasa focused most of his attention on running the family business while William went on to become a United States congressman, then the governor of Rhode Island, then a U.S. Senator. His blossoming political career would be cut short when Amasa was murdered back home.

It was December 31, 1843, and Amasa was about a mile away from the mansion, checking on his cattle near the Pocasset River. He had started to cross a footbridge when one or more men jumped him. His mangled body was found

Amasa Sprague

on the banks of the river and carried back to the mansion, where it was most likely laid out in the front parlor of the mansion for his wake and viewing.

Accusing fingers pointed at an Irish immigrant named Nicholas Gordon and his brothers. Nicholas's store, near the Sprague mill, had a liquor license that mill workers took advantage of, and Amasa used his influence to ensure that the license would not be renewed. A few days before the murder, several witnesses observed an argument over the license between Nicholas Gordon's brother John and Amasa. This circumstantial evidence, plus a confused witness and anti-Irish sentiment of the time, was enough to convict John Gordon of Amasa's murder. He was hanged in 1845, the last victim of capital punishment in the state of Rhode Island. The public was outraged, and those close to the Gordons knew that John didn't murder Amasa Sprague.

So who did?

Some think it was William himself. The brothers had differed on how the business should be run; and with Amasa gone, William expanded the Sprague Print Works company to become the largest calico-dyeing plant in the nation. Profits soared. Did William have his own brother murdered to make an already wealthy family even richer?

The Sprague fortune continued to grow until the Panic of 1873, when banks called their loans, people everywhere sold off their stocks, and the economy collapsed almost overnight. The Spragues were impacted, and by 1888, they had sold their mansion and holdings and faded off into the yellowing pages of history. Their legacy is not forgotten when one walks inside the Sprague Mansion today.

Andrew Laird is founder and director of The Rhode Island Paranormal Research Group (TRIPRG). The group has conducted more than a half dozen investigations at the mansion, including a preliminary walk-through in 2004. "We were in the front parlor where Amasa had been laid out, though we didn't know this at the time, and all of our meters and everything else were going off," Laird said. "We experienced all kinds of stuff that night. We heard things downstairs near the wine cellar. I felt a tap on my shoulder, and when I turned around no one was there."

The Cranston Historical Society is headquartered in the mansion. Lydia Rapoza, curator since 1996, and Dr. Michael Bell, a member of the Cranston Historical Society's board of directors and a folklorist and author, explained how in the 1960s the mansion was in bad shape and was going to be torn down. Local resident Viola Lynch helped raise the $100,000 necessary to buy the property and preserve the Spragues' legacy (and possibly their ghosts). Mrs. Lynch and her family have also become part of the ghostly legends here.

In 1968, Viola's son Robert was working as a caretaker for the mansion. He and some of his friends constructed a Ouija board and sat down to reach out to the ghosts of the house. Robert explained to a *Providence Journal* reporter that the pointer on the Ouija board spelled out MY LAND. MY LAND. When they asked the spirit, "What would you want done to have your spirit at peace?" the board answered, TELL MY STORY. The spirit identified itself as CHARLES.

So who was Charles . . . or Charlie, as he's become affectionately known?

"We don't know," Rapoza said. "The Ouija board said he was a butler here."

According to one of the legends, Charlie's daughter was supposed to marry one of the sons of the mansion owner. It is unclear if it was a Sprague or one of the families who lived there after them. Local lore says things didn't work out with the engagement, and Charlie has been upset ever since that his family didn't marry into wealth and power. Since 1968, people inside the mansion have joked about Charlie, though no one has ever seen him . . . well, not conclusively.

Rapoza mentioned one worker who had a strange run-in with something unexplained near the main stair-

125

case. "This guy was fixing up the doll room and he sees this white filmy thing up there," she said. "He didn't want to work here alone after that."

The doll room is easily the creepiest room in the house. The size of a walk-in closet, it's located off a small landing halfway between floors. The room is full of old dolls from the 1700s and 1800s. One doll has no eyes, while others stare off in a lifeless and eerie fashion.

Andrew Laird mentioned the experience of a guest during one of the Halloween parties held at the mansion. "This lady showed us a video of one of the guides giving the mansion tour," Laird said. "They were in front of the doll room. The guide was talking about the dolls, and just as the guide is turning around to point to one of them, you can hear this EVP [electronic voice phenomenon] of a little girl's voice saying, 'Leave my doll alone.' It's as clear as a bell."

Other unexplained events have happened during Halloween parties. "It was the night of the first Halloween party," Lydia Rapoza said. "There were twenty-eight people here."

Dr. Bell added, "Some of the ladies who came decided they wanted to try out the Ouija board. So they got the board and they were in the front parlor and it spelled out . . ."

"'. . . Tell Bob I need him,'" Rapoza finished. "And it was signed by V. L. and they had no idea who Viola (Lynch) was, or who Bob was. Bob was her husband and he was still alive at the time."

"This was October," Dr. Bell said. "She'd died about a year before that and he was painting her over and over." One of these paintings now hangs in the front parlor.

"The poor guy was heartbroken, and doing these paintings kept him alive," Rapoza said. "So this was October, and then in February they find him dead in his house."

At the 2004 Halloween party, photographer Cyril Place and about five others were among the last to leave. "We had come downstairs and we were standing right in the foyer by the front door at the foot of the stairs," Place said. "All of a sudden we heard the music box—which was up on the third floor. This was very strange because Lydia had already locked it up—she's meticulous with that. It played for about a minute.

"Lydia was with us in the foyer. She said, 'Nobody's up there. Nobody's been up there, and everything is locked up.' And then the music ended at that point."

The main staircase has also been the site of a ghostly female figure who has been reported floating down the stairs. Many paranormal investigations

focus on the foyer and staircase because the area is the central part of the house—it ties the building together—and whether a long-ago butler is still performing his duties or whether some belle is still trying to make her grand entrance, the staircase seems to be a hotspot.

Another supernaturally active location within the house is the wine cellar—a dark storage room in the basement. Strange noises have been heard inside, and the room contains one artifact that sends chills up the spines of those who read the old, dusty wine bottle label. The vineyard name is Gordon, a not-so-subtle reminder of the man who was hanged for Amasa Sprague's murder.

127

Ms. Rapoza claims she's never seen any ghosts here, but she did capture a strange blur in one of her photos that she took in the ballroom back in 2001.

Though she hasn't seen a ghost, she certainly feels that the spirit of Amasa Sprague is always nearby. "I talked to Amasa on the Ouija board," Rapoza said about one night in April 1999. "We had a board meeting . . . I was fooling around with a Ouija board, and I said, 'Who are you?' And it spelled out 'Amasa Sprague.'"

The Sprague Mansion is now on the National Register of Historic Places. It represents the result of Yankee ingenuity and entrepreneurship that helped form an industrially prosperous state. Against the odds, the mansion survives, and the Sprague story is told again and again with the ghosts and spirits watching from inside.

GOVERNOR SPRAGUE MANSION
1351 Cranston Street, Cranston RI 02920

THE
OTHERWORLDLY
OUTDOORS

While yet a boy I sought for ghosts, and sped
Through many a listening chamber, cave and ruin,
And starlight wood, with fearful steps pursuing
Hopes of high talk with the departed dead.
—Percy Bysshe Shelley, *Hymn to Intellectual Beauty*

IN SOME ACCOUNTS of haunted houses, neighbors often report seeing the living occupants running out of the house in terror. But who's to say that the outdoors is somehow a haven? That once outside, you're safe from the spirits who wander the spaces between four walls? After all, there are countless reports of ghosts who like to crunch leaves in the woods and kick up winds and weather. And more than a few ghosts have lurked just beyond the edge of the campfire light.

The stories in this chapter focus on the ghosts of the natural world: forests, fields, rivers, caves. An invisible boater plies the Blue River in Indiana. A nineteenth-century farmer plows the Florida earth he once cultivated. Hunters in Wisconsin repeatedly encounter the spirit of a long-dead hermit. A man is shaken by the energy given off by an ancient Hawaiian heiau where humans were sacrificed to the gods. And plenty of visitors to Mammoth Cave—the largest cave system in the world—have learned that ghosts have more than enough room to roam.

The next time you take a walk in the woods, breathe deeply and soak up the wonders of nature. But you also might want to stay on your guard. Most likely, that snapping twig you hear is caused by something living . . . but who really knows?

WORLD'S LARGEST HAUNTED PLACE

by Troy Taylor

LYING BENEATH THE FORESTS and hills of central Kentucky is the largest known cave in the world. Mammoth Cave became a National Park in 1941 and now welcomes some two million visitors annually, but humans first explored its endless paths, passages, and tunnels as long ago as 12,000 years. Indigenous peoples used the cave as a burial place for their dead, and several mummies have been unearthed here over the years.

The first owners of the land mined the cave for saltpeter (essential to the production of gunpowder) until demand dropped off at the end of the War of 1812. It was then that the owners opened the cave to tourists, and it became more and more famous as the nineteenth century progressed.

It's hardly surprising that an underground world of dark corners, shadowy crevices, and black waters has given rise to a number of ghostly tales, and those said to have taken place in Mammoth Cave span several generations. For every tourist who has no understanding of the natural phenomena of caves and consequently interprets an occurrence as "weird," there is a knowledgeable park ranger, guide, geologist, or spelunker who has encountered things that cannot easily be explained.

I've visited Mammoth Cave several times and have talked with many of the people who work there. Most of the park rangers are reluctant to discuss ghost stories, but a few don't laugh off the odd tales and will share their observations of strange phenomena. Among those are three ghosts who are particularly noteworthy: a slave who had the distinction of being the first man to map the cave system, a girl spurned by her beau, and a onetime owner of the portion of the cave system known as Crystal Cave.

THE SLAVE STEPHEN BISHOP

In 1838, landowner Franklin Gorin introduced Stephen Bishop, a sixteen-year-old slave, to the cave. Bishop would become the first man to explore and map

the cave system. He served as an expert guide there for the rest of his life, and so loved this dark underground world that he purportedly turned down a chance for freedom because it would mean leaving Mammoth Cave behind.

Science teacher Larry Purcell, of Bowling Green, Kentucky, worked as summer guide at the cave for a number of years and had some strange experiences, one of which could have been connected to the ghost of Bishop.

One day, Purcell was on a tour when the group stopped as another guide delivered his regular talk. The lights were all off, and it was Purcell's job to go down the path and turn them back on.

132

"As I was walking along, I saw a black man with a woman and two children," Purcell said. "The man had on white pants, a dark shirt, a white vest, and a white Panama hat. The people were real enough that I walked around them. But when I turned on the lights, they were no longer there." The late 1880s attire worn by the vanishing man was from Bishop's time, so who knows whether Bishop might have been in the mood to conduct a family tour of the cave.

Purcell isn't the only one who may have encountered Stephen Bishop. Other visitors have reported seeing a man of the former slave's description and have assumed him to be part of a historic tour, perhaps playing the part of Bishop. When they've asked about the man or have looked for him again, he is gone.

SPURNED MELISSA

Another cave ghost is even more famous, probably because her story was told in "A Tragedy in Mammoth Cave," an article that appeared in *Knickerbocker* magazine in February 1858. The central character is a girl named Melissa, who lived near Mammoth Cave. The article states that she told the entire tale on her deathbed before succumbing to consumption—the affliction now known as tuberculosis.

Melissa had fallen in love with her tutor, a young Bostonian named Beverleigh. But the tutor rebuffed Melissa's affections and began courting a neighbor girl instead. So Melissa plotted her revenge.

Familiar with the twists and turns of Mammoth Cave, she lured Mr. Beverleigh there for a "tour." At Echo River, an underground stream deep in the cave, she vanished into a side passage, leaving the poor man to find his own way out.

Days passed without any sign of Beverleigh. A despairing Melissa, who had intended only to play a cruel trick, began to make daily treks underground. She searched and called out to the object of her affection until she was hoarse, but Beverleigh would never be seen again.

A few years after the tragedy, Melissa was diagnosed with consumption and died a short time later. It is said that she never recovered from her guilt over her tutor's death. Many believe that her ghost is still seen and heard in Mammoth Cave, desperately searching for the unfortunate Mr. Beverleigh.

The story has its share of melodrama, but don't dismiss it too quickly. Gary Bremer, a former Mammoth Cave guide, says there may be something credible about the tale. Several years ago, Bremer and four others were in a boat on Echo River. One of the men left to get another paddle for the boat, and Bremer

133

remembers what happened next: "Those of us in the boat all heard a woman calling out. It wasn't screaming. It was more like she was looking for someone." It wasn't until the next day that Bremer first heard the story of Melissa.

This wouldn't be Bremer's last encounter on the Echo River. A short time later, he was there with a new employee who had never seen the river before. She suddenly turned and grabbed his shoulder. "Did you hear a woman cough?" she asked. Bremer felt a cold chill. Melissa had died of tuberculosis, he remembered.

The other employee verified Bremer's version of the experience and added that she had also heard garbled voices wafting through the cave, and on another night believed she heard someone whisper her name.

A GHOST NAMED FLOYD

Not all of the weird tales from Mammoth Cave are set in areas accessible to the public. Many of the strangest come from Crystal Cave, once believed to be a separate cave and operated as a private attraction. It is no longer open to the public, yet the stories that surround this portion of the cave are too mysterious to ignore.

Most of these legends involve the ghost of W. Floyd Collins, an avid cave explorer and the former owner of Crystal Cave, which he had discovered by accident in the winter of 1916–17. He and his family opened the cave in 1918,

A MEDIA CIRCUS

THE DETERMINED but failed attempt to rescue Floyd Collins became a national sensation even without the aid of TV. Radio and the press were enough to keep the public fascinated by what was happening. In fact, it could be said that the story reached historic proportions. Louisville *Courier-Journal* reporter William Burke ("Skeets") Miller, who interviewed the trapped man several times, won the Pulitzer Prize for his coverage. Years later, the drama surrounding Collins's death inspired the 1951 movie *Ace in the Hole* (originally titled *The Big Carnival*), and famed author Robert Penn Warren based his novel *The Cave* (1959) on the event.

Two years after Collins died, his family sold Crystal Cave to a local dentist, who would cash in on the media circus surrounding the death in a rather macabre way.

As part of the property transfer, the dentist gained the right to exhume Collins's body and move it to Crystal Cave. It was placed in a glass-covered, bronzed metal coffin that would be set in the middle of the tourist trail leading to the cave's main concourse. Thereafter, guides recounted the former owner's exploits as wide-eyed tourists gazed at Collins's waxen face.

In 1989, W. Floyd Collins—cave explorer, businessman, promoter—found his final resting place at nearby Flint Ridge Cemetery. Today his memory lives on in the Floyd Collins Museum, located in Cave City on Old Mammoth Cave Road.

after which Collins constantly sought a commercially exploitable hook that would ensnare tourists.

His explorations led him to a hole on a nearby farm that the press would later call the Sand Cave— in reality, a series of narrow, twisting crevices that Collins sought to expand. What he thought could be a commercial boon actually became his undoing. While working at the site on January 30, 1925, he was trapped in a small passage after part of the cave collapsed and his foot became wedged under a rock.

Despite a massive effort, constantly shifting earth prevented searchers from rescuing Collins, who was trapped for two weeks before he died.

A few decades back, a group of Mammoth Cave employees was on an after-hours excursion in Crystal Cave when they noticed an old whiskey bottle resting on a rock ledge. One of the men in the group picked it up, looked at it, and put it back in the same spot. The group then walked on deeper into the cave.

Later that evening, one of the men was walking back toward the cave entrance and was passing the bottle when he heard something. "It was just behind my ear," he stated. "I heard a sound as though someone had flicked a finger against glass . . . a clink. I turned around just in time to see the bottle hit the ground."

Another man who was with him jumped back in shock. He claimed that the whiskey bottle hadn't fallen but instead had come straight out from the ledge and just dropped! "The little clink was loud enough to make me look back toward the ledge," he remembered, "and as I did, the bottle actually came out and then went right down in front of me. It was very bizarre."

Could the ghost of Floyd Collins be responsible for this strange occurrence? The men involved wondered whether this was the case, but a later event that took place in the area would have a more direct connection to the man.

In July 1976, a former Crystal Cave employee named George Wood filed a report saying that he and another employee, Bill Cobb, spent a day checking springs for a study on groundwater flow. They didn't make it to the last spring, which was near the abandoned Collins house on Flint Ridge, until after dark. Cobb went to the spring while Wood waited near the truck. After a few moments, Wood heard the sound of a man crying out. At first, he thought it was his friend calling for help, but the voice seemed too high-pitched. It was

135

THE PLAYFUL GHOST

AN EXPERIENCED Mammoth Cave tour guide named Joy Lyons tells of a tour taken a few years ago. When the large group and two additional guides reached a point on the trail known as The Methodist Church, all of the lights were turned off as usual, allowing visitors to experience what the cave was like in total darkness. Lyons was standing at the back of the group when the lights went out and the lead ranger began his talk.

All of a sudden she felt a strong shove against her shoulder, hard enough that she had to step forward to keep from falling over. She turned to the ranger who was supposed to be standing next to her and whispered to him to stop clowning around. A moment later, after the lead ranger had ignited a lantern, Lyons saw that her fellow ranger was actually about seventy feet away. There was no way he could have shoved her and then walked so far in the pitch-black darkness.

"There was no one near me," she said, "but it was a playful shove. There are many of us who feel things in various parts of the cave. The incident wasn't frightening, but it's just proof that some things that happen in the cave can't be explained."

also so faint that he had to listen carefully to hear what it was saying.

The voice called out over and over again: "Help me! Help me! Help me, I'm trapped! Johnny, help me!"

As Wood stood there on the edge of the dark road, he felt a cold chill as he recalled hearing about how Floyd Collins was trapped—and where he was trapped: in Sand Cave, only a short distance away.

A few minutes later, Cobb returned to the truck and Wood asked him if he had been calling for him. Cobb said no, and that he had heard nothing while at the spring. But after hearing his friend's account of the cries, Cobb admitted that he too was spooked. The two men didn't waste any time before driving off.

Could the spectral voice have really belonged to Floyd Collins? And if so, could the "Johnny" heard in the mysterious cry have referred to Johnny Gerald, a friend of Floyd's and the last person to speak with him before the cave collapse sealed him off from rescue? Is his spirit still trapped in the cave, or could the sound have been merely an eerie echo of yesterday?

MAMMOTH CAVE
1 Mammoth Cave Parkway, Mammoth Cave KY 42259

THE MOUNT TOM BEAR
by Linda S. Godfrey

ONE OF THE FIRST LESSONS learned by those who step into the world of
the supernatural is that things in the spook dominion are seldom what they
seem. The case of the Mount Tom Bear is no exception. You'd think it was an
animal story, but this tale isn't about a bear—at least, not the kind with fur and
fangs.

I heard it from a retired Wisconsin hunter who encountered the Mount
Tom Bear firsthand, and more than once. Although no longer up to stalking the
land as he once did, Pat Taggart was a true old-school outdoorsman in his day.
And it was a passion for hunting that led to the strangest experience of his life.

"Back in 1960," Pat told me, "I had just graduated from high school in
Racine, and my good friend Jeff and I were very much into the outdoors,
especially hunting and fishing. We even took up archery and learned to shoot
the longbow. We spent literally all our spare time in the field, learning animals
and their ways and their tracks and their migrations, and we got to be pretty
good at hunting. We didn't get jobs until a year after we graduated, and we
took a liking to trying to understand the night creatures—the coon, the fox, the
coyote."

Pat and Jeff themselves became creatures of the night, prowling the countryside around Racine and Kenosha, scouting for likely hunting spots, and
getting on the friendly side of the farmers who owned the woods and fields.
They also hunted fields owned by relatives—old farmers with land that had
been in the family for generations around the communities of Burlington and
Eagle Lake.

The pair perfected their night hunting skills on a relative's farm a few miles
east of Burlington in the rustic area near a wooded hill known as Mount Tom.
Pat's elderly great-uncle Michael owned 100 acres there, about half of it in
open field. The rest was a dense forest of ancient hardwoods, behind which
rose Mount Tom.

Jeff and Pat would leave home after supper and hang out in Michael's
woods until two or three in the morning, teaching themselves to hunt rac-
coons without dogs. The nights were black as tar in the isolated rural area, so
they used flashlights that were especially effective at "shining" the reflective
eyes of nocturnal animals.

137

Their favorite time of year was late fall, after the leaves had dropped and dried. The pair would get into the woods just at dusk while it was very quiet and settle in, listening until they could hear the animals waking in the woods around them. At the sound of approaching paws on dry leaves, they would ready their flashlights, then suddenly click them on to see what kind of creature stood frozen in their beams.

"Not much scared us," said Pat. "We got to understand what was out there. Those were beautiful quiet moments, hearing the guttural sounds of coons and of the night forest."

WHO (OR WHAT) GOES THERE?

One late October night, Pat drove into his great-uncle's field and stopped just outside the edge of the woods. "Not too long after I sat down," Pat recalls, "I could hear something coming from deep inside the woods. It was on two feet, like you'd hear if you were walking in the woods yourself. It was coming straight for me from way out, and took several minutes to get just to the other side of the brush line, which was about fifteen feet from me. Jeff and I both had our flashlights off, but I could still tell where it was moving because of the dry leaves.

"I held my position quietly, and so did it."

As Pat's heart hammered inside his chest, he flicked on his flashlight and quickly scanned the brush. Nothing was there. Puzzled, he used the flashlight to signal Jeff that he had heard something. About ten minutes later, Jeff signaled back that he, too, had heard something, only just now. The two men ran to meet. Like Pat, Jeff was sure something on two feet had walked up to him, and in exactly the same way.

With the incident behind them and nothing else out of the ordinary happening, the two quickly hunted down the first raccoon they could find and went home.

The next weekend they returned—first stopping, as they usually did, at Great-uncle Michael's little farmhouse. Pat and Jeff never thought about telling Michael of their strange experience, but headed back to the field.

They took approximately the same positions outside the woods as they had the last time. "And lo and behold," said Pat, "it happened again. Those eerie footsteps. So I said to myself, 'I'm gonna be ready for it this time.'"

Pat forced himself to listen in complete silence as the footsteps crunched rhythmically on the crackly leaves, the sound growing steadily louder as the unseen presence approached. Pat could feel sweat pop out on his brow in spite of the cool night air.

The footsteps suddenly stopped on the other side of the bushes, just as they had before. Pat immediately switched on the brilliant, square flashlight beam, and again saw nothing but the trees against the blackness. "If it was a night creature," said Pat, "its eyes would reflect because the light was strong."

THE MYSTERY EXPLAINED?

The next time Pat and Jeff dropped by the farmhouse before a hunt, Michael stopped them before they headed out to the field. "Oh, by the way, boys," he said, casually. "Have you guys run into the Mount Tom Bear yet?" Feeling uneasy, Pat asked his uncle what he was talking about.

The old man told the boys that a long time ago an old fellow, almost a hermit, lived in a shack in the woods near Mount Tom. Because he was wild-looking and was generally described as "grizzly," folks started calling him the Mount Tom Bear. One day, Michael said, the shack caught on fire and the hermit was trapped inside. He burned to death, and as time went on people began encountering what they believed was the hermit's ghost. 139

"Michael just told us about it without Jeff or I ever saying anything to him," said Pat. "The explanation of what had been happening to us came without any prompting."

As the pair continued hunting in those woods, the Mount Tom Bear seemed to retreat. Then one night when Pat brought along his brother Dennis, the unseen presence "did his thing" yet again. It was as if the spirit of the old hermit wanted to check out the new person invading his turf.

In all, Pat said, he experienced the phenomenon four times. Dennis heard the phantom steps several other times on his own. The three men stopped most of their nighttime hunting expeditions around 1967, since by then they were married and had families.

"I never saw the Mount Tom Bear," said Pat, "but I knew it was only fifteen or twenty feet away from me. We never heard it leaving and never picked it up in our lights. There was no smell, no vocalization. My senses were keyed then to pick up on anything, and I could hear a mouse at fifty feet in those dry leaves.

"This is the one and only thing in my whole life that's totally unexplainable. If there's such as thing as hauntings, then this spirit really does haunt those woods. And it could still be out there."

THE GHOST WHO DROVE A PLOW

ON SEPTEMBER 11, 1892, the Chicago *Tribune* ran a story headed "Strange Apparition That is Now Puzzling Florida Farmers," transcribed here by Charlie Carlson.

A respectable farmer named Peterson, who owns a place a few miles from Fernandina, brings in a curious story of a ghost that haunts his cornfield and plows by moonlight. He says that he first noticed the apparition about a month ago when sitting up with a sick child. He happened to look out on the field about the hour of midnight, and to his amazement he saw the figure of a man guiding an ox team over the ground. The animals, man, and plow were all as plain to be seen as if it had been daylight, though the rest of the field was in comparative gloom.

Not knowing what to make of this singular sight, he called his eldest son to go and see who the stranger was. The boy went at once, and his watching father was further amazed to see the lad walk right through the plow and man as if there was nothing there. When the boy returned, he declared that he had found nothing and nobody in the field.

Mr. Peterson himself now resolved to go, and did so, but he could see no trace of the man and team, though on returning to the room from which he

had seen the sight he found them as plain as before. The man was dressed in the clothes of a laborer and wore a large broad-brimmed hat, which completely concealed his features. He seemed intent on his work and never raised his head; when he cracked the whip he carried over the backs of the oxen, there was no noise.

Since this time, Mr. Peterson says he has repeatedly seen the phantom plowman, and has called in neighbors to see it with him, though always on going into the field nothing was found. The people declare that the figure is that of the farmer who owned the place before Peterson bought it, and who early one morning was found dead in this field—by his own hand, it was thought.

THE CAMP MORGAN THING
by Jody Noller

WHEN I WAS 14, I spent my summer at Camp Morgan, a YMCA camp located near Washington, New Hampshire, in the foothills of the White Mountains. I was among the many campers sleeping in canvas tents at Lumberjack Village, about a quarter of a mile away from the base camp. It was here that we awoke one night to something terrifying.

It was a typical night in the mountains—cool, clear, and quiet, with no wind to speak of. At around 2:00 a.m., I was awakened by the sound of heavy footsteps crashing through the leaves in the forest near my tent. I heard brush being swept aside and a kind of low-pitched wailing I couldn't identify. I was familiar enough with forest animals to know that it wasn't the sound of a bear, raccoon, coyote, or wolf. Nor did it sound like a teenaged camper playing a prank.

I grabbed my flashlight and woke up my buddy Bruce, who was sharing the tent with me. He too was puzzled by the crashing and wailing sounds.

Both wide awake and scared, we opened the tent's rain fly, switched on our high-powered flashlights, and beamed them in the direction the sounds were coming from. It was an area where no tents stood—just woods and nothing else.

All of a sudden the leaves and branches were being pulled off trees and thrown around, as if something very large and invisible was deliberately destroying the trees. Unable to tell who or what was the cause, we screamed for our counselors Jim and Jay, asleep in a tent about sixty feet from ours. They yelled at us for waking them up and said that if we were joking we were in deep trouble.

Emerging from his tent, Jim beamed his flashlight at the same spot we had. When he saw the branches and leaves being violently tossed around for no apparent reason, he yelled at us to stay quiet (which we did) and to get back in our tents (which we didn't because we wanted to see what happened next).

ROCKS GO FLYING
We saw Jim go back into his tent. He must have assumed, as we did, that no camper could have been behind this, because when he came back out he was carrying a 20-gauge shotgun. Jay followed, holding a light.

Jim and Jay crept to about twenty feet away from the ruckus, after which Jim aimed and fired into the woods. Tree bark and branches blew apart, but nothing was there.

141

He fired again. Tree bark and leaves blasted into the air just as before, but nothing else was hit.

It was at that moment that small- and medium-sized rocks went flying toward our tent. One hit me right in the head, hard enough to hurt badly. Rocks flew in our direction several times, hitting different tents. Between the gunshots and the flying rocks, all of the other kids had woken up and were screaming at the top of their lungs. Who could blame them?

We heard something moving back into the deep woods—something that made the same strange wailing sounds I heard earlier. Then it was again dead quiet.

By now it was 3:00 a.m. Nobody could sleep, so we built a large campfire and sat around it trying to figure out what had been going on. Jim had gone back to the base camp and called the state police and camp director. They arrived at Lumberjack Village in the next forty-five minutes or so and started to search the woods. All they found was lots of ripped-apart branches and saplings on the forest floor.

For the next several nights, the camp director camped out right in the middle of Lumberjack Village, along with several counselors armed with shotguns. But whatever "thing" had caused the ruckus never returned. To this day I have no idea how to explain the incident, but I do know that I've never experienced anything as frightening in my life.

THE GHOST OF FIDDLER'S ROCK

A Tennessee tale adapted by Craig Dominey

BACK IN THE LATE 1800S, Martin Stone was the most popular young fiddle player in northeastern Tennessee. For years he wandered the mountainous back roads of Johnson County, playing at every social event that would have him—church picnics, weddings, barn dances, even funerals. It was a good living, allowing Martin plenty of leisure time to do whatever he wanted.

In the summertime, Martin liked to take Sunday off and sit up on a rocky bluff near the top of Stone Mountain. There he would play his fiddle and watch the sun come up over the green, rolling hills. Sometimes he would spend all day up there, playing reel after reel until the sun dropped from the sky.

THE SNAKE CHARMER

One day, Martin was playing a slow, leisurely tune on his fiddle when a rattlesnake slithered out from under a rock, curled up in the sun, and watched him play. Then another came out and joined him, followed by yet another. Before Martin knew it, the surrounding rocks were filled with rattlesnakes. Most people would have fainted dead away in terror at that point. But Martin was fascinated because the snakes made no move to strike. Instead, they swayed back and forth to the music like scaly reptilian metronomes.

As the sun went down and dark shadows filled the valley, the snakes slipped back into their nests. Martin packed up his fiddle with a chuckle, and made plans to come back next week—but with a surprise.

The next Sunday, Martin climbed to the rocky overhang and began to play his fiddle. Again, the rattlesnakes slithered out from beneath the rocks and listened to him, hypnotized. Martin put down his fiddle and picked up a shotgun. He began blasting away at the rattlesnakes, picking them off one by one as some of the snakes hurriedly slid back to their nests.

Martin stopped shooting and laughed as he collected the dead snakes in a burlap sack. This is too easy, he thought to himself—I can make even more money by selling rattlesnake hides!

Every Sunday for the next few weeks, Martin returned to the bluff, played his fiddle until the snakes came out, and then began shooting. It became a sport to him, and soon he became known around the county as the Fiddlin' Snake Man. Whenever someone wanted a snakeskin to wrap around his hat or

143

to make into a belt—or even a rattle for their babies—Martin was the man to see.

TABLES TURNED

One Sunday toward the end of summer, Martin returned to the bluff as he had done many times before. As the sun rose, he began to play a soft waltz on his fiddle. Once again, the rattlesnakes wiggled out from underneath the rocks and listened, swaying back and forth to the music.

144

Martin stopped playing, reached for his shotgun—and then stopped. Something in the snakes' eyes caught his attention. On his previous trips, the snakes' black eyes seemed to glaze over from the soft, gentle notes of his fiddle. But today, the snakes glared at Martin with fiery red eyes. Martin was hypnotized in their glare. As hard as he tried, he couldn't reach for his gun.

The snakes surrounded Martin and attacked, their sharp fangs ripping into his flesh. All Martin could do was scream—a horrifying scream that resounded throughout the valley.

A few days later, a search party found Martin's lifeless body sprawled across the overhang, his fiddle by his side. They looked with horror at the bite marks that covered his skin. Even more of a mystery was the loaded shotgun leaning against the rock, well within Martin's reach. Why didn't he try to defend himself?

To this day, some Johnson County residents refuse to climb to the rocky overhang at the top of Stone Mountain, which they now call Fiddler's Rock. For in the lazy summer months, when the sun rises over the hills, they say you can hear the faint notes of a fiddle, followed by a high-pitched screeching sound—the scream of Martin Stone as the snakes take their revenge.

INCIDENT AT ILI'ILI'OPAE HEIAU
by Rick Carroll

A FEW YEARS AGO, a friend named Michael and I flew from Honolulu to the island of Molokai to see Ili'ili'opae, the great heiau where Hawaiian kahunas practiced rites of human sacrifice only 150 years ago. We hired a car at Ho'olehua Airport and drove to where the island became lush, green, and tropical. We then turned down an unmarked red dirt road toward the sea and entered the cool, shady oasis of Mapulehu, a mango grove steeped in perfume so strong it stung our eyes.

Under sheltering trees, we stood blinking in half-light as two galloping horses rounded a corner pulling a wagonful of screaming children. They disappeared in fine red dust that settled on the mango trees and all over us.

Out of the dust, a smiling Hawaiian woman appeared to welcome us with a warm "Aloha!" I've forgotten her name, but not what she told us—that Mapulehu once was a pu'uhonua, a place of refuge, where in ancient savage days an errant subject could avoid death by gaining access. The location was appropriate, since Ili'ili'opae—the biggest, oldest, most famous heiau on Molokai—was a short hike up the hill.

We'd missed the wagon to the heiau, the woman said, but we could go on foot if we liked. She pointed toward Mount Kaunolu, the 4,970-foot island summit. "If you see a rainbow over the valley, look out for the waikoloa," she said.

"What's the waikoloa?" I asked.

"A hard, wet wind that comes suddenly down the valley," she said before she left us.

PRICE OF A TRESPASS
We followed the dry streambed uphill past an abandoned house. It was a steep hike and we arrived at the heiau hot, sweaty, and a little light-headed.

No words prepared me for the bulky reality of Ili'ili'opae. Nearly three stories high and as long as a football field, the heiau looked more like an early Roman fortification than a Hawaiian temple of doom. It rose in four tiers on the hill overlooking the green mango grove and four fishponds on the south shore of the island. Boulders big as Volkswagens had been fitted so expertly that the temple had been held together for centuries not by mortar but by its own mass.

145

Even under the glaring tropical sun, the heiau is a very eerie place. Heat waves shimmer off the flat surface rocks. I felt like someone was watching me.

From reading what happened here long ago, I knew how people were summoned by the beating of drums on the twenty-fourth to the twenty-seventh day of the moon, how the sacrificial victim–always a man–was carried into the temple and tied to a scaffold, how victims were strangled and then cremated.

I stepped out onto the heiau, walked right out on the flat table-size rocks to gain a sense of the whole. I meant no disrespect. I only wanted to get closer–to what? The primal past, the secrets of the heiau? I don't know what compelled my trespass. I knew better, yet I kept walking out farther on the heiau, drawn by something larger than curiosity.

Midway across and dizzy under the hot sun, I turned back and felt my foot slip between rocks that opened and shut around my ankle. Something had hold of me. I yelled for help. The rocks moved again and I was free. No spirits, no ghosts–only a misstep on wobbly rocks.

It was then that I saw a rainbow beginning to glow high on the ridge above the heiau. "It's the waikoloa!" I shouted, remembering what the Hawaiian woman had said.

As the rainbow grew brighter, a flash flood sent water coursing down Mapulehu's dry streambed. Rain pounded the hot rocks of the heiau, sending up clouds of steam as rainwater seeped around old smooth stones and trickled

VISITING THE HEIAU

A HEIAU is an ancient Hawaiian temple. According to the Hawaii Chamber of Commerce's Web site, Ili'ili'opae Heiau, on the island of Molokai, is "the second largest and possibly the oldest religious site in Hawaii." Legend says Ili'ili'opae was built in one night by a human chain of ten thousand men who passed rocks by hand up and over the spine of the nearly mile-high island from Wailau Valley, ten miles away over a narrow trail.

Built in the thirteenth century as a school for sorcerers, the huge stone platform (320 by 120 feet) that can be seen today "is probably only a small portion of the original structure, which could clearly be seen by canoes approaching from Maui, making it a very formidable sight." The heiau is on private property, but you can call 800 670-6965 or 808 558-8132 for permission to visit.

down to the soul of the temple, where relic ashes repose.

Michael and I scrambled down a streambed awash with runoff. Water ran through the rocks and across the highway and into the mango grove and over the beach, staining the fishponds and the sea blood red. The entire south coast of Molokai oozed that redness the next morning when Michael and I flew back to Honolulu.

I don't know if one thing had to do with the other. I am sure it was all coincidence that a rainstorm and rainbow occurred just after I'd trod too far on sacred ground. I do know it was good to visit Ili'ili'opae heiau, but it was better to leave.

THE HEADLESS BOATMAN
by J. B. Smith

MY FAMILY LIKED TO CAMP in the hilly farm country between Fredericks-burg and Milltown, Indiana, along the banks of the Blue River. In the 1970s and '80s, campers could choose from campgrounds ranging from KOAs to the much more interesting mom-and-pop operations out in the backcountry, including our campground of choice: Recreation Unlimited. The campground lay between the river and the cornfields of the property owner. It was an area that had been farmed for more than a hundred years, and some echoes of the past still thumped and bumped down that river on a regular basis. In other words, the river had a ghost.

One of the worst floods on record struck the Ohio River Valley in January 1937. In a matter of a few days, over nineteen inches of snow, rain, and sleet fell across the region. The Ohio and its tributaries, including the Blue River, rose thirty-three feet above their normal banks, inundating much of the surrounding lands. Hundreds died.

THE UNLUCKY FARMER
When the weather started turning nasty, a farmer who lived in the vicinity of what eventually became our campground climbed into a flat-bottom longboat and paddled along the river to drive his prize cattle to higher ground. He underestimated the power of the storm, and on his return he encountered a river gone mad. It was twenty feet above flood stage and roaring along at over 35 miles per hour. He tried to make for safety on the shore, but his boat was thrown under a driftwood logjam with such force that he was decapitated. His smashed boat and headless body were found along the icy river several weeks later.

It was then that the legend of the Headless Boatman of the Blue River took root. It was said that you could hear the farmer's ghost as he paddled along the river in search of his missing head.

I myself heard the hollow *thump . . . swish . . . thump . . . swish* of a phantom boat being paddled down an empty river many times, as did my cousins and various friends. It became a game for us to see whether the sounds we heard belonged to the living or the Boatman as boats came down the river.

Early on many evenings, we'd hear a boat come around the bend, only to see nothing there. We'd run through the woods alongside the river, following the sounds of the paddle to confirm what we didn't see. After close calls with poisonous snakes, natural pitfalls, and other dangerous obstacles, we stopped chasing the phantom boat. I thought at the time that something might be warning us to stay away.

A Phantom Blaze

Many things changed along the Blue River as I hit my late teens. Indiana declared it a "wild river" to protect it from development, leading to restrictions on river access and usage. As a result, the owner of the campground decided not to renew leases on the individual campsites. Luckily, my family had just renewed our lease, so we would be among the last campers to leave this bucolic home away from home.

On our last weekend, we moved some of our possessions off the campsite. We finished in early evening and were chatting with our neighboring campers when we heard that familiar *thump . . . swish* sound–this time very close by.

The sound was followed by something completely unexpected.

About two campsites down, we saw a fire spring to life inside a wooden shack used to shelter the fire pit. One moment there was nothing, and in the next the entire shack seemed to be illuminated by a roaring fire. Fearing the worst, several of us grabbed shovels and fire extinguishers to try to contain the blaze.

As we ran toward the shack, we had to drop down into a small ravine and detour around several trees bisecting the path. By the time we got to the campsite, all signs of the fire had vanished. No burn marks, no smoke, and the welded steel-plate fireplace was stone cold.

We all confirmed to one another that we hadn't been confused and that we had seen a fire blazing away not two minutes before. It was then we heard the familiar paddling noise, moving away from us down the river. Could it be that the Boatman was giving us one last thrill and leaving us with a memory to keep for the rest of our lives?

GHOSTLY
GRAVEYARDS

The fence around a cemetery is foolish, for those inside can't get out and those outside don't want to get in.
—Arthur Brisbane

WE BEG TO DIFFER with Mr. Brisbane's quote—at least on the part about "those outside" not wanting to get in. Some of us on the outside do want to get in, not in a coffin but as walking, talking visitors able to leave whenever we choose.

Some cemeteries are so historic and beautiful they become tourist attractions. Others are long forgotten and attract visitors who are up to no good. What all cemeteries have in common is their abundance of stories—not only the stories of the individuals who've been laid to rest there, but often of tales of the spirits of the dead who wander among the tombstones.

It could be that many of these spirits just want to stick close to their mortal remains. Others may want to protect their turf, and do so by becoming aggressive—sometimes terrifyingly so. In other cases, what is perceived as a ghost could merely be a product of the imagination.

To paraphrase a common epitaph, "What I am now you will soon be." In other words, the places where we bury our dead also serve as reminders of our own mortality. If we imagine that those who lie buried covet mortality, we could easily further imagine that maybe they're jealous of us living folk—jealous to the point of popping up to remind us that we shouldn't take life for granted.

The places of rest in this chapter run the gamut from abandoned cemeteries to those with vacancies yet to be filled. A word to the wise: Whatever the nature of a graveyard, always respect the dead. We never know what they might do if we don't.

THE BLACK ANGEL'S EYES

by Ali Garaets

GROWING UP IN IOWA CITY, IOWA, I never put much stock in ghost stories. Sure, my town had its share of legends and weird happenings, but I didn't take any of them seriously until the summer of 2000, when I was sixteen.

Late one night that summer, I was at a backyard bonfire with a group of my friends when we decided we wanted to go do something we'd never done before. We voted to visit the Black Angel.

The Black Angel, located in Oakland Cemetery, is a huge statue standing over the graves of the Feldevert family. The Angel, once gleaming bronze, became covered by a black patina. Supposedly, if someone crossed her path, made her angry, or did anything impure, the Angel would strike that person down.

I never believed the stories, and they didn't stop me from joining my friends as we set out at 2:00 a.m. Four of us drove to Prairie du Chien Road and

153

down toward Hickory Hill Park. After we parked the car and took a quarter-mile walk up the hill to Oakland, we climbed its south wall and began to move quietly through the huge graveyard.

I'm not sure how long it took us to find the Black Angel, but she was suddenly right there before us. Dwarfing us all, she stood with one wing outstretched by her hand, the other draped behind her shoulder. I remember that we stared at her for the longest time, not knowing what to say.

It's rumored that if a virgin receives her first kiss before the Angel, she'll die; they also say that if you touch the Angel you'll suffer a horrible ailment or even death. So, being stupid teenagers, we dared each other to touch her. Finally, one of the guys reached out a hand and brushed the base of the statue with his fingertips. We then all glanced up at the Angel's face,

which the moonbeams had given a hellish halo. Even scarier were her eyes: They were silver in the moonlight, and not because of the reflections from the moon. She looked positively demonic.

Terrified, we ran out of the cemetery as fast as we could, scrambling up and over the wall. As we ran down the hill toward our car, we heard what sounded like loud screams coming from the cemetery. We couldn't explain it away as the wind, since there wasn't any wind to speak of. Relieved to make it back to the car, we quickly peeled out of the Hickory Hill parking lot.

My Return

I went back to the cemetery for the first time four years later, wondering if I would witness anything to confirm what I know I saw earlier. I stood in front of the Angel and I looked up into her face, but I saw nothing to be afraid of. Before leaving the cemetery, I left fresh flowers for the family of Feldeverts lying below my feet. I like to think that the Angel is just protecting them.

I don't know what it was that my friends and I saw that night, but I do know that I now keep a much more open mind about these things. When I hear people talk about the Angel, I tell them, "It's true. Don't make her angry. Don't go up there." A few years back, some kids died after vandalizing the cemetery. Could she have had anything to do with it?

If you go to see the Black Angel, be respectful and understand that she's watching over the whole cemetery.

OAKLAND CEMETERY
1000 Brown Street, Iowa City IA 52245

GHOSTS OF GREENWOOD

by Troy Taylor

EXACTLY WHEN PEOPLE were first interred at what is now Greenwood Cemetery in Decatur, Illinois, remains a mystery. First used as a burial ground for native peoples, it began to be used as a graveyard by settlers sometime in the 1820s. It also may be the site of the graves of runaway slaves. In 1857, the cemetery was officially incorporated into the city of Decatur, and by 1900 it had become the place to be buried. But its prominence was short-lived and in 1920 the cemetery went bankrupt. The grounds soon became overgrown and the graves fell into disrepair.

It was the desolation of the oldest part of the cemetery that led to the stories and legends that would haunt Greenwood for years to come. When the city of Decatur took charge of Greenwood in 1957, it also took responsibility for maintaining the cemetery. Still, the graveyard's reputation stuck. Stories of ghosts and the unexplained mingle fact with fiction and are told to this day. Following are two of the best known.

155

THE GREENWOOD BRIDE

The story of Greenwood's most famous resident ghost, the Greenwood Bride, is set in the early 1930s and concerns a young couple engaged to be married. The young man was a reckless bootlegger who in no way was approved by his future bride's family. One summer night, the couple decided to elope; the plan was to meet just past midnight, as soon as the young man could deliver one last shipment of whiskey and pocket enough money for a wedding trip. But the marriage would not come to pass. During the delivery, the man was murdered by rival businessmen who dumped his body into the Sangamon River, where fishermen found it the next morning.

The young woman had gone to the arranged meeting place and waited until daybreak for her lover. She was worried when she returned home, and then utterly devastated when she learned he had been killed. Crazed with grief, she began tearing at her hair and clothing. Even though the family doctor sedated her, she disappeared later that night, taking only her wedding dress with her.

She was found the next day in the dress, floating face down in the river near where her lover's body had been pulled ashore. She had taken her own life, perhaps hoping to find him in eternity.

Her body was laid to rest on a hill in Greenwood Cemetery, but there is reason to believe she doesn't rest there in peace. As time passed, witnesses began reporting encounters with an apparition that's come to be called the Greenwood Bride. They claim the ghost of a woman in a glowing bridal gown can be seen weaving among the tombstones on the hill. She walks with her head down, a scrap of cloth gripped tightly in her hand. Occasionally, she raises it to her face, as if wiping away tears.

Prisoners of War

If other visitors to the cemetery are to be believed, the Greenwood Bride has company: soldiers who were buried in a mass grave on a high, desolate hill in the far southwest corner of Greenwood Cemetery.

During the Civil War, Decatur was on a direct line of the Illinois Central Railroad, which ran deep into the South. The line continued north and connected to a railroad that went to Chicago. Here, it reached Camp Douglas, a

prison for Confederate soldiers. Many trains came north carrying Union troops bound for Decatur and beyond. Soldiers aboard these trains were often wounded, sick, and dying. Occasionally, deceased soldiers were taken from the trains and buried in Greenwood Cemetery, which was very close to the train tracks.

In 1863, a prison train holding more than a hundred Rebel prisoners pulled into Decatur. Many of them had contracted yellow fever in the diseased swamps of the South. The Union officers in charge of the train had attempted to separate soldiers who had died in transit, but to no avail. Many of the men were close to death from the disease, and it was hard to tell who was alive and who wasn't.

The bodies were removed from the train and taken to Greenwood Cemetery, where they were unloaded and stacked at the base of a hill in the southwest corner—possibly the least desirable spot in the cemetery. The hill was so steep that many of the gravediggers had trouble keeping their balance. In a portent of what was to come, perhaps, it was the last place anyone would want to be buried.

The men hastily dug shallow graves and tossed the bodies of the Confederates inside. It has been said that without a doctor present, no one could have known if all of those buried were actually dead. Some may have been inadvertently buried alive—no doubt the reason why this is said to be the most haunted section of Greenwood.

Decades of reports tell of ghosts and strange energy lingering about the hill. Visitors, many of them knowing nothing of the hill's bizarre history, have seen mysterious lights and heard voices, footsteps in the grass, whispers, and cries of torment. Some even claim to have been touched or pushed by unseen hands. There are also reports of soldiers returning from the other side of the grave, with visitors seeing what they described as transparent men in uniform walking among the tombstones.

Could the Confederate soldiers who were buried so haphazardly on the hill be determined to make themselves known to the living?

157

GREENWOOD CEMETERY
606 S. Church Street, Decatur IL 62522

"DO NOT GO ALONE!"
by Greg Bishop

SOME FOURTEEN MILES WEST of the wine mecca of Paso Robles, on California's central coast, is a historic burial ground that plays host to a tragic but harmless spirit—and, so they say, any number of more sinister ones. The graveyard can be found in the community of Adelaida, first settled in the late nineteenth century. Pioneers flocked to the area for the perfect weather that seemed to make everything grow. A post office was established at Adelaida in 1887, and Mennonite Christians of German origin soon became a presence in the town.

It is said that the cemetery's most famous ghost is that of Charlotte M. Sitton, supposedly a Mennonite woman who met with horrible misfortune when both of her children died in a diphtheria epidemic. Most accounts say that Sitton was so distraught over the loss of her children that she committed suicide. (While this makes a good story, there has been no evidence uncovered that lends credence to the tale.) Several other accounts have Sitton sinking into a depression from which she never recovered and taking her own life a few years later by either hanging herself in the schoolhouse or taking poison.

Many youngsters' graves in the cemetery give 1887 as the date of death—probably the year the diphtheria epidemic raged through the little town. Sitton, who was nineteen when she left the world of the living, died in 1889.

Charlotte is supposed to make her appearance every Friday night, anywhere from 10:00 to 11:30, either drifting through the tall grass and weeds in a white dress or wandering about the headstones weeping for her children.

MRS. SITTON'S COMPANIONS

Because the Adelaida Cemetery sits atop the summit of a commanding hill amid thousands of acres of fog-shrouded vineyards, it's hardly surprising that the lonely hillside has attracted the attention of amateur parapsychologists for years. And they are not often disappointed.

On entering the cemetery, the first thing a visitor notes is the thick strands of Spanish moss hanging from the oaks, as if the place were decorated for some sort of year-round Halloween party. Ghost hunters and run-of-the-mill thrill seekers alike have reported seeing shadowy human-shaped mists and furtive

glowing red eyes and hearing the sound of footsteps. Newly bought or fully charged batteries fail, and EMFs (electromagnetic field meters) go wild. Cold spots come and go, and hooded black figures chase the adventurous.

Daniel Barry, an investigator who made at least two trips to the area, stated that the hooded specter appeared in his bedroom three weeks after a visit to Adelaida.

Perhaps the last word should be left to Mr. Barry: "If you go to this cemetery to investigate these findings, DO NOT GO ALONE. . . . There seems to be an evil presence in the grove of trees at the center of this cemetery. Red eyes are normally connected to a poltergeist, which can be very harmful."

ADELAIDA CEMETERY
Klau Mine Road, Paso Robles CA 93446

THE PINEWOODS SCRATCHER
by Evan De Georgio

PINEWOODS CEMETERY is located in Brunswick, New York, a small town east of Troy that's less than an hour's drive from my hometown of Clifton Park. Its real name is Forest Park Cemetery, but most people who live in the Albany/Troy/Schenectady area call it Pinewoods after a road that runs alongside it. I had heard all the stories about the cemetery long before I visited it, but nothing prepared me for what happened when I went there with a group of friends.

It was a Saturday night, and my friends and I were looking for a thrill—and thought Pinewoods might be the place to find it. So we drove to the cemetery and parked on the road outside the entrance. We were all a little apprehensive, but that didn't keep us from walking right in.

As soon as we entered, we heard strange sounds that could have been voices. But we kept walking. I held the flashlight as we ventured toward the remains of a large mausoleum in the middle of the cemetery.

When we stopped in front of the mausoleum, we heard something moving near the spot where my friend Jay was standing. The flashlight showed it to be a tree, its branches creaking and cracking as if someone were climbing it. But no one was. Nor was there any wind that night to rustle the branches.

We just stood there, too scared to move on. Finally Jay said, "Okay, who here has guts?" He then began to walk toward the path that leads to some headless statues in a different part of the cemetery, and my younger brother Adam and his friend Troy started to follow him.

Just as they struck off, we heard a loud sound from the mausoleum. Jay, Adam, and Troy doubled back to join those of us who'd stayed behind. Even with the flashlight on high beam, I couldn't see what it was; but it sounded like it was coming toward us. Jay came up next to me and said, "Whatever it is, it's right there in those trees."

UNEXPLAINED GASHES

The flashlight must have been casting some light on my face, because Nicole pointed toward me and told my fiancée, Candi, to look.

Candi turned and said, "Oh my God."

Then the rest the group looked at me and started shouting that my face was bleeding. In fact, it did burn a little, and I ran toward the road and our cars. Everyone else followed, still screaming.

When I got to my car, I felt like I was about to throw up. Someone shined the flashlight on my face again, and everyone got even more upset. We jumped into our cars and peeled out. As we drove away, I took a quick look at myself in the rearview mirror and was shocked to see two bloody gashes on my left cheek.

To calm down, we headed to a nearby bar. There we met two strangers, Dennis and Phil. They asked about the scratches on my face but were skeptical when we told them what had happened. They said they were familiar enough with the cemetery to know that the route we'd taken had no low-lying trees or branches that could have gashed me. So, foolishly or not, we all went back to the cemetery to investigate further.

The eight of us walked close together as we entered. I didn't hold the flashlight this time, thinking maybe that was the reason I'd gotten scratched. I also put the hood of my sweatshirt up to protect my face.

We walked closer to the mausoleum than we had before and began to hear the same strange noises. Dennis, who was holding the flashlight, said he saw eyes up ahead. My brother Adam saw them too, once Dennis pointed them out.

Barely five minutes had passed when Troy looked at my face and very calmly said, "Evan, let's go back to the road now." Then, when everyone else looked at me, they took off running.

Thinking Troy had roped the others into playing a joke on me, I wanted to punch him. But as soon as we got to the road, a girl pulled a small mirror out of her purse and someone shined the flashlight on my face. What I saw were five new scratches—this time, on my right cheek. Two of the scratches were in the shape of an "X." I felt like crying as we started back toward the cars.

As we drove home to Clifton Park, Troy said that he had been watching my face as best he could for the whole time we'd been there. He saw blood forming on my face, he said, but not anything that could have scratched it. And just like the first time, I felt nothing when it happened.

But that's not all that happened that night. The whole way back home, the

A CEMETERY'S HISTORY

FOREST PARK CEMETERY is located in Brunswick, New York. It has no strange history of its own—no mass murders, no graves left under pricey new homes, no surreptitiously buried slaves or colonial soldiers. It was originally planned to cover two hundred acres and designed by the first African American graduate of the Rensselaer Polytechnic Institute. The most impressive feature of the cemetery was a large granite receiving tomb, which according to the Upper Hudson Library System's Web site originally featured a "rolled copper roof and domed glass skylight" and contained "128 marble catacombs."

Forest Park was incorporated in the late nineteenth century and went bankrupt twice before finally being abandoned in the 1930s. By the 1990s, it had shrunk to less than twenty-two acres, some of which run along Pinewoods Avenue—the reason so many locals refer to the graveyard as Pinewoods. The skylight and roof are long gone from the receiving tomb, and the rest of the structure is covered in graffiti. There have been attempts to restore and maintain the cemetery, but as with many places that are allowed to decay, people take notice, imaginations run wild, and the curious arrive in droves—the reason the cemetery is now open only to those whose friends and loved ones are buried there.

Most of the cemetery's rumored hauntings don't revolve around ghostly figures. Instead, statues bleed and disembodied babies cry. The cemetery even has its own versions of the bloody hook and Resurrection Mary stories. How true they are is anybody's guess, but the fact that they exist leads to this conclusion: Take one abandoned cemetery and throw in a few overactive teenage imaginations, and you've got the fodder for plenty of ghostly legends.

162

lights inside the car went on and off, over and over again. I said out loud to whatever I hoped was responsible, "I'm sorry we went to the cemetery and bothered you. Can you please leave us alone?" After I spoke, the lights stayed on, but we couldn't get them to turn off until miles later.

The scars from the scratches on my face are still visible today. Whenever anyone asks me what happened, I just say I got into a fight. And why not? No one would believe me if I told them the truth.

FOREST PARK CEMETERY
(Pinewoods Cemetery, Forest Park Cemetery)
Access prohibited to all but family members.
Pinewoods Avenue, Brunswick NY 12580

THE WITCH'S BALL

by James A. Willis and Andrew Henderson

IN MYRTLE HILL CEMETERY in Valley City, Ohio, a spherical marble stone marks the grave of a woman who was a tormented soul. What form the torment took varies from story to story, but all portray the woman—a Mrs. Stoskopf—as suffering mental and physical abuse at the hands of her husband and young sons.

Finally, the woman plotted her revenge. She decided to poison the family's water supply, the well in the backyard. She killed her entire family, then dumped them all into the well.

With her family missing, it didn't take long for the neighbors to become suspicious of Mrs. Stoskopf. The bodies were eventually discovered and the woman was arrested. She was deemed unfit to stand trial and instead was committed to a state mental hospital for the rest of her life. Upon her death, her remains were relocated to Myrtle Hill Cemetery and buried beneath the heavy round stone.

163

A variation of the legend says the woman in question was also a witch, who turned to the dark side to seek her revenge. She's said to have practiced her craft in and around the cemetery, including the nearby woods. It is also said that after the bodies of her husband and sons were discovered, the townspeople stoned the woman to death. Her body was then buried under the heavy sphere to keep her from rising from the grave.

Such precautions did little good because the woman's spirit is said to have found a way to escape the grave and return to the places where she practiced her magic. It is also believed by many that the stone itself has soaked up some of the woman's evil, explaining why it feels warm to the touch in the winter and freezing in the summer. It is said that snow and leaves don't fall near the monument, suggesting that even nature is fearful of the Witch's Ball.

MYRTLE HILL CEMETERY
Myrtle Hill Road, Valley City OH 44280

ROSE HILL'S PERSISTENT PHANTOMS
by Mike Marinacci

ROSE HILL CEMETERY, a small burial ground above the nineteenth-century ghost towns of Nortonville and Somersville, California, bears silent testimony to the hardships and tragedies of life in this coal-mining region, formerly populated by hundreds of Welsh immigrants. Tombstones mark the resting places of men killed by mine disasters and black lung, of women who died in childbirth, of infants and small children felled by typhus and smallpox. Some of the headstones are lettered in Welsh, flowery Celtic epitaphs to the dead.

But the sleep of the dead has been disturbed here. In recent years, vandals have opened graves and have toppled, smashed, or stolen headstones. Many of the beautiful tombstones that once graced the cemetery are either missing or broken.

The White Witch et al.

Such wanton desecration, some local psychics say, is what causes the eerie phenomena in and around Rose Hill Cemetery. Ghostly laughter, cries, and the tolling of bells are sometimes heard coming from the graveyard. On still days, a windlike sound occasionally whispers through the cypress trees on the hill. Some people have seen a glowing cross hover silently above the night-darkened cemetery. And in one incident, a photographer in the graveyard was knocked down and menaced by an invisible force.

Rose Hill's best-known phantom is the White Witch. Also referred to as the Glowing Lady and the Gliding Woman, she's a luminous white specter who glides above the field of headstones. One night, a couple who had driven to the cemetery for a tryst was terrified when she floated right over to their parked car. Considering the damage the cemetery has endured, one can hardly blame her for chasing off the living.

It seems that the Rose Hill phantoms are a persistent, unforgiving lot. Though each of the 119 known gravesites has been exorcised, the disturbances continue to this day.

Perhaps the living can yet make amends to the dead here. The Oakland-based East Bay Regional Park District is currently trying to track down missing headstones, repair damaged ones, and generally help restore Rose Hill Cemetery to its prevandalism state. These good works may achieve what exorcism couldn't—bringing peace to the cemetery once again.

THE LADY IN GRAY

by Andrew Henderson

A MELANCHOLY GHOST haunts the rows at Camp Chase Confederate Cemetery, on the west side of Columbus, Ohio. Known as the Lady in Gray, she usually weeps quietly over the grave of one Benjamin F. Allen, a private in the 50th Tennessee Regiment, Company D. Allen's grave is number 233 out of 2,260 Confederate soldiers laid to rest in this two-acre plot in the capital city of a very Northern state.

The cemetery in Columbus's Hilltop neighborhood marks the place where a prisoner of war camp stood more than 140 years ago, though at the time the location was well outside the city limits. In May 1861, a Union military training ground named Camp Jackson was established here. By July of that year, when the first prisoners were admitted, its name was changed to honor President Lincoln's Secretary of State (and later Chief Justice of the United States), Hamilton County native Salmon P. Chase.

165

At first, Camp Chase took only officers as prisoners, with enlisted men imprisoned at Fort Warren, near Boston Harbor. A large number of the officers were captured during 1862 Union victories at Fort Donelson, Tennessee, and Mississippi Island No. 10. But by the beginning of 1863, some 8,000 men of every rank were incarcerated behind the high staked walls of the camp, necessitating the building of a stockade on Johnson's Island in Lake Erie. Most of the officers imprisoned at Camp Chase were transferred to Johnson's Island once the stockade was completed.

During the smallpox epidemic of 1863, some 500 of the imprisoned soldiers died in the month of February alone. Overcrowding forced two or three men to share single bunks and led to severe shortages in food, medicine, clothing, and blankets. Malnourished and cold, the men were highly susceptible to disease.

Near the end of that deadly year, a cemetery was built at the camp. As a result, the Confederate dead who had been buried in the city cemetery were moved back to Camp Chase, buried under cheap wooden markers in a plot surrounded by a low fence.

When the war ended in 1865, most of Camp Chase itself was dismantled. Some of the cabins where POWs had been housed were used as shanties for a few years; but for the most part, every trace of Camp Chase would soon be gone—except for the graveyard, which was left to deteriorate until it was restored and used as a gathering place for patriotic speeches in the 1890s.

Today the small cemetery is picturesque and well maintained, its wooden headstones replaced with granite. Its centerpiece is an arch constructed from granite blocks. Atop the arch stands the statue of a Confederate soldier facing south, and on the keystone below his feet is engraved a single word: AMERICANS.

WHO'S THAT LADY?

166 So many men died miserably here at a young age that it's surprising the Lady in Gray is the only ghost who haunts the place. She is described by witnesses as wearing a flowing gray dress and a gray veil hiding her face. Is she Benjamin Allen's Tennessee bride, weeping over the reunion that never happened?

Visitors to the cemetery and even those passing by the gates have reported seeing this woman walking among the seemingly endless line of tombstones. Once in a while, she is even seen walking through the locked cemetery gates at night. But more often than not, she is spotted standing over two specific graves—that of Benjamin Allen and one of an unknown soldier.

Researchers of the paranormal have yet to figure out who the ghostly woman is and why she chooses to mourn where she does. She doesn't appear to be the spirit of any known relative of Mr. Allen's, and her concern for an unknown soldier further compounds the mystery. Perhaps the Lady in Gray isn't connected to these graves at all but is simply eternally mourning the atrocities of war in general.

| CAMP CHASE CONFEDERATE CEMETERY |
| 2900 Sullivant Avenue, Columbus Ohio 43204 |

GHOST SIGHTINGS AT FORT BOISE

IN IDAHO is another military cemetery where strange goings-on have been reported—the one at Fort Boise, on Mountain Cove Road in Boise. Idaho Spirit Seekers, a group of paranormal researchers based in nearby Nampa, investigates the cemetery on a regular basis. While that group has yet to find evidence of any hauntings, members Marie Cuff and Julie Decker here relate some of the stories surrounding the cemetery.

"The story of Idaho and its beginnings is contained within the fences of the Fort Boise Military Cemetery. Enlisted men, officers and their families, and some civilians now rest there as a testament to the difficulties of pioneer life

"Some of the residents of the cemetery seem to think that they still have work to do. Ghostly soldiers patrolling the perimeter of the cemetery have been seen by many people over the years, and one man even got a picture of two soldiers in Civil War uniforms marching down the side of the cemetery.

"A psychic visiting the cemetery heard the restless ghost of a soldier speaking to her about a girl. 'It was obvious,' the psychic said, 'that he loved this pretty little girl very much and was worried about whether she was all right.' A tape recording of the conversation, made by the psychic on her visit, captured an EVP [electronic voice phenomenon] of the ghost saying 'Marge' in a labored voice.

"Local stories tell of a girl who hanged herself from the cemetery flagpole years ago. An attempt by some teenagers to contact the girl through a Ouija board was stopped short when a few of the girls suddenly felt unable to breathe. As soon as they walked away from the flagpole, their breathing returned to normal."

Are these incidents real or imagined? Marie and Julie still don't know, but say that they hope the military cemetery's haunted history will enable them to "someday run into one of the patrolling soldiers—and ask him whether he knows Marge."

A WOMAN CALLED INDIAN EVE
by Holly J. Thomas

SOME PEOPLE FIND CEMETERIES frightening just by their very nature, and the Messiah Lutheran Church's cemetery in Bedford County, Pennsylvania, can be particularly unnerving—and not just because the tombstones of the old graves are damaged, fallen over, or leaning. More disquieting is the long-standing belief that a ghost haunts this hallowed ground: the spirit of a woman who came to be known as Indian Eve.

Ironically, the grave of this woman is in fine condition and includes a quaint wooden plaque. The tombstone reads "Indian Eve, Wife of Adam Ernst," and the story behind her nickname is one of murder, kidnapping, and a long journey home.

Eve Hillebart (or Imler, according to some records) was married to Adam Henry Ernst in November 1757, when she was seventeen years old. The couple would be blessed with six children. In 1775, the happy family moved into a log cabin built by Adam on the banks of Dunnings Creek.

A mere two years later, tragedy would strike. On a morning in September 1777, Adam and two neighbors sat in the cabin preparing to spend the day splitting logs for fencing. Eve was puttering about in the kitchen with four-year-old Henry and baby Michael, and the four older children were still asleep in the loft.

The sun had barely come up when a band of Indians attacked.

SPIRITED AWAY

After ramming in the door, the Indians killed and scalped Adam and his friends right before Eve's eyes, then set fire to the cabin. The older children escaped by sliding down the roof of a shed attached to the cabin, then hid in the woods. But a different fate awaited Eve and the two youngest children. The Indians abducted them as the cabin went up in flames. Afterward, grieving relatives, though they found no remains, had no choice but to presume that Eve, Henry, and Michael were dead.

After a yearlong journey from Indian village to Indian village, Eve and her children were taken to Fort Detroit, where the Indians ransomed them to the British for rum and money. They remained there as prisoners for eight years, after which they were transported to Fort Duquesne in Pennsylvania. Another year passed before they were released. Only then could Eve and her children return home, with the boys riding a pony and Eve walking the whole way.

After enduring nearly nine years of captivity, Eve and her sons were finally reunited with the family they thought they would never see again. Some of her other children were now married with families of their own.

FOREVER MOURNFUL?

Home at last, Eve remarried, and she and husband, Conrad Samuel, settled on a farm at Dutch Corner, no more than ten miles from the log cabin where her first husband was slaughtered. (Today, the graves of the three men murdered in the raid can be seen on the banks of Dunnings Creek, marked by small fieldstones.) Eve reclaimed her life, put together the pieces of a family torn asunder, and forever after became known as Indian Eve, a legend in her own time. She passed away in 1815 and was buried at the Messiah Lutheran Church Cemetery, where she would later be joined in death by some of her children.

People say that Indian Eve's spirit haunts the cemetery, and some have even seen her apparition. She tends to appear on nights when the moon is full and bright, most often in summer or autumn.

If you happen to encounter this wandering soul, you'll likely see her near her own tombstone after sunset, gazing into the distance in a state of eternal unrest over the murder of her first husband. Or perhaps this devoted mother haunts the crumbling graveyard so she can watch over the spirits of her beloved children.

MESSIAH LUTHERAN CHURCH CEMETERY
741 Messiah Church Road, Bedford PA 15522

THE GHOST OF LITTLE GRACIE
by Abby Stillman Grayson

170   THE IDEA THAT children should be seen and not heard did not hold true for Gracie Watson when she was alive, and it doesn't hold true now. In fact, now it's just the opposite—Little Gracie makes herself heard but not seen. She is said to haunt the site of her parents' famed soirées, the former Pulaski Hotel in Savannah, Georgia.

The Watsons ran the Pulaski Hotel in the early 1880s, and Gracie was born in 1883. Northerners who longed to fit into Savannah society, the Watsons began inviting the city's elite to elaborate parties, with Gracie as an adored pint-size "hostess." Her father's pet, she charmed the upper crust until she became bored, at which point she would wander off to play under a stairwell at the back of the house.

When Gracie died at the tender age of six after a bout with pneumonia, she was sorely missed. Her father had a statue commissioned in her likeness to mark her gravesite in Bonaventure Cemetery. A marker at the grave tells the story.

Little Gracie Watson was born in 1883, the only child of her parents. Her father was manager of the Pulaski House, where the beautiful and charming little girl was a favorite with the guests. Two days before Easter, in April 1889, Gracie died of pneumonia at the age of six. In 1890, when the rising sculptor John Walz moved to Savannah, he carved from a photograph this life-sized, delicately detailed marble statue, which for almost a century has captured the interest of all passersby.

GONE FOR GOOD?

It's not just Gracie's gravesite that captures the interest of people in Savannah. Little Gracie, it has been reported, is still out and about. While the Pulaski

Hotel building still stood, it was said that a child could be heard playing under the stairwell, yet no child was in sight. In the new building that went up after the Pulaski was razed in 1957, the area around its former staircase became the site of the ladies' room—and many a surprised restroom visitor is said to have been startled by Gracie's antics.

171

Now that the new building houses a bank, it remains to be seen whether Gracie will continue to haunt the premises. Without the familiar din of people eating, laughing, and talking, will Little Gracie feel at home? Perhaps she will wander off in search of more entertaining diversions, as she was long ago known to do.

THE TOMBSTONE LEI

by Rick Carroll

THE OLDER WOMAN, pale and wheezing, looked about ready to die.

"Can I help you?" I asked.

"There's nothing we can do," her daughter answered.

We were waiting at Kahului Airport for the Honolulu plane one windy day in March or maybe April (one month seems like the other on Maui) when I noticed the older woman's distress.

"What happened?" I asked.

"It's so strange," her daughter said. "We stopped at that little Hawaiian church by the sea, the one with cats playing in the graveyard."

"Near Makena Landing?" I asked.

"Yes," she said, "that's the one, on the coast, past Wailea. We went for a drive. My mother wanted to stop at the church because the tombstones were strung with flower leis."

"What happened?"

"I touched one," the daughter said, "and the plumeria lei I was wearing around my neck just died; it shriveled up and fell in dust to the ground. We should have left right then, but my mother took a lei from a tombstone—the flowers were so beautiful—and put it around her neck. It happened immediately: Her face turned white, pale white. Something was strangling her. She couldn't breathe."

172

"THANK YOU"

Concerned, I asked, "What did you do?"

"I took the lei off her and put it back on the tombstone, and we left right away for the airport."

"How long ago?" I asked.

"About an hour," her daughter said.

Her mother fanned her face with her plane ticket. I got her a cup of water and told her that she'd either had an allergic reaction to the flowers or encountered a spirit in the graveyard. If a spirit were the cause, I told her, she probably would be all right if she told the island she was sorry. It was all I could do.

"Thank you," mother and daughter said. "Thank you."

After we deplaned in Honolulu, I saw them again. Mother was breathing easier. Daughter looked less anxious. I bid them Aloha, and they smiled and waved good-bye. I like to think the mother had taken my advice and apologized.

When I later told my Hawaiian pal Sam Henderson about the incident, he shook his head. "She's lucky," he said. "Never take someone's lei. Especially if they're dead." *173*

WELCOME TO SPOOKSVILLE
by Jenifer Parastschenko

WHEN I WAS A JUNIOR in high school, my best friend was my next-door neighbor Sara. One night we planned to hang out with her boyfriend Craig, his friend Matt, and Matt's neighbor Vinny. Matt picked us all up and decided to take us to a cemetery in Sussex County, New Jersey—a graveyard the locals call Spooksville.

Sara and I thought the guys only wanted to scare us into sitting on their laps and crying. Thinking this would make them feel better about themselves, we decided to play along with their plan.

I sat up front with Matt, who during the whole trip told me stories of ghost sightings at the cemetery. After we drove down a wooded road and passed over a one-lane bridge spanning a swamp, we finally got to the chained-off cemetery at about 10:00 p.m. It's not visible from the road, since it's set about fifty yards away in the middle of a hayfield surrounded by trees and underbrush.

Matt stopped his car near the cemetery entrance, and Craig got out to relieve himself and walked into a ditch on the side of the road.

After a minute or so, I turned to look down the road behind us and saw someone in white clothing walking toward the car. I assumed it was Craig, since he was wearing a white T-shirt and light-colored blue jeans.

I got out of the car and yelled, "Craig, what the hell are you doing all the way out there?"

Just then, a voice right next to me said, "I'm right here. Who are you talking to?"

I looked on the driver's side of the car and there was Craig, standing in the ditch and zipping up his pants. I looked at him. Then I looked at the apparition, which was getting closer by the second. "If you're here," I said, "then what the hell is that?"

THE FLOATING FIGURE

Matt saw what I saw, then looked at me with eyes as wide as saucers. We jumped back into the car and told Matt to step on it. Matt tried, but the car's engine shut off all of a sudden. We would have thought the battery had died if the headlights hadn't stayed on—but they did. The radio, which had been playing music up until that moment, now transmitted only static.

Sara turned around and looked out the back window. The figure was only a few yards away from us now. Sara started to cry, Craig was yelling at Matt to get going, and Vinny was curled up on the back seat saying Hail Marys. I was not only dumbfounded but also scared out of my wits.

The figure was so close I could tell that it was a female with long dark hair, a white flowing nightgown-style dress, and piercing deep-set eyes. What shocked me was that she had no feet. She was floating toward us! Now almost up to the car, she reached out her left arm as if to touch us. At just that moment, Matt's car started.

We tore off, but after about fifty yards we had to stop. Blocking our escape was an old farmer sitting on his tractor with the headlights off in the middle of the road. He jumped off the tractor, came up to the driver's side window, started yelling at us, and demanded to know why we were near the cemetery.

Matt just stared at him, so I told the farmer we'd just seen a ghost. The old man spit his tobacco and said, "That's what you kids get! I keep telling the locals to stay away from here because you little punks keep on stirring things up!"

Our jaws dropped. The farmer then yelled, "Now get out of here before I call the cops." He sure didn't have to tell us twice! We were out of there before he could finish his sentence.

It has been almost ten years since that night. Sara and I remain friends and still talk about our experience every once in a while, even though it freaks us out. I don't know the real history of the cemetery and why such strange things are supposed to happen there. But I do know that I saw something that night, and so did four other people. What that farmer said was even stranger, making me wonder whether he guards the spirits from people, and vice versa.

If you're looking for a place that will give you a good scare, it's definitely the cemetery they call Spooksville. Just don't let the old farmer catch you!

KATIE LIKES FLOWERS
by Joanne Austin

MANY ABANDONED BITS of civilization are found in the woods in the part of New Jersey where I live—towns that simply disappeared off the map for one reason or another. Their remnants include foundations of buildings, mine shafts, and graveyards—and the closest I've ever come to a haunting was in one of these forgotten graveyards.

Cherry Ridge Cemetery is located somewhere off the New York–Tennessee gas pipeline that runs through the area. According to local lore, the graveyard is haunted, and you can hear strange noises, moaning, and even music and laughter there. The cemetery served families in the area until they were bought out by the state so that a reservoir could be built to supply the city of Newark with clean drinking water.

One day I was hiking along the gas pipeline with friends. The pipeline is buried, and there's a large clearing around it that makes for a wide trail that's unobstructed except for the occasional boulder or marshy spot. We had come to a place that was high up on a hill, and we could look ahead at the other hills along the pipeline—a vista that brought to mind a roller coaster. We stopped here for a little while to rest.

A MYSTERIOUS URGE

As a hiker who subscribes to the "take only pictures, leave only footprints" philosophy, I don't normally pick wildflowers on a trail. But today was different. There were these pretty little purple flowers growing just off the pipeline. And something made me pick some. I thought I could either put them in water or press them in a book when I got home—again, not things I normally do. My friends kidded me about my breach of hiking protocol.

We finished resting and decided to head back the way we had come. We had planned to visit Cherry Ridge Cemetery, which we knew was somewhere on our way back. But we weren't sure exactly where.

When I came to a certain spot along the trail, I had a hunch the graveyard was off to our right. Even though nothing indicated the graveyard was nearby—no trail, no markings—I slipped into the forest. The rest of the group followed, and we scuttled around for a short time in the dry leaves and undergrowth. Then I saw the graves, most of them sunken and with headstones long

gone or broken. I felt myself being drawn to the back corner of the graveyard.

There I found the gravestone of Katie Rome, one of the youngest known occupants of the graveyard, having died in 1880 when she was only three. Buried next to her was her mother Lucretia, who died only a few years after Katie.

As I stood there, I suddenly knew why I had picked the flowers. I crouched and put most of the flowers on Katie's grave, then left the rest with her mom. Michelle, one of the friends I was hiking with, said to me, "Oh, that's so sweet of you!"

Maybe so, but I can't help wondering how much of my kindly gesture was really under my control that day. Perhaps I had some help from a small, long-deceased child who in life enjoyed pretty little purple flowers.

HOSTEL
ENVIRONMENTS

You can check out any time you like
But you can never leave . . .
–The Eagles, "Hotel California"

HOTELS, INNS, AND RESORTS are places where the weary traveler can safely rest, kick up his feet, and check out the minibar offerings or order room service. Where she'll find fresh sheets, tiny towels, and a toilet that has been sanitized for her protection. Maybe even a mint on the pillow, if it's a classier establishment. In short, a home away from home.

But not really like home. There's a transient quality to these places. After a sleepover on the road, a business meeting, a convention, or a vacation, lodgers head home with at least a few toiletries and possibly a satisfying outcome to their endeavors. The rooms they stay in are cleaned up and set aside for the next living bodies, a process repeated ad infinitum.

Not all hotel guests discussed in this chapter turn in their keys or plastic room cards at the end of a stay, nor do some of the proprietors ever leave. Rather, they hang around after they've departed this life. Guests in a South Dakota hotel have met the icy gaze of the town's first sheriff and luxury hotel owner. The ghost of a "loose" woman likes to steal guests' underwear in a Georgia inn. Little girls haunt hotels in Oregon, Oklahoma, and Ohio. A deadly domestic dispute plays out over and over again in an empty room in a Nevada hotel, and a door-knocking spirit harasses female hotel guests in Alabama.

So hang your DO NOT DISTURB sign on the door, if you dare, and get ready to check into some of the scariest hotels in the United States. We'll leave the lights out for you!

THE BULLOCK HOTEL

by Scott A. Johnson

DEADWOOD, SOUTH DAKOTA. The very name evokes images of the Old West, cowboys, and hard-drinking, hell-raising good times. Though the ruffians of the past are gone, landmarks remind visitors of days gone by—especially in those places where the smell of cigar smoke and the sound of clinking poker chips still waft down the halls, and shadows shift and ebb.

In one of these historic places— the Bullock Hotel—cowboys whose lives were cut short by their revelries continue the party in the afterlife. And lest the party get too out of control, steel-gray eyes cut through the darkness, stopping many in their tracks and sending chills down the spines of the living.

181

When Deadwood was still in its infancy, it gained a reputation for unbridled bawdiness. Miners, transients, gamblers, gunfighters, wild men, and prostitutes made up most of the town's population, making nights rowdy and, as often as not, soaked with blood. There was money to be made from the trade of vice and sin, and for a time those who owned businesses simply counted the money coming in and paid little attention to their customers' antics. But when Jack McCall shot and killed James Butler "Wild Bill" Hickok (McCall was supposedly seeking revenge for the death of his brother at Hickok's hands), the need for law and order became apparent.

Seth Bullock, who owned a successful hardware store in town, was appointed the first sheriff of Deadwood—a role he seemed made for. He cut an imposing figure: tall, with a stare that could, according to all accounts, stop fights without a word spoken. According to his grandson, Bullock could "outstare a mad cobra or a rogue elephant." In fact, during his time as sheriff, Bullock never killed a single man. Yet his reputation and demeanor brought peace and order to the once rowdy town.

When fire broke out and claimed the Deadwood Hardware Store in 1894, Bullock bought the land and built the 64-room Bullock Hotel on its ruins at a cost of nearly $40,000. Construction took two years; but when the hotel finally opened, it was the finest of its day, with steam-heated rooms and a bath-room on every floor. It also boasted a 24-hour casi-no on the ground floor.

Seth Bullock

Bullock remained a colorful person for his entire life, enlisting with Theodore Roosevelt's Rough Riders and winding up appointed by Roosevelt as the state marshal of South Dakota. When he died in 1919 of cancer, it was in room 211 of his beloved hotel. He was buried in Mount Moriah Cemetery alongside Wild Bill Hickok and Calamity Jane. However, soon after he died, it became clear that while his body may have been laid to rest, he wasn't about to leave the hotel that bore his name. And he wasn't the only one, either.

A Posse's Worth of Ghosts

Just how crowded with ghosts is the Bullock Hotel? More than you'd imagine. Some paranormal investigators and psychics have estimated at least thirty-seven separate entities. Few other hotels in the world can boast the kind of paranormal activity present in the Bullock, and many of the phenomena sound as if they come straight out of the movies—in this case, both old westerns and horror films.

Eight of the hotel's rooms have a history of strange happenings. Guests' items are often reported to have moved inexplicably from one place to anoth-er, while others have simply disappeared, only to be found later in other loca-tions. Lights and electrical devices in the rooms have suddenly turned off and on, often when they're unplugged. The restaurant has also had its share of activity, with plates and glasses shaking, flying off the shelves, and smashing to the floor before guests' and employees' startled eyes. Even bar stools and cleaning carts move all by themselves, in full view of many witnesses.

Objects aren't the only things in the hotel that provide evidence of the unknown. The second and third floors are where most people report feeling a strong presence, often accompanied by phantom footsteps and even voices calling out guests' names in whispers. Some report hearing a low, lonely whistle coming down the hall, passing them and then fading as the unseen whistler goes about his way. Many declare that they have been tapped on the shoulder, and then turned, only to see an empty hallway.

Of the apparitions, the most frequently seen include shadows that dart in and out of the peripheral vision, leaving many witnesses with the uneasy feeling that they're being followed. Photographs taken in room 211, where Seth Bullock died, have often revealed misty apparitions hovering over the bed. There is even a little girl who people claim appears and disappears with alarming regularity in the hotel.

SETH'S SPIRIT

By far the most often seen—and most famous—apparition is that of Seth Bullock himself. Those who see him never forget his icy stare and imposing demeanor. Whether he stalks the hallways to keep the peace or an eye on his investment, those who see him claim they couldn't mistake his gaze. Still, it seems that Bullock isn't always the gritty character he was in life. On at least one occasion, a child became lost in the hotel, and according to the boy, it was Sheriff Bullock who led him back to his room.

The oldest hotel in Deadwood, the Bullock Hotel is not only still open for business but was completely restored in the 1990s. There has never been any documentation of the times of year when paranormal phenomena occur in the hotel, and an investigation performed in July 2003 yielded very few results, capturing only one anomalous spike in electromagnetic energy. However, because Bullock died in the month of September, it stands to reason that this would be the most likely time for visitors to brave the steely gaze of the Deadwood lawman.

As for the rest of the entities, sightings are both random and constant, depending on which apparitions decide to make their presence known. According to the staff and many guests, not a day goes by when something strange doesn't occur in Deadwood's most famous old hotel.

183

THE BULLOCK HOTEL
633 Main Street, Deadwood SD 57732

THE 17 HUNDRED 90 INN
by Scott A. Johnson

A MAN IS AWAKENED from a dead sleep in the middle of the night by fingers caressing his face and tugging at his blankets. In his sleep-induced stupor he smiles, rolling over to kiss his wife who, for whatever reason, seems very affectionate. It isn't until he rolls over and sees the empty pillow beside him that he remembers: He's not home; he's in a hotel in Savannah, Georgia, and the room is empty. As he whirls his head around the room, looking for the mysterious lover who woke him, he sees a thin streak of mist by the window. It seems to turn toward him, revealing tear-reddened eyes in a young woman's face, and then leaps out the window of his room with an ear-splitting scream.

Savannah has often been called the Jewel of the South, and its rich history reflects as much tragedy as glory. It seems a person can't go ten steps without hearing one story or another of deaths, either wrongful or self-inflicted, in any given building. But while many of the buildings purportedly house specters, few people know exactly who they are and why they choose to stay around. One such place is an old inn named for the year it first opened its doors: 17 Hundred 90 inn.

The inn was originally used as a boardinghouse. Because Savannah was a popular fishing and shipping port, rowdy sailors and pirates and their ilk frequented such places, some of which had less than savory reputations. One such person was a young woman—a girl of seventeen years, really—named Anna Power.

By all accounts, Anna was a woman of questionable moral fiber; in a word, she was loose. Whether fairly or not, her family felt she was a disgrace and turned her out on the streets. Miserable, she came to the boardinghouse, attempting to make her way in the world. It was there Anna found the man she believed to be the love of her life.

MAKING HER PRESENCE KNOWN

There are no records that state the name of the young sailor with whom Anna fell in love—and by whom she became pregnant. For the first time in her life, she felt happy. When she finally revealed to the sailor that she was with child, she fully expected him to quit the seafaring life and marry her. After all, they were in love, weren't they?

The sailor, it seemed, had other plans, and they didn't involve Anna Power. He set sail one evening with the tide, letting her know that he would probably never come back. From the third floor of the boardinghouse, Anna watched as the sails of her love's ship faded into the horizon. She then leapt from the window, ending her life and her suffering. Or so it would seem. Shortly thereafter, the room from which she jumped to her death became the site of some truly strange goings-on.

Eerie occurrences have been reported as late as 2003. A couple assigned to Anna's room arrived and went to unlock their door, but it wouldn't budge even after they'd done their best with the key. It seemed the deadbolt, which could only be operated from the inside, had been turned. They then sought out the manager, who had a passkey and assured them he would have no trouble getting them in. When they all returned to the door, it freely swung open.

While several spirits are said to still haunt the 17 Hundred 90 inn—including a man who seems to frequent the bar area and a woman who was reported to practice voodoo in the kitchen—it is the ghost of Anna Power that is the dominant soul of the place. Since the day of her death, Anna has roamed

the halls and particularly her room, causing mischief and letting lodgers know that she and her broken heart never left.

Many of the lodgers have reported hearing the cries of a baby at the top of the stairs, thought to come from Anna's unborn child. Others have told of flickering lights and mysterious footsteps. But what makes this haunting unique is even stranger.

One gentleman, who chooses to remain nameless, reportedly got into an argument with his wife while staying in Anna's room. The tiff became so heated that the wife banished her husband to the small couch for the night. Fast asleep, he was awakened by his wife, whom he thought wanted to "kiss and make up." The next morning, he rose from the couch and thanked her for being so understanding, only to have her glare at him and ask what he was talking about. The man swore that his encounter with a caressing woman was no dream.

On another occasion, a group of friends gathered in the tavern for dinner. When one of them brought up the subject of Anna Power, a woman in the party scoffed, claiming that ghosts couldn't possibly exist. She then excused herself to go to the ladies room. Once inside, she found herself pelted with half-empty tubes of toilet paper from an invisible assailant. She left the bathroom shaken—and no longer so skeptical.

ANNA THE PILFERER

Perhaps the thing that sets the haunting of the 17 Hundred 90 inn apart is that its ghost seems to have a sense of humor. In addition to locking doors from the inside and making advances to unsuspecting lodgers, Anna Power likes to steal things. Patrons have appeared at the front desk complaining of stolen wallets and keys. But there's one thing Anna seems to favor pilfering above all others: underwear. No one's knickers are safe, with Anna blamed for dozens of pairs of purloined pantaloons. All the stolen items—including the burgled bloomers— eventually turn up, most of them found in planters and at the back of shelves. But that hasn't kept some patrons from checking out of the inn immediately. The staff, on the other hand, think of Anna and her companions as family.

There seems to be no rhyme or reason to Anna's appearances; she simply comes and goes as she pleases. But most of the "fun" happens in room 204, where the young woman lived and loved. If you're lucky enough to book this prized room, just be sure to watch your undies!

---

17 HUNDRED 90
307 East President Street, Savannah GA 31401

THE GOLDEN LAMB

by James A. Willis

A VISIT TO THE GOLDEN LAMB in Lebanon, Ohio, is like stepping back in time. For more than two hundred years this restaurant and inn has been offering guests and weary travelers warm beds, delicious food, and spirits—spirits of all sorts.

In 1803, Jonas Seaman, formerly of New Jersey, applied for a license to "keep a house of public entertainment" at his residence. Raised by a father who was an innkeeper, Seaman wanted to try his hand at the trade. The idea was to use his two-story log cabin home as a place to offer fine food and lodging to those passing through the area. Seaman's wife, Martha, would handle the cooking duties.

Shortly after officially opening for business, Seaman's luck took a turn for the better when, in 1805, the first courthouse in Lebanon was built right across the street from the inn. Soon after, Seaman's little tavern became the spot for everyone to meet for lunch. In or around 1815, the first brick structure (now the lobby) was added to the log house. To meet the demand for lodging rooms, a third floor was added in 1834.

A dizzying array of famous people visited the inn in the ensuing two centuries, including Mark Twain and Charles Dickens. Twelve United States Presidents—among them James Garfield, Martin Van Buren, and Ronald Reagan—also stopped by. And if the stories are to be believed, some guests still roam the halls to this day.

LITTLE SARAH'S ANTICS

The first ghost believed to have haunted The Golden Lamb is Judge Charles R. Sherman, father of General William Tecumseh Sherman. Judge Sherman died in the building in June 1829. Guests have reported seeing a tall, gaunt figure walking the halls at night or smelling pipe tobacco inside the building, a nonsmoking establishment.

The most famous ghost at the inn is nonetheless shrouded in mystery. Although rarely seen, she makes her presence known by moving objects around in rooms, knocking things off walls, or causing ruckuses of other sorts. Perhaps for this reason, people began to refer to the ghost as that of a little girl.

She was given the name of Sarah, after the niece of inn manager Isaac

OHIO'S OLDEST HOTEL

IN 1940, the Daughters of the American Revolution officially established The Golden Lamb as Ohio's oldest hotel. Today the hotel that grew from a log cabin built in 1803 is on the National Historic Register, and the Ohio State Historical Society lists The Golden Lamb as Ohio's oldest continuous business. The current hotel boasts a dining area with over 450 seats and eighteen comfortable guest rooms.

Where the name The Golden Lamb comes from is unclear. An 1820s advertisement for the inn refers to the building as The Ohio and Pennsylvania Hotel at the Sign of the Golden Lamb, with the questions surrounding the name counting as a little mystery of its own.

188   Stubbs, on the assumption that she could be the mischievous ghost. Of course, in the world of ghost lore, fact and fiction tend to intermingle, and in reality Sarah lived well into adulthood.

Another theory about the ghostly girl is that she is actually Eliza Clay, the young daughter of Ohio statesman Henry Clay. Eliza died at The Golden Lamb from a fever in 1825. Local lore holds that her ghost first appeared after some of her effects were moved up to a fourth-floor room to be put on display. Apparently, the display wasn't to Eliza's liking and her ghost began moving items and "adjusting" photographs on the wall.

Today, the room is closed off to the public, although visitors to the fourth floor of The Golden Lamb can peer through the Plexiglas window installed in the door to see if anything has moved inside the room. The legend of the ghost is also printed there for all to read. Confusingly, the room Eliza Clay is believed to haunt is called "Sarah's Room." Apt, perhaps. Because in the end, who knows?

THE GOLDEN LAMB
27 South Broadway, Lebanon OH 45036

THE SILVER QUEEN HOTEL

by Janice Oberding

MARK TWAIN NEVER OWNED a cell phone. And if he could get by without that modern marvel, I reasoned, I could surely spend the night at the Silver Queen Hotel, which offers neither phones nor televisions in any of its twenty-nine rooms.

Built in Virginia City, Nevada, in 1876 when the Comstock Lode was dispensing silver to prospectors like bubble gum from a machine, the Silver Queen is famous for a painting adorning its walls: the floor-to-ceiling "silver dollar lady" in a dress made of 3,261 silver dollars. Tourists from all over the world snap shots of the buxom lady in the very expensive gown.

The sidewalks roll up early around here, considering there's not much to do but window-shop or hang out at a few saloons once the sun goes down. But that was okay with me. After dinner and a play at Piper's Opera House, I was ready to call it a night. With a long drive ahead of me the next day, I needed some rest. I fell asleep as soon as my head hit the pillow.

I might have slept the night away if not for the couple in the next room. This was the night they chose to argue. Because the hotel's transoms and walls were built in a different era, the argument would not be private. I rolled over and looked at the clock: 2:30 in the morning.

In the next room, the fight was on. He said something cruel; she snapped back. He replied, and she started whimpering.

"Come on you two," I said. "No one wants to hear your fights."

Wham! It sounded like he had shoved her against the wall. She was crying and begging his forgiveness. That was it! He was shoving her around and she was begging for forgiveness. He needed to go to jail and she needed help . . . more help than I could give her. I jumped up, ready to call the front desk.

But what was I thinking? This was a small hotel in a tiny town, and those who manned the desk were probably home somewhere sleeping like babies.

I would call the sheriff. No, I wouldn't, because there was no phone in this room—and like Mark Twain, I had no cell phone.

ASLEEP AT LAST

Then the name-calling began; he reeled off every vile name I have heard in my life—and believe me, I've heard plenty. She kept crying.

Why don't you just leave him? I silently asked her. Anything has to be better than what you're enduring. He pushed her against the wall again. She whimpered and promised never to do it again. What could she have done that warranted this kind of abuse? Nothing. He was a cruel monster, and I was going to report him first thing in the morning.

Silence. Had they kissed and made up? I wondered as I glanced at the clock. It was a little past 3:00, and if the couple next door stayed quiet, I could still get a few hours sleep. I pulled up the covers and drifted off.

The sun rose over the top of Sugar Loaf and shone through my window at 7:30—not as early as I wanted to get up, but I intended on reporting the man in the next room before he checked out. After breakfast, I found the manager and dutifully shared what I had heard last night from the other side of the wall. She looked at me as her brow furrowed. "You're kidding me, right?"

Kidding her! I don't kid about people being treated like that, and I told her so.

"There was no one in that room last night," she said.

"So they sneaked in?" I asked.

"Well, not exactly . . ." She gently led me away and out of earshot of anyone who might overhear us.

"What you heard were our ghosts. A man murdered his girlfriend in that room a long time ago, and . . ." She stopped at my expression of disbelief. "No one could possibly have been staying in that room last night. Come on, I'll show you."

I followed her up the stairs and she opened the door. Except for a ladder, a drop cloth, and other paint supplies, the room was empty. It was so cold I shivered.

"As you can tell, there's no heat on in here either," she said, smiling.

THE SILVER QUEEN HOTEL
28 North C Street, Virginia City NV 89440

THE HALLOWEEN WAITER
by Rick Carroll

DURING A STAY on the island of Lanai, I sat down to dinner one Halloween evening at The Lodge at Koele, and the waiter appeared at my elbow. I couldn't help but notice how stiff and "un-Hawaiian" he looked in his white dinner jacket, holding a burgundy leather menu.

"Good evening," he said—not "Aloha."

"Hello," I replied, and smiled.

He handed me the menu and the wine list.

"I can't tarry," I said. "I'm reading from my books after dinner."

"I know you are," the waiter said. "I've got a spooky story to tell you."

"I'd like to hear it."

"Certainly, sir."

It was the perfect place to be on Halloween, since The Lodge at Koele was built on or very near an old graveyard. The waiter began to tell me how when the plush resort first opened, an advertising agency hired a beautiful young woman and a handsome young fellow to pose as rich honeymooners.

"They stood outside their suite on the second floor and looked down into the Great Lobby," the waiter said. "The photographers took lots of pictures. When the brochure came out, there was the young couple, but standing behind them were faint outlines of other people. Not shadows, other people. They threw away the brochures. Tossed 'em. Junk. Took new pictures."

"I'd like to see a copy of the original brochure," I told him.

"I have one at home," he said. "I'll bring it tomorrow."

The next day, the waiter called my room to say he'd looked everywhere and couldn't find the brochure but that he would keep looking and would call me when he found it. But I never heard from him again.

I told the young Filipino woman at the concierge desk the story I'd heard at dinner, and she just hugged her arms, looked around to see who was listening, then said almost in a whisper, "There are many ghosts here."

A few days later, I called the Lodge to ask the waiter if he ever found that brochure. But when I asked for him, I was told that nobody with that name had ever worked there.

Hmmm . . .

191

THE CHARLESGATE HOTEL
by Christopher Balzano

THE FORMER CHARLESGATE HOTEL stands in the vicinity of Boston's Kenmore Square. After incarnations as a hotel and a college dormitory, it has now been converted to expensive condominiums. It also has a reputation as one of the most haunted buildings in Boston, and over time its history has fallen into myth and urban legend.

The Charlesgate was built in 1891, and bad luck seems to have followed it almost from the beginning. It was rumored to be a haven for criminals and illegal activity. Many Bostonians still believe mobsters built it, although there has been no connection between the original contractor and architect, J. Pickering Putnam, and organized crime. The top floor isn't visible from the street because of high awnings and decorative structures, fueling speculation that this was where much of the illegal activity took place.

Other design elements make people scratch their heads. One side of the building curls in, cutting off the interior windows from the street and closing

the building off to the public. Eerily odd faces, some more obvious than others, are sculpted around the windows and in the metalwork. Scratches on the building's façade that at first glance appear to be random spell out expressions like "No Exit," "Hell," and "Gone" on closer examination. Over the past century, new owners have each put their own physical stamp on the place. During one remodeling, rooms were boarded up or cut off by drywall, creating a number of spaces with no windows.

In 1947, the Charlesgate became a Boston University dorm. The university sold the dorm in 1973 and it became a tenement, serving some of the most unsavory of Kenmore's residents. At that time, a number of college students began to move in as well, creating an interesting mix of college kids and sketchy adults.

Emerson College bought the building in the 1980s and renovated it. Its ominous look and sordid history were all the students needed to connect it to every college urban legend. Most tales were more than a little embellished as they passed from older residents to incoming freshmen. One tale was of the "Old Tenant."

Said tenant had taken a rent-controlled apartment when the Charlesgate was a tenement. When Emerson bought the building, the college was unable to evict her. The woman hated the students and stayed put in her room, smoking cigarettes and coming out only late at night to go shopping.

Everyone avoided her, and when the Old Tenant died, it was two months before the smell of death overcame the stench of her cigarettes and her body was discovered. The smell of smoke remained for the next twenty years, but every once in a while, the door to her former apartment would suddenly open and slam shut, and a foul odor would linger in the air.

Other legendary spirits include several horses that died in the basement when it contained stables. And a little girl is said to haunt the elevator in which she died.

193

SPIRITS, OUIJA BOARDS, AND MORE

For every legend, there are documented experiences. At night, residents could hear scampering in the ceilings that sounded too big to be rats, but too small to be humans. They would also hear voices and have problems with lighting in their rooms. A few students saw a gurney roll down the corridors.

In the 1970s, it was reported that in one room an alarm clock would go off at exactly 6:11 a.m., even though it wasn't set. The room had been the site of a suicide.

Three girls moved into a room on the sixth floor that had a big closet—most likely one of the vacant spaces created by partitioning off walls. Although each of the girls had wanted to use the closet after moving in, they all had unusual sensations when they approached it. As a result, they decided to leave it unused. Research later revealed that another suicide had occurred in the closet.

In still another incident, a student once woke to see a spirit hovering over him. A resident assistant who ran in to see why the student was screaming also saw the ghost.

Although Ouija boards were banned in the building, in the early 1990s every student seemed to have one. What's more, every user tended to contact a strong spirit. Spirits were known to predict fire alarms (or set them off), and it's said that one spirit summoned by the board even tried to kill a resident. These spirits would consistently give details about the people living in the room—and not just those using the board. One group of students contacted a spirit calling itself Zena. Zena said it was born of a spell cast in all the doorways by the original building contractor to protect the people inside.

So what happened after the Charlesgate was converted into a fancy condominium? One person currently living in the building says he never has had anything happen and that few of his neighbors know the unusual past of their new home. But the Charlesgate has never stayed quiet for long, and it may be only a matter of time before the next wave of hauntings and storytelling begins.

THE CHARLESGATE HOTEL
now private residences

A (S)LIGHT CONCUSSION

DURING ITS TENEMENT PHASE in the 1970s, the Charlesgate was home to a college student who lived in a basement-level studio apartment with one window opening onto the courtyard. Here, he tells what made him pack up and leave.

"One night I finished reading at around one o'clock, put out the lights, and settled into sleep. But then I suddenly was jerked awake by a noise coming from the lone window. Normally, no outside lights filtered in from the window, yet I could see a very faint light coming from it, barely detectable but growing stronger.

"I also realized the noise I was hearing became louder. It was a muffled voice, complaining or whining, and then changing to a desperate sob.

"I was afraid to move toward the window or even reach for a light. Finally, something in me broke and I leapt out of my bed and charged up to the window. I was angry, though why anger should be my reaction I can't understand to this day.

"I pounded on the window's frame and found myself shouting, 'Leave the guy alone, damn it!'–an exclamation that didn't form in my mind but just came out of the blue.

"To say I perceived the folly of challenging whatever was out there is an understatement. To add to my terror, I could see the light from the window wobbling and forming a sort of shape directly in front of my face, just on the other side of the glass. At the same time, the sound of the voice changed; it was darker and rather angry. This new sound wasn't the whiny one I'd first heard, but something much bigger.

"*BAM!* Something slammed the window frame hard enough to rattle and crack the glass in one corner. I turned and ran back toward the bed. But in the near total dark, I managed to slam headfirst into the opposite wall and blacked out.

"I awoke with a slight concussion. In the faint morning light–the real thing–I could see that wind and rain were coming from the new crack in the window. I washed up, packed my few things, and left. And I never set foot in the Charlesgate again."

THE TUTWILER

by Alan Brown

IN THE YEARS just prior to World War I, Birmingham, Alabama, was the largest city in the South. It grew rapidly, due in large part to the discovery of nearby coal and iron-ore deposits in the late nineteenth century. Every day, more than a hundred passenger trains arrived and departed from Birmingham's train station, which was located at 25th Street and 5th Avenue North. Ironically, even though Birmingham had been dubbed the Magic City, none of the dozen or so hotels that sprang up around the train stations were "grand" in any sense of the word.

When representatives from U.S. Steel began visiting Birmingham, the lack of first-class hotels became something of a problem. As a result, local businessmen invested in the construction of a luxury hotel on an available lot at the corner of 5th Avenue North and 20th Street. Christened the Tutwiler after the hotel's major stockholder, Major E. M. Tutwiler, the hotel first opened its doors on June 14, 1914.

For almost sixty years the hotel—known from 1923 on as the Dinkler-Tutwiler after the lease was sold to the Dinkler Hotel Company of Atlanta—was at the center of Birmingham's social, business, and political activity. Throughout most of its history, it was the place to see and to be seen in the South. Hundreds of celebrities and politicians visited the 450-room grand hotel, attracted by its private baths, its thousand-seat ballroom (the scene of a Charles Lindbergh press conference in 1927 and movie star Tallulah Bankhead's wedding reception), and its luxurious meeting rooms.

By the 1960s, downtown Birmingham deteriorated as businesses relocated to the suburbs, and the Dinkler-Tutwiler fell on hard times. Despite repeated attempts by civic leaders to save the bankrupt hotel, it was forced to close its doors for the last time on April 1, 1972. After sitting vacant for a year, the hotel became the second building in U.S. history to be destroyed by implosion.

Eleven years later, the original Tutwiler was "resurrected" when a banking firm began converting the Ridgley Apartments, on 21st Street North, into a new version of the luxury hotel. At the time, the eight-story building, which also had been built and financed by Major Tutwiler in 1914, was still owned by the Tutwiler family and was listed on the National Register of Historic Places. When the new incarnation of the Tutwiler opened for business in 1986, the red brick building had been totally refurbished. Today the Tutwiler Hotel is managed by Wyndham.

"Good Night, Major Tutwiler"

Although the original hotel is no longer with us, some people believe that the spirit of Major Tutwiler still is. If stories told by some are to be believed, guests at the new Tutwiler Hotel occasionally receive more than they expect. The bell captain, who has been employed there since August 2004, claims that in the past two years at least seven people have had encounters with an entity he calls "the knocker."

In November 2004, a female guest in room 604 asked the bell captain to come up to her room immediately. "It was very strange," he said. "I could tell that something really scared her." The woman told him she had heard someone knocking very rapidly on her door. When she opened it up, no one was standing there. At least six other sixth-floor female guests reported having had the same thing happen over the next year and a half.

The bell captain suspects that the hotel has been haunted for a long time. "Some women who've been staying at the hotel for the past ten or fifteen years tell me about the ghost knocking on their door or the door of someone they've stayed with," he says. One of his informants told him that she suspects that the ghost is a male.

The bartender at the Tutwiler Hotel not only agrees that the hotel's ghost is a male, but he thinks he knows the name of the ghost as well. Late one night in 1995, the bartender began turning off the lights and the stoves, just as he'd done for many years. After he clocked out, he took one final look at the restaurant and was shocked to see that all of the lights and appliances had been turned back on. He repeated the process four times before finally giving up and going home.

The next morning, the bartender told the general manager that something had prevented him from turning off the lights, only to be scolded. For five nights, the bartender was unable to turn off the lights in the restaurant and received a verbal reprimand as a result.

On the morning of the sixth day, the general manager called the bartender and said, "Come to the restaurant, quick! I've got something to show you." Expecting to be upbraided once more as he followed the manager into the restaurant, the bartender was shocked to find that someone had cooked a full-course meal, drawn the curtains, and removed an old bottle of wine from the cabinet.

The two men conducted a full investigation; but after they failed to come up with a logical explanation, the bartender concluded that the ghost of Major Tutwiler had set the table. After this incident, the bartender never closed up the restaurant without saying, "Good night, Major Tutwiler. Please leave the lights and stoves off, and don't make a mess." The bartender's nightly entreaties seem to have appeased Major Tutwiler, given that no nocturnal disturbances have occurred in the past decade.

If the ghost is indeed the spirit of Major E. M. Tutwiler, one wonders why he haunts the former Ridgley Apartments but didn't appear at the original Tutwiler Hotel. The answer might lie in the fact that at one time Major Tutwiler actually lived in the building that housed the Ridgley Apartments. Quite possibly, his spirit simply wants people to acknowledge his presence in the place he used to call home. After all, everyone craves a little attention now and then—even, apparently, ghosts.

THE TUTWILER HOTEL
2021 Park Place North, Birmingham AL 35203

THE STONE LION INN

by Scott A. Johnson

FOUL PLAY IS AFOOT. Guests walk the halls of the Stone Lion Inn in Guthrie, Oklahoma, their inquisitive minds trained on finding a murderer. Of course, it's all a game, right? They signed up for Murder Mystery Weekend in an old historic inn. Tensions are high, but the stakes aren't real. Then again, who was the little girl, lurking on the third floor, one moment there and gone the next? Or the older gentleman in period dress in the basement? Surely they're nothing more than hired actors. No, say the employees. The people who once lived in the inn long before it started taking boarders startle the guests by making their presence known.

Within the walls of a stately inn, history is remembered not just by the staff but also by those who played a part. The memories of certain buildings are embodied in their memorabilia, relics of the past that present-day owners find quaint or fascinating. Others have a different reminder of days gone by: the souls of those who once dwelled there.

199

EERIE ECHOES

The Stone Lion Inn was built in 1907 by F. E. Houghton as a home for his large family, sited right next door to the house they had outgrown. When they moved in, Houghton and his wife had twelve children, including a daughter named Augusta, a very playful child whose games and toys were mostly confined to the third floor.

Tragedy struck when Augusta was eight years old and she contracted a case of whooping cough that left her bedridden. Medicines of the day were often laced with opium and codeine, and the child died of an accidental overdose.

The devastated family lived in the house for many more years until some time in the 1920s, when they leased it out as a funeral home. The imposing Victorian mansion was actually owned by the Houghton children until 1986, when Becky Luker bought it. With the help of her sons, Luker was determined to fix it up and turn it into Guthrie's first bed-and-breakfast.

Things took a strange turn as the new owners began their renovations. During the night, they could hear the sounds of someone walking around upstairs and up and down the back staircase. On several occasions, Luker

called the police, but no intruders were ever found. The large third-floor closet, where her son stored his toys, was routinely ransacked by an unseen presence.

Luker found some other occurrences to be odd as well, until a visit from Houghton's children offered an eerie insight. They told her about the death of sister Augusta and identified the chest in the third-floor closet as one they had used in their youth to store toys. They also related that they would often creep along the back staircase for some late-night playing after their parents had fallen asleep.

While several restless souls seem to inhabit what is now a stately B&B, none is as famous as the little girl named Augusta. Several guests have reported a childlike figure tucking them into bed at night or touching their faces to wake them in the morning. Some have complained that the child played on their bed as they tried to sleep. The most common manifestations of Augusta, however, come in the form of footsteps up and down the back stairs, the sound of giggling, and the clacking of a wooden ball being rolled across the third floor.

PIPE TOBACCO AND PHANTOM LAUGHTER

It appears that Augusta is not alone. Many people claim that F. E. Houghton himself haunts the basement. Many have seen him, but more have sensed his presence in other ways. Though the Stone Lion Inn is a non-smoking establishment, the scent of pipe tobacco pops up from time to time, with seemingly no source.

Phantom voices, including the laughter of an unseen woman, also have been reported. While some guests find these phenomena fascinating, others are frightened to the point of leaving.

Several paranormal investigative groups, including The Oklahoma Paranormal and Research Investigations team and GHOULI (Ghost Haunts of Oklahoma & Urban Legend Investigations) have investigated the house with interesting results. Among the evidence found are electronic voice phenomena (EVPs) of a young girl's voice and that of an older man. Electromagnetic field meters have gone off in places with no discernible source, and cold spots have been felt throughout the inn.

The spirits of the Stone Lion Inn seem to enjoy their house to this day, considering that they still make themselves known to guests. Augusta is most often found sneaking up and down the back staircase between the hours of 10:00 p.m. and 12:00 a.m. The laughing woman is most often heard around 4:00 a.m. Mr. Houghton, however, seems to appear at random, keeping to no schedule but his own.

THE STONE LION INN
1016 W. Warner Ave., Guthrie OK 73044

WHISPERS AT THE FARNSWORTH INN
by Barbara Klein

MY HUSBAND AND I once spent the night at the Farnsworth Inn in Gettysburg, Pennsylvania. Supposedly one of the most haunted hotels in that area, it still has bullet holes in the south wall, remnants of the famous Civil War battle. The inn, which was built in 1810 and added onto in 1833, housed Confederate sharpshooters during the battle. It was named for Brigadier General Elon John Farnsworth, who died at Gettysburg along with sixty-five of his men on July 3, 1863.

We stayed in the Jenny Wade Room, named for the only civilian to die at Gettysburg. Twenty-year-old Jenny was baking bread in her house on Baltimore Street when a single bullet ripped through two wooden doors and killed her instantly.

From the minute I stepped into the Jenny Wade Room and saw that it had a closet door that opened up to a brick wall, I was spooked. Despite the glass of wine I'd had earlier to relax me, I tossed and turned and couldn't sleep. I finally drifted off around 4:00 a.m., only to be awakened by someone whispering in my ear. Thinking it was my husband, I turned over in the bed—but he was sound asleep.

I was awake for the rest of the night, praying for dawn. I could hear someone walking up and down the corridor outside our room and thought he or she was having trouble sleeping as well. The next morning at breakfast, I met a couple who were staying in a room near ours. When I mentioned the constant walking I'd heard in the corridor, the man said that he had heard it too.

A Boy's Tricks

A few weeks after our trip, we were watching a TV show about the most haunted hotels in America, and they featured the Farnsworth Inn. They reported that when another woman and her husband had slept in the Jenny Wade Room, she was awakened by someone tickling her ear.

The show revealed that a young boy was hit by a horse and carriage outside the Farnsworth and was taken to the room that would later be named for Jenny Wade to undergo medical care. The father of the boy paced the floor outside the room all night, but to no avail. The little boy died, and it is his spirit who supposedly likes to play tricks on women who sleep in that room by tickling their ears or whispering to them.

I had goose bumps after watching the show. And needless to say, I'll never forget the night when someone unseen whispered into my ear at the Farnsworth Inn.

THE BALSAMS

by Joseph A. Citro

MOST NEW ENGLANDERS have heard about The Balsams resort in Dixville Notch, New Hampshire. Deep in the North Country wilderness, ten miles from the nearest town, it is a city unto itself. There's something surreal about this magnificent grand hotel in such a remote and wild setting, almost as if some kind of giant Victorian spacecraft had touched down in the great north woods.

Of course, many people know that Dixville Notch's residents are the first to cast votes in presidential primaries—and, in fact, the voting booths are here in the hotel. Besides national politicians, you can also expect to see notables from the entertainment industry at the hotel, along with the less recognizable elite from every walk of life.

What you don't expect to see are ghosts. And if there were ghosts, you'd expect the well-trained staff to be sworn to secrecy. Yet when I visited two years ago, I was delighted to discover The Balsams has a wonderfully active otherworldly population.

I was even more surprised to learn then president and managing partner Stephen P Barba—who had worked at the hotel since 1959—not only talked about the ghosts, but has also been documenting their activity for years.

THE VANISHING BEAUTY

"The number of reports [of ghosts] has greatly increased since we began our renovation program fifteen years ago," Steve told me.

Although he's never seen a wandering spirit himself, Steve doesn't discount the testimony of the many employees and guests who've had supernatural run-ins. "There are several staff members who report seeing ghosts," Steve told me. "We have a bellhop who will never go to the third floor. . . ."

In the summer of 1997, Steve said, doorman Wesley Richardson was heading up to room 439. Halfway up the last flight of stairs, he looked up and saw a beautiful woman sitting in a chair on the third-floor landing. At first he thought she was a guest, but when he considered the hour (almost midnight), her clothing (a long, black old-fashioned dress), and her fixed stare, he wasn't so sure. When she didn't seem to notice him or the sound of his footsteps, he finally realized what he was seeing: not a guest but a ghost.

Just as Richardson began to turn away, the beautiful woman vanished.

A similar encounter involved a young businessman visiting the hotel. Thinking he was alone in the John Dix social parlor, he was surprised to hear the delighted laughter of a young woman. Enchanted, he began looking around for her. Much to his disappointment, she was nowhere to be seen. Later, returning to his room, he passed a large mirror in the corridor. In its dim depths he saw the reflection of someone behind him—an extraordinarily beautiful young woman in a long formal gown. She and the clothing she wore seemed strangely old-fashioned.

The young man quickly turned to face her, but the hall was empty.

This lovely apparition has been reported many times in many parts of the hotel. Though she is often glimpsed in mirrors, she is also spotted sitting in chairs, standing in dark corners, and on occasion in plain sight. She has even appeared in the main lobby.

THE NAKED MAN

Steve took me to room 120, one of the several allegedly haunted guest rooms. When we arrived, a housekeeper who had just finished cleaning was locking the door from the outside. Though we all knew the room was empty, we could plainly hear movement and talking within. Steve smiled, placing his ear against the door.

"You hear that?" he said.

Unbelievably, I did.

Just to be sure no one was there, Steve knocked before unlocking the door. Sure enough, the room was empty.

After we stepped inside, he told me what had happened there.

At 12:30 in the morning of February 17, 1995, a lady awoke to find a naked man at the foot of her bed. Moonlight revealed that he was dripping wet from head to toe. At first she thought it was her husband, fresh out of the shower. She called to him, "Honey, are you all right?"

The answer came from under the bedclothes right beside her.

She quickly understood that the intruder was not corporeal. He faded away as she watched. Just before the apparition vanished completely, her husband, a sergeant in the Massachusetts state police, glimpsed it too.

Afterward, Steve Barba did a little research that revealed two possibly relevant details. First, back in the era of the big bands—the 1930s—bandleaders routinely stayed in room 120. Second, a certain bandleader had drowned in Lake Gloriette, which is located on the grounds of the hotel.

AND OTHERS . . .

Jacques Couture, an occasional employee of the hotel, is convinced that the place has not one, not two, but a small population of ethereal residents, some of whom he has personally seen. On November 15, 1995, for example, he was standing in the Captain's Study talking with hotel employee Diane Hall. As Jacques looked over Diane's shoulder in the direction of the Sun Room, he saw an apparition materialize right before his eyes. It appeared slowly, he said, standing directly in front of the door leading outside. Though the ghost's features were indistinct, Jacques was pretty sure it was a man.

Without saying anything, Jacques tried to signal for Diane to look, too. But before he could touch her shoulder, the apparition vanished. Jacques also reports an accompanying physical sensation, saying he felt very cold.

These are but a few of the myriad curious encounters at New Hampshire's most venerable haunted hotel. Nature? Supernature? Who knows? Both worlds seem perfectly intertwined at The Balsams.

THE BALSAMS GRAND RESORT HOTEL
1000 Cold Spring Road, Dixville Notch NH 03576

EDGEFIELD
by Jefferson Davis

EDGEFIELD, ONLY A QUARTER-HOUR drive from Portland, is an oasis set on thirty-eight acres at the mouth of the Columbia River Gorge. Legions of Portlanders go there to escape the busy life of Oregon's largest city for get-aways that include golfing, wine tastings, and other relaxing activities.

Many hotel guests would be surprised to find that a complex so comfort-able and varied—complete with European-style rooms, fine dining, beautiful gardens, a microbrewery, and an onsite glassblower and potter—began as a working farm for the poor. Built in 1911 as the Multnomah County Poor Farm, it was once home to residents who raised hogs and poultry and grew vegeta-bles and fruits. They also operated a dairy, cannery, and meatpacking plant.

The Poor Farm was later renamed the Multnomah County Home and Farm before the farming operation was shut down in the late 1950s. In 1962, it was renamed Edgefield Manor and served as a nursing home until it closed down in 1982.

The buildings sat vacant until 1990, when Mike and Brian McMenamin bought the complex and converted it into a resort. The buildings are now full of good cheer, but in some places the past sometimes escapes into the pres-ent—especially on the third floor. Following is a synopsis of what I learned when I set out to investigate claims of paranormal activity.

A PLAYFUL GHOST

On the third floor of Edgefield's centerpiece—a Georgian-revival manor that has been designated as a National Historic Landmark—is the Althea Room, named for a past resident. According to guests and employees, the spirit of a little girl haunts it.

I was told by hotel staff that groundskeepers have seen the little girl look-ing out the third-floor window many times as they've worked on the property nearby. Yet the room was always empty when employees investigated. It is speculated that the ghostly girl was the daughter of a past administrator of the Poor Farm, and that she had died in childhood.

Several times, guests staying in the Althea Room have awakened in the middle of the night to see a little girl standing at the foot of the bed. Sometimes she simply faded away, while at other times the girl sang nursery rhymes and

asked the startled guests to play with her before she suddenly disappeared. I asked why the guests woke up in the first place, and was told it was because they felt someone rubbing their feet.

One of Edgefield's staffers, Allyse, gave me a tour. Allyse told me that although she's a skeptic, she believed there was something different about the Althea Room. As we walked upstairs to the room, she started chanting. *"One two, buckle my shoe . . . won't you come and play with me."*

As she continued to recite the nursery rhyme, I looked into her face. Her expression was normal, but her voice had a dreamy, detached quality. When we reached the top of the stairs, I finished the rhyme for her. My guess was that Allyse had just been imitating the ghost—but I was wrong. Startled, she turned to me and asked why I had spoken. I answered that she had begun the rhyme and I simply finished it.

Allyse was visibly shaken. She said she had been thinking of the rhyme but wasn't aware she had spoken it aloud. She also told me she felt a presence in the room, and seemed eager to leave once I had taken a few pictures.

MY OWN EXPERIENCE

Sometime later, my wife and I stayed in the Althea Room. It was winter, and the damp air had caused the door on the second floor landing—the one opening on the stairs that led up to the Althea Room on the third floor—to swell and stick shut. I had to brace my foot at the bottom of the door and tug hard on the doorknob to open it.

My wife and I didn't get much sleep as we waited for something to happen. We took several photos and hours of videotape, but nothing out of the ordinary took place that night. Perhaps we were trying too hard, we thought. It was only after we relaxed that something strange occurred.

Early the next morning, I awoke and left my wife dozing in bed. The bathroom was on the second floor, and I went down the stairs and tried to be as quiet as possible. It wasn't easy—the stairs creaked, the door hinges squeaked, and the door itself scraped as I opened and closed it. Still, I believe I managed not to wake up any of the other guests. The building stayed quiet while I showered and shaved.

I was just finishing when I heard the sound of footsteps coming down the stairs from the Althea Room to the second floor. The stairs were on the other side of the wall from the bathroom, so I heard each footstep clearly. I thought that my wife must be coming down to take a shower, and since she wasn't strong enough to open the stuck door on the landing, I hurried out of the bathroom to open it for her. Yet when I popped the door open, I saw that there was no one on the stairs. I quietly called out for my wife, but there was no answer.

I paused a more few seconds, listening. Perhaps someone else in the building was up and moving around. But I heard no other sounds. I walked upstairs and found my wife still sleeping. I woke her up and told her about the footsteps, but she was too sleepy to be interested.

DOES ALTHEA HAVE PETS?

ALTHEA'S ROOM isn't the only place at Edgefield where hauntings have been reported. In other rooms, guests have seen, heard, and felt the ghosts of past residents. And not all the ghosts are human. A spectral black dog sometimes jumps up on the bed in one room at night, and one guest reported hearing a cat meowing to be let out of a bathroom. When she opened the door, the noise stopped but no cat was found.

Could the vanishing feline have been the mysterious black cat that has been seen in and around Edgefield's wine-tasting room? Maybe only Althea knows the answer.

I didn't think she was trying to pull a prank on me; but just in case, I walked up and down the stairs to see if I could climb them without making any noise. I couldn't. It had taken me less than fifteen seconds to go from the bathroom and open the door on the landing, meaning that if my wife or anyone else had tried to trick me, they wouldn't have been able to walk back up the stairs or hide without my hearing them.

So, who was the little girl? I haven't heard of any children dying in the Althea Room and I never saw the ghostly girl, but I've met other people who have seen her. They and others continue to visit Edgefield to relax and perhaps do a little ghost hunting. In fact, the front desk keeps a book where guests can write down their experiences. Needless to say, it makes for an interesting read.

McMENAMINS EDGEFIELD HOTEL
2126 Southwest Halsey, Troutdale OR 97060

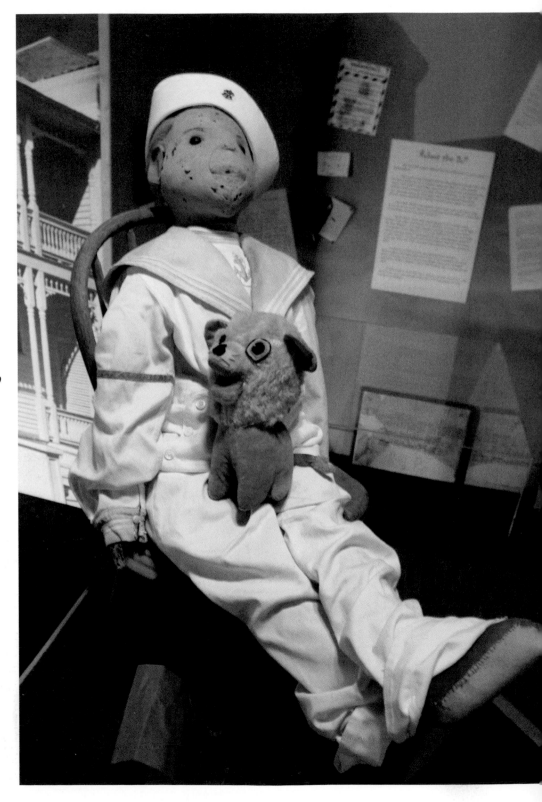

ROBERT THE DOLL

by Scott A. Johnson

A CHILD OF TEN awakens in the middle of the night and finds one of his favorite toys, a stuffed doll, staring at him from the foot of his bed. There is something unnatural about its glassy eyes, its expressionless face. It sits piercing the child with its gaze, somehow threatening. For no reason he can understand, the child is paralyzed with fear.

Across the house, the child's mother is awakened by her son's screams and the sound of furniture being overturned. Rushing panic-stricken to his room, she finds the door locked. On the other side of the door, she can hear the sounds of chaos and giggling, broken only by the screams of her son calling out to her. When at last she wrenches the door open, she finds her son still huddled in his bed, his room wrecked, and the doll sitting at the foot of his bed. "Robert did it," says the boy in a frightened whisper.

211

FRIEND OR FOE?

It's not uncommon for children to have imaginary friends. Often a mischievous child will blame some wrongdoing on a spectral presence or a favorite doll, a claim parents usually attribute to an overactive imagination. But what happens when the doll begins to torment the child and terrorize anyone else who lives in the house? Such is the strange case of Robert, the evil doll of Key West, Florida.

A well-off man named Thomas Otto and his wife built the structure known now as the Artist House in 1898. By many accounts, they were abusive to their servants. One serving girl who'd been badly mistreated and was apparently versed in the arts of voodoo gave their son, Robert Eugene Otto (called Gene by his friends), a straw doll that stood about three feet tall and was dressed in a crisp sailor suit; in a finishing touch, the doll clutched a stuffed lion.

The doll would be Gene's companion and friend throughout his childhood. Gene gave it his first name, Robert, and took him along everywhere. It is said that Gene's parents often heard him upstairs talking to the doll and answering in an entirely different voice.

Strange mishaps began to occur as misfortunes befell the family, and always Gene would appear, holding the doll and proclaiming, "Robert did it." While to outside eyes the spilled paint or uprooted shrubbery would be the work of a rambunctious child, close friends of the family agreed that it was in fact the doll that was somehow to blame. Many claimed to hear giggling coming from the doll or to have caught a glimpse of him running up the steps or staring out the turret-room window.

When his parents died and Gene inherited the house, he discovered Robert in the attic. Almost from the moment Gene laid eyes on him again, he could feel Robert's influence. His wife found the doll unsettling, insisting she'd seen the expression on its face change—but Gene would hear none of it. When his wife locked the doll back in the attic, Gene flew into a rage, shouting that Robert needed a room of his own where he could see the street. It wasn't long before Gene's sanity came into question.

After a number of inexplicable occurrences, Gene decided to put Robert back in the attic. Robert, it seemed, had other plans. Dinner guests could hear something walking back and forth in the attic, even though no one was up there. Several times, demonic giggling interrupted a quiet evening.

Even the other residents of Key West knew about Robert and his evil habits. More than once it was reported that the doll watched passersby and mocked schoolchildren from the window of the turret room. On one occasion, Gene insisted that Robert was in the attic and was surprised to find him in the rocking chair by the turret-room window. He grabbed the doll and took it back to the attic, only to find it reseated in the rocking chair when he came back down.

When Gene Otto died in 1972, many locals thought that Robert's misdeeds would cease. Evil, however, never dies. Robert waited patiently until another family bought the house. When the ten-year-old daughter found Robert in the attic, she claimed him for her own. In the process, she unleashed hell, and the girl swore to her parents that the doll had tortured her. Now, more than thirty years later, the still traumatized woman steadfastly claims that the doll was alive and wanted to kill her.

While evil doll stories aren't uncommon, the case of Robert is unique in that so many people claim to have witnessed his shenanigans firsthand. Visitors report they have seen his expression change into a menacing smirk, and a plumber once fled from the house swearing that he heard the doll giggle.

Robert isn't the only restless soul associated with the Artist House. When

212

Robert was finally removed, it is said that Anne, Gene Otto's late wife, took up residence in the turret room to guard against the little monster's return.

ROBERT AS MUSEUM PIECE

Today, Robert lives comfortably in a glass case at Key West's Fort East Martello Museum. Visitors are welcome to see him, though taking pictures has proven to be difficult. Cameras tend to stop working when pointed at the doll, only to resume normal function outside the museum walls. The Artist House, too, is open to the public, having been turned into a bed and breakfast. Visitors who stay in either the turret or attic rooms often report strange occurrences and sounds, as though someone is pacing the floor or watching them while they sleep. The staff just smiles and nods, knowing that it's actually Anne standing guard.

Robert, still dressed in his white sailor suit and clutching his stuffed lion, has also reportedly pulled pranks aplenty on those who care for him. A museum employee once cleaned Robert and left for the evening, locking the doors behind him and shutting off the lights. When he arrived the next day, several lights, including the one near Robert's case, were on. Also, Robert was positioned differently than when the employee last saw him; stranger still, the bottoms of Robert's shoes were coated in fresh dust as though he'd been walking around the museum. More than once, employees have reported hearing a sound like someone tapping on glass as they pass Robert's case. When they turned to look, Robert's hand was pressed against the glass.

Though Robert receives visitors year-round, the museum staff recommends that you introduce yourself during the month of October, when Robert is taken from the Martello Museum and housed in the historic Custom House a few blocks farther down. October is said to be the time when Robert is most active, and the employees leave a bag of peppermints in his case to cajole him into behaving. They swear that many of the candies are gone the next morning.

FORT EAST MARTELLO MUSEUM
3501 South Roosevelt Boulevard, Key West FL 33040

CUSTOM HOUSE (KEY WEST MUSEUM OF ART AND HISTORY)
281 Front Street, Key West FL 33040

THE ARTIST HOUSE KEY WEST
534 Eaton Street, Key West FL 33040

213

EERIE EATERIES, SPOOKY SALOONS

Death is coming in and leaving the tavern,
death leaving and coming in.
— Federico García Lorca, *Malagueña*

I N VIRTUALLY EVERY CULTURE, ghosts like to wine and dine. The Chinese hold the Hungry Ghost Festival, a time when the living try to appease their ancestors' needs by burning replicas of material goods: cars, homes, and food. The Mexicans have *El Dia de los Muertos,* the Day of the Dead, when bread is baked especially to share with the dead at their graves. The living perform these rituals and ceremonies to assure themselves that the dead won't bother them—at least for another year.

While ghosts have a place at some tables, they're probably the last thing on your mind when you just want to tuck into a nice dinner at a fancy restaurant or tip back a few beers at your local bar after work. But ghosts haunt these places, too. In fact, sometimes things that go bump in the pantry have as much drawing power as the food and drink offered by an establishment.

The ghosts featured in this chapter might not be so easily appeased with burnt offerings or bread or other cultural icons. Instead, all they might want is a little companionship from the living in the places where people tend to relax and let their guard down. Consider a few who appear in the following pages.

In Texas, a ghostly madam likes to hang out in the restrooms of buildings that were once part of her successful bordello. A prankster ghost nicknamed Lemonade laughs at living patrons in a Delaware bar. In New Jersey, Revolutionary War soldiers haunt an inn near a major battle site, and a bloody dress awaits its ten-year-old owner in the attic of a Massachusetts inn.

So have a seat while we serve up some ghostly fare and lively spirits. Care to hear about the specters—er, specials?

STONE'S PUBLIC HOUSE

by Scott A. Johnson

WHEN PEOPLE think of hauntings in Massachusetts, Salem usually comes to mind. However, there are other places whose histories are just as bleak and dark—not just in towns but also in buildings. And one of those buildings is Stone's Public House, a bar in Ashland.

The original proprietor, John Stone, was a giant of a man. The rough-hewn farmer had quite a reputation, not only as

a captain of the militia but also as a savvy businessman.

He realized that land was the key to a man's success, and bought up much of the town of Unionville, which would become Ashland.

His instincts paid off. In the 1830s, Stone discovered that a railroad was to be built right through the center of town, which was in fact his land. Sensing money to be made, the shrewd businessman built an inn right alongside the tracks.

The Railway House, as it was called, was an instant success, opening to a large and merry crowd on September 20, 1834. Anyone who traveled the railway began to stay at the hotel, playing card games and enjoying the finest food Stone could provide. Stone's enterprise was so successful, in fact, that he remained in charge for only two years, after which he continued to live on the property and leased the place to a long string of innkeepers. John Stone died in 1858, a wealthy man.

It was during the tenure of a later innkeeper that a tragedy of the worst kind occurred. Ten-year-old Mary J. Smith was playing near the tracks alongside the inn when the train rolled into town. Shocked patrons who witnessed the horror of her body being struck by the train quickly rushed to help her and

217

take her inside. Though a doctor was called, he arrived too late. On June 11, 1862, the little girl died of her injuries.

Nearly thirty years later, another death occurred at the inn, though this one was less dramatic. A local fellow named Burt Phillips loved the Railway House and its relaxed atmosphere so much that he spent many evenings drinking himself into a stupor in the bar downstairs. Local lore says that he often refused to leave. His wish to stay on was fulfilled in 1890, when he died at his favorite inn.

A COMPLEMENT OF GHOSTS

Over the next few decades, the inn's reputation changed. The Railway House was no longer a haven for the weary traveler, but rather a place for railway workers to spend their paychecks on all sorts of excesses. The building's façade began to reflect the business dealings inside, falling into disrepair. It seemed for a while that Stone's inn would be allowed to deteriorate beyond repair.

In 1976, Leonard "Cappy" Fournier recognized the historical importance of the old inn and bought it; he would then spend the next several years restoring it to its former glory. It was when renovations began that Fournier started to notice strange happenings. Despite the expert craftsmanship that had gone into the new doors, they would unlatch and swing open. Lights began to turn themselves on and off even though new wiring had just been installed.

Fournier didn't discuss the strange phenomena at first, thinking he might have just imagined them. But three years after buying what he had renamed Stone's Public House, he felt he had to tell others what was happening.

He also began to dig deeper into the inn's early days. Fournier learned that the upstairs function room had a long history of negative feelings, and with a bit of research he discovered that the room had been the scene of a card game between a New York salesman named Mike McPherson and John Stone. McPherson, it seems, was the big winner of the evening, which led Stone to believe he'd been cheated. Stone ordered several servants up to McPherson's room, telling them to club him over the head, take his money, and drag the body out back.

It is unclear whether the gambler's death was in fact intentional, but he died nonetheless. Still, it isn't McPherson who roams the halls but Stone himself, along with a maid named Sadie, Sam Thompson the cook, and a bartender named Will. According to psychics who have investigated the building, the four are bound in remorse for their heinous act and continue to walk the hall-

ways, waiting for absolution that will never come.

Stone has been blamed not only for crashing dishes and plates but also for roughly grabbing unsuspecting people by the back of the neck and dragging them toward the door. A portrait of Stone hangs on one of the pub's walls, and some patrons swear they can feel the eyes in the painting staring at them.

Then there are those other unfortunate souls who met their end in the building. Mary Smith, the girl killed by the train, has been seen over the years staring out the kitchen window toward the train tracks. Some question the veracity of the story, thinking it to be no more than a colorful legend. Such doubts are usually quelled by a trip up the stairs to the attic, where lies a bloodstained dress of the correct size for a ten-year-old girl.

The other patron who refuses to leave is Burt Phillips, whom the employees characterize as a fun-loving prankster. He's often blamed for water faucets that won't turn off or that turn themselves on. Also, he's notorious for tapping unsuspecting patrons on the shoulder. When they turn, they find no one there.

Resident ghosts notwithstanding, Stone's Public House is a thriving business with excellent food and a welcoming staff. The four-story structure has been extensively renovated and preserved, giving patrons the feeling that they've stepped back in time. Still, even the assistant manager has been quoted as saying he wouldn't be caught dead staying alone in the house at night.

John Stone and most of the other ghosts appear frequently, though diners aren't likely to notice them during the dinner rush. Little Mary, it seems, most often makes her presence known in the month of June, around the date when the train took her life.

STONE'S PUBLIC HOUSE
179 Main Street, Ashland MA 01721

THE LEMP MANSION
by Troy Taylor

THE LEMPS CAME TO PROMINENCE in the mid-1800s as one of the premier brewing families in the country. By the 1870s, Lemp's Western Brewery was the largest of the thirty breweries in St. Louis, with E. Anheuser Company's Bavarian Brewery (later Anheuser-Busch) coming in second. Yet today the Lemp family is largely forgotten, remembered more for the house they built than for the beer they once brewed. That house stands today as a memorial to wealth, tragedy, and suicide.

In 1977, the house was converted into a restaurant, and bed-and-breakfast accommodations followed in the year 2000. Yet the past lives on. By day, the mansion bustles with diners and employees; but at night, after the doors have been locked tight, something still walks the halls.

Are the ghosts of the spirits of the Lemp family still unable to find rest? Quite possibly, for this unusual family was as haunted as their house is purported to be today.

220

BOOM, BUST, DEATH

Adam Lemp, a German master brewer from Hennen, immigrated to America in 1836, settled in Cincinnati, and moved to St. Louis in 1838. There he opened a small grocery store whose wares included his homemade vinegar and beer. Two years later, he founded a brewery that produced some of the nation's first lager. Success followed, and his son William inherited the company on Adam's death in 1862.

By the mid-1890s, what had become the William J. Lemp Brewing Company was known all over America, having been the first brewery to distribute beer coast-to-coast. Its success was echoed by the Lemp family's mansion, which would eventually boast 33 rooms, elegant artwork, handcrafted wood decor, ornately painted ceilings, large beautiful bathrooms, and an elevator.

William J. Lemp

Over time, the family's happiness and success gave way to despair. A combination of competitor mergers, bad equipment, the growing temperance movement, and the arrival of Prohibition in 1919 proved devastating. The brewery's introduction of a nonalcoholic malt beverage called Cerva kept it hanging on for a while, but one day the employees arrived at work to find the giant plant's doors and gates locked. What had been the nation's third largest brewery in its heyday was no longer in business. In 1922, the plant was auctioned off to the International Shoe Company, which would operate there until it sold the complex in 1992.

The brewery's decline was paralleled by the tragic deaths of five Lemp family members over a forty-eight-year period. The first was of Frederick Lemp, William Lemp, Sr.'s, favorite son and heir apparent, who died in 1901 at the age of twenty-eight from heart failure.

A sad chain of suicides, three of which occurred in the Lemp Mansion, followed Fredcrick's death. The first was that of his still grieving father, in February 1904. William senior shot himself in the head with a .38-caliber Smith & Wesson revolver, and no suicide note was ever found.

William J. Lemp, Jr.

The March 1920 suicide of daughter Elsa Lemp Wright—considered the wealthiest heiress in St. Louis—didn't occur at the mansion; but she, too, failed to leave a note. When William Lemp, Jr., (Will) and his brother Edwin arrived at her house after the suicide, Will said, "That's the Lemp family for you."

Truer words were never spoken: The next suicide was Will's, in December 1922. At the time, he was at work in the Lemp mansion, which had been converted into offices. Though seemingly cheerful and full of plans for the future the week before, Will was depressed over the collapse of the brewing dynasty and had become nervous and erratic. While his staff was elsewhere in the building, he shot himself in the heart with a .38-caliber revolver. And like his father and sister, Will left no suicide note. His son William III ran into his father's office after it happened and knelt beside his father's body. "I was afraid this was coming," he cried.

Will's brother Charles was the last family member to commit suicide. After moving back into the Lemp mansion in 1929, when it again became a private residence, he grew more bitter and eccentric the longer he lived. In May 1949, a servant discovered Charles dead from a bullet wound to the head. He was the only one of the family who left a suicide note, in which he had written, "In case I am found dead, blame it on no one but me."

In the interim, William Lemp III died of a heart attack in 1943, at the age of forty-two—yet another death in a family stalked mercilessly by the Grim Reaper.

The Hauntings Begin . . .

It didn't take long for stories of hauntings of the newly vacant mansion to begin circulating. Shortly after Charles's suicide in 1949, a young girl and her friends managed to get in and started up the main staircase to the second floor. Just as they reached the first-floor landing, they looked up and saw a filmy apparition coming down the steps. The young girl later described it as an almost human-shaped puff of smoke.

Later, after the mansion was sold and converted to a boardinghouse, residents often complained of hearing ghostly knocks and phantom footsteps. Soon it became hard to find tenants, and the old Lemp Mansion was rarely filled. Like the surrounding neighborhood, it slowly deteriorated.

Richard "Dick" Pointer and his family purchased the mansion in 1975 and worked to turn it into a restaurant. They soon discovered they weren't alone in the house. Workers reported strange occurrences, including feelings of being watched, vanishing tools, and strange sounds. Many of the workers left the job site and never came back.

A painter who worked on the ceilings stayed overnight in the house while he completed the job. He claimed he heard horses' hooves on cobblestones outside his window, even though there were no cobblestones outside. The Pointers dismissed the claim until Dick Pointer later discovered a layer of cobblestones beneath the topsoil just beyond the painter's room and realized that this portion of the grounds had been a driveway to the carriage house.

Another artist, brought in to restore the painted ceiling in one of the front dining rooms, was lying on his back on the scaffolding when he felt what he believed was a "spirit moving past him." It frightened him so badly that he fled

222

the house without his brushes and tools. Later, after the Lemp Mansion restaurant had opened for business, an elderly visitor told the staff that he had once been a driver for the Lemp family. He explained that the painting on the ceiling in the dining room had been papered over because William Lemp hated it. On hearing the story, staff members noted that the artist restoring the painting had gotten the impression that the "spirit" he encountered was angry. Had the late William made his contempt known?

. . . AND CONTINUE

During the renovations, Pointer's son Dick junior lived alone in the house. One night he was lying in bed reading when he heard a door slam in another part of the house. No one else was supposed to be there, and he was sure he had

THE SLIDING CANDLE

THE WRITER OF THIS STORY, Troy Taylor, had no firsthand experience with the strange goings-on at the Lemp Mansion until 2004, when he, his wife, and a group of friends spent the night there. Here, he reports what happened.

"In hopes of contacting one of the lingering spirits in the house, several of us went up to the attic and attempted to open communications with an old-fashioned Ouija board. We hadn't been the first to try this, and at some point a previous party had left behind a number of small candles in holders on the floor, as well as a small table and chairs.

"We placed the board on the table and spent the next hour or so vainly trying to get the spirits to speak. After a while, when it became obvious to us that the Lemps weren't interested in talking, we sat around talking for a while and then made another serious attempt with the Ouija board. A friend and his fiancée were using the board but soon grew tired and gave up. 'Maybe someone else should give this a try,' he sighed.

"No sooner had he spoken than we heard a sliding sound on the wooden floor. We quickly turned our flashlights in the direction of the sound and saw that one of the abandoned candles had slid across the floor from one side of the room to the other. No one was standing near it at the time—so could the Lemps have had something to say after all?"

locked all the doors. Fearing that someone might have broken in, he and his dog, a large Doberman, decided to take a look around. They searched the entire house and found no one there. All the doors had been locked, just as Dick junior had left them. The same thing happened again about a month later; but again, the young man found nothing.

Ever since the restaurant opened its doors, staff members and customers alike have had odd experiences. Glasses have been seen to lift off the bar and fly through the air, unexplained sounds are often heard, and people have glimpsed apparitions who appear and vanish at will. Some visitors claim that the doors lock and unlock on their own, the piano in the bar plays by itself, and voices come from nowhere.

Late one evening when Dick junior was bartending, the water in a pitcher began swirling around of its own volition. Pointer thought he was just seeing things, but the customers who were still there swore they saw it, too. Then one night in August 1981, Dick junior and an employee were startled to hear the piano start playing a few notes by itself. Not only was nobody near the piano at the time, but there was no one else in the entire building.

On one morning, a waitress encountered an unusual customer. Though the restaurant hadn't opened for business, she spied a dark-haired man seated at a table in the rear dining room. Surprised, she went over to ask if he would like a cup of coffee. He simply sat there and didn't answer. She frowned and looked away for just a moment. When she looked back, the man had vanished.

PLANCHETTES AND A SÉANCE

Not surprisingly, the Lemp Mansion has attracted ghost hunters from around the country. Guests can be entertained at the establishment's Murder Mystery Dinner Theatre and also sign up to attend the annual Halloween party.

The hauntings first gained attention after an investigation was conducted in the mansion in October 1979 by St. Louis "Haunt Hunters" Phil Goodwilling and Gordon Hoener. At the time, they taught a class on ghosts at St. Louis University, so they brought their students and even a local television crew along.

The students were divided into groups of four and given writing planchettes for contacting the spirits. Like the Ouija board, the planchette is used to spell out messages from ghosts.

One of the groups asked, "Is there an unseen presence that wishes to communicate?"

"Yes," the pencil tip of the planchette scrawled on the surface.

The students asked another question: "Will you identify yourself?"

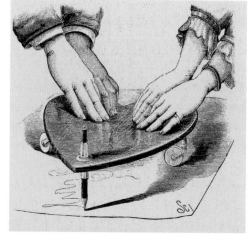

A planchette

The planchette scratched out "Charles Lemp."

After the name was revealed, the spirit added that he had taken his own life. Asked why he did this, the spirit replied in three words: "Help, death, rest."

Goodwilling later noted that the students who received this message were the most skeptical in his class. He also noted that no one in the room that night, with the exception of Dick Pointer, had any idea that Charles Lemp had committed suicide; the history of the house had yet to be widely publicized.

In November, the Haunt Hunters returned to the house, bringing along a camera crew from the television show *Real People.* Goodwilling and Hoener participated in a séance with two other people, neither of whom had any idea about the past history of the mansion.

Once they made contact with the spirit who identified himself as Charles Lemp, they asked him why he had committed suicide. Among the words that could be made out in his reply were ". . . damn Roosevelt." Apparently, the Lemps had been less than fond of the politics of FDR.

The séance continued with the next question from the group: "Is there a message for someone in this house?"

The answer came: "Yes, yes. Edwin, money."

Goodwilling felt that if the spirit was indeed Charles Lemp, he probably became active because of the remodeling in the 1970s or perhaps because he had something to tell his brother Edwin. During the séance, Charles may have believed that Edwin was still alive and was trying to pass along a message about money. Could this be what caused Charles's ghost to remain behind? Could there be a secret treasure hidden somewhere in the house? If so, it has yet to be found.

226

THE LEMP MANSION TODAY

Is the Lemp Mansion still haunted? Most visitors, especially the ghost hunters, will tell you that it is. One of the owners, Paul Pointer, considers the ghosts as just another part of the mansion's ambience. "People come here expecting to experience weird things," he said, "and fortunately for us, they're rarely disappointed."

Paul sometimes tells visitors of his own observations and eerie encounters, but he prefers to let them experience the hauntings on their own. Many guests have reported feeling ghostly cold chills, seeing moving objects, and hearing creaking footsteps. Just as many have taken bizarre photographs in the house— photos with images that seem to have no explanation. Given the evidence, it seems that the once triumphant but ultimately defeated Lemps—or some of them, at least—just can't bear to leave their family home.

LEMP MANSION RESTAURANT AND INN
3322 DeMenil Place, St. Louis MO 63118

GHOSTS OF MARKET SQUARE

by Fiona Broome

THEY SAY EVERYTHING'S BIGGER IN TEXAS. And when it comes to ghosts, that may be true. Downtown Houston boasts more than one haunted house. It has an entire haunted block–namely, the 800 block of Congress Street.

It all started in the mid-1830s, when Pamelia Mann came to town. People whispered that she'd been a popular prostitute in New York City but had to flee after she caused mortal injury to a rival by pushing her down the stairs. They also said she'd shot a customer when she ran a brothel in New Orleans, and had to leave town when she learned her victim was the son of a politician.

So when Mrs. Mann opened a "boardinghouse" called the Mansion House hotel on the corner of Congress and Milam streets, people expected a good, if risky, time. They weren't disappointed. In a time when Houston had only a couple of two-story buildings and most of its residents lived in tents, the Mansion House offered a dining room serving elegant meals on real china dishes with German silver cutlery.

Upstairs, customers could enjoy clean beds with feather pillows, and the company of an attractive woman . . . for a price. Pamelia's "girls" were among the most celebrated in Texas. Legend has it that even Susanna Dickinson–she who went down in history as one of the few survivors of the Battle of the Alamo, during which she was widowed–was among the Mansion House's "ladies."

The customers were equally noteworthy, and included congressmen, army officers, and Tonkawa chiefs. Sam Houston–for whom the city was named–was a regular guest.

As the city of Houston grew, the Mansion House expanded to

227

meet demand. It was a huge success. At the end of 1838, Pamelia Mann's tax bill was the third highest in Houston. By 1840, she had bought most of her city block and the block across the street, opening a livery and other businesses. As the city grew, this area became the commercial hub of Houston known as Market Square.

Pamelia was famous for her wit and her wild ways. She almost always carried a knife and a gun, and had used both on several occasions. In fact, she had a remarkable police record, but also friends in high places. In 1839, she was found guilty of forgery, a hanging offense in Texas. The day after she was sentenced, the president of the then Republic of Texas, Mirabeau Lamar, pardoned her, and the notorious Mrs. Mann was set free.

Unfortunately, nothing could save her from yellow fever. In 1840, just a few months after the death of Pamelia's fourth husband—a man only six years older than her eldest son—the legendary madam succumbed to the deadly disease.

The parties at Mansion House continued after Pamelia's death, as the "hotel" changed hands several times. And even though the Mansion House closed its doors by the early twentieth century, its parties aren't exactly over.

Enter the Ghosts

About twenty years after Pamelia Mann's death, John Kennedy—a baker from Ireland—bought a quarter of the block that had been home to the Mansion House. The land brought him luck, as it had Mrs. Mann. Kennedy opened a steam bakery and he was soon one of the most successful businessmen in Houston.

When the Civil War began, he leased one of his nearby buildings to the Confederacy for an ordnance depot. As a result, Kennedy's bakery served hot biscuits to hungry Civil War soldiers, adding to his business. The Congress Street site was also a Pony Express station, an Indian trading post, and the "mission" from which Kennedy distributed goods and money to the poor, supported by a Franciscan missionary named Father D'Asti.

Perhaps Kennedy had a premonition when he donated land for St. Vincent's Cemetery, the first Catholic graveyard in the city, considering that in 1878 he was shot dead at the front door of his bakery. Since then, things have changed at Market Square. The Mansion House was replaced long ago, after a fire swept the block in the 1850s, trapping countless people inside the buildings. According to local lore, many of the victims haunt the 800 block of

---

WHO LURKS ABOVE?

ALTHOUGH La Carafe's upstairs is generally closed, it's not unusual to hear footsteps overhead, as well as other sounds from the haunted wine bar's otherworldly guests. Bar staff and regulars agree that the second floor and the stairs leading to it are the most haunted parts of the building. Employees and guests alike have heard the ghost of a young boy bouncing a ball on the floor upstairs, but, when the curious go upstairs to find the source of the noise, it stops—and neither hide nor hair of anyone is ever seen.

One frequently told tale took place a few years ago, when the upstairs was open to customers. A couple was relaxing at an upstairs table when, without warning, the man bolted down the stairs and out the door. His companion followed, wondering what had happened. Apparently, the frightened guest had felt icy hands on his back. When he looked around and saw no one there, he was convinced that he had just encountered a ghost.

British-born Gladys Burrell is another charming spirit at La Carafe. On a wall opposite the counter, her larger-than-life oil portrait is a tribute to the early-twentieth-century beauty. According to La Carafe manager Gavin Connor, Gladys likes the people in the other pictures on the wall to tilt toward her in deference, as if she's their queen. When a new employee straightens the smaller pictures on either side of Miss Burrell's portrait, their frames tilt back toward the beauty by morning.

229

Congress Street, looking for the warm welcome and boisterous parties that Pamelia oversaw.

Although new businesses have opened on the northeast corner of Congress and Milam streets, many wasted no time in closing their doors. The ghosts are very picky about who stays in the neighborhood.

It is said that Pamelia has been spotted strolling down Congress Street after dusk, usually in a white gown. She's also been seen in "men's attire." Late at night, her girls sometimes appear at upstairs windows, apparently unaware that the building where the Mansion House once stood now houses offices.

THE HAUNTED WINE BAR

A few doors away, John Kennedy's brick building still stands at 813 Congress Avenue. It is not only listed in the National Registry of Historic Places but is also Houston's oldest bar, oldest commercial building, and oldest structure on its original plot of land. Kennedy's former bakery is now the home of La Carafe, a comfortable wine bar named one of *Men's Journal*'s 50 Greatest Bars in the United States. More recently, the *Houston Chronicle* described it as "one of the prettiest, most unique bars in all of Texas."

It's definitely pretty—and uniquely haunted. In addition to memorable red and white wines, La Carafe provides other kinds of spirits.

A few of La Carafe's ghosts are surely Pamelia's former customers, including Sam Houston. But one of the wine bar's favorite ghosts is Pamelia Mann herself. She may not have had fancy indoor plumbing when she owned the Mansion House, but she revels in it now. She's most famous for visiting the ladies rooms in the businesses around Market Square, especially at La Carafe. This has earned complaints from guests who want to enter the restroom yet have to wait for Pamelia to leave. It seems they don't realize that she is a ghost.

The former baker and owner of the building, John Kennedy, supposedly pays regular visits to La Carafe as well. He sometimes appears as a dark figure just outside the bar or around the first floor. He has occasionally been seen climbing the stairs, wearing a fedora and a Sherlock Holmes cloak-style coat. Witnesses report that Kennedy is more often a fleeting shadow seen out of the corner of the eye.

Psychics and ghost hunters frequent La Carafe, most of them sensing the haunting but comfortable energy. Many guests describe the ghosts in detail from their impressions and sightings. Photos around the stairs and near Gladys Burrell's portrait often reveal ghostly orbs of spiritual energy.

At least one visitor attempted to cleanse the energy in the bar. After he lit a smudge stick (sage incense, reportedly a spiritual purifier) and successfully smoked the downstairs, the smudge stick went out, and then wouldn't relight upstairs.

Despite the smudge stick, ghosts have remained in the brick building. Apparently they like La Carafe and wish to enjoy the popular bar as much as its patrons do.

LA CARAFE
813 Congress Street, Houston TX 77002

ENCOUNTER IN A POWDER ROOM
by C. Chrissy

IN THE TOWN of Tannersville, nestled in the Poconos of eastern Pennsylvania, stands an old stagecoach house now called the Tannersville Inn. The food served in the restaurant is good, and the bar is nice as well. The owner and staff are friendly. With live music on some weekends and the overall atmosphere, it's a cool place to chill.

One afternoon about three years ago, my mom and I drove there to meet my cousin and grandmother for lunch. At one point, I excused myself to go to the restroom in the back of the inn. I knew the Tannersville Inn had a history of hauntings, so I wasn't completely surprised when I immediately felt that I wasn't alone in the restroom.

The room was small, and felt even smaller because I wasn't the only one occupying its space. My breathing was quick and shallow, as if air were scarce. My skin felt funny, but not like goose pimples; it was just supersensitive, as if each cell was alive and tingly.

I know this may sound ridiculous, but I spoke to whatever entity was in that restroom. I said out loud, "I know you're here, and if you'd like to talk, I'm not afraid. But I'd like some privacy until I'm done using the toilet. Thank you."

As I washed my hands at the sink afterward, I still felt a presence, so I began talking to what I felt was a "her." I started with my name and told her she was safe to show herself to me if she'd like to or needed to. I now feel silly confessing that I did this, but during that moment it all felt as if those were the words that needed to be said.

A Spectral Hand

I stood next to the sink drying my hands when it happened. A hand began to appear between the bathroom door and me, at about shoulder height. It was a soft grayish-white color and was waving slowly, like a bird fluttering its wings. I noticed how pretty and delicate it seemed.

I felt that the ghost and I were comfortable with each other, frozen in time in the restroom—neither in the present nor the past. And just as I began to see more of the spirit's arm, my cousin came through the door. The ghost disappeared as my cousin burst right through her wispy form. I was very disappointed. I didn't even tell my cousin, since what had occurred seemed so private and so based in trust. Had I done so, I felt, I would have betrayed whomever I had encountered.

THE OLYMPIA SAILOR AND FRIENDS

by Jefferson Davis

THOUGH I HAVE EXPERIENCED many strange things during my several years of investigating anything paranormal, I've never seen a ghostly apparition. Yet many of my fellow investigators have a knack for attracting spirits. One of the few friends I knew who had consistent insight into the paranormal was Janet. Most of the time, I took her along to haunted locales, but there were a few times when she invited me and we shared interesting adventures.

Janet's family had real estate holdings near Olympia, Washington, which ranged from rental homes to a grocery store to a small restaurant. Janet's job was to maintain the rental properties, taking care of everything from having new carpeting installed to, yes, conducting spiritual cleansings. She kept an office at the family restaurant, which was believed to be haunted and was going to be sold.

232   The restaurant started life as a large house, and if more money had been poured into the original building, it would have been called a mansion. It was built on the side of a rather steep ravine, and the main dining room and a long cedar deck looked down on a tree-studded creek below. Summer patrons sat on the deck, enjoying the view of Puget Sound. Janet told me that one of the owners had been a sailor, and I could see why he might like the view.

I made coffee as Janet prepared to cleanse the restaurant of spirits before its final sale. Patrons and employees of the restaurant sometimes complained of cold spots in certain places. Some also reported the sensation of someone blowing on the back of their neck or touching their hair from behind. One employee watched a candle—which was set in a fixture on the fireplace mantel—unscrew itself, float across the dining room, and land on a table in the middle of the room. The sailor may also have been the source of a disembodied voice that some of the employees heard swearing late at night.

Janet told me that several entities haunted the building, and that the primary spirit was a sailor—possibly the original owner. She and others had heard him walking through the main dining room several times. He also liked to rearrange table settings and move furniture around. Even though the sailor's ghost could be irritating, he liked everything shipshape and kept the other spirits under control; for example, most of the time he kept the less powerful spirits from entering the dining room.

JANET'S TAKE

Janet had the impression that the property had a mix of ghosts, some of whom were children. The house was built on land once inhabited by Native Americans, and Janet felt that several spirits from ancient tribes had remained nearby. They stayed outside most of the time, but went inside if a customer attracted them.

She told me that she once left her son alone in the office for a few minutes. When she returned, he reported that he had watched a piece of paper rise off the desk and float around the room for several seconds before drifting back down on the desktop.

Jane said that as a gesture of good faith to the incoming owners, she promised to cleanse the building of all the spirits. Some she would "send to the light," and others she would convince to go somewhere else.

She also told me that the spirits knew why she was there. During renovation, they apparently guessed the building had been sold. Most of them had left the building and retreated to the edges of the property. She pointed through the French doors at the deck. "The sailor's out there waiting for me to leave. He doesn't want to go," she told me, and giggled. 233

I went to the doors and looked outside. It had rained hard earlier, and the deck was a soaking mess. The roof had just been reshingled, so tarpaper and cedar shingles were scattered over the deck. I tried the door, but it was locked. It also looked like it was going to rain again, so I decided it wasn't worth my time to go outside.

THE CLEANSING—AND MORE

After I finished my coffee, we went to the basement because Janet wanted to clear the building from the bottom up. To start, she sat down in the middle of an empty room and meditated. She explained to me that she began by centering herself spiritually, drawing in to herself and concentrating her spirit energy. She would then light a smudge stick made of sage and sweetgrass.  Using the smoking stick as a focusing tool, she would sweep through the building, forcing the spirits out through the front door.

As Janet sat quietly, I took a few pictures and waited for her to begin. It was then that I heard the sound of a door opening on the floor just above us—the locked French door that led to the deck. I heard three or four footfalls, and then silence. The footsteps had been heavy and steady and didn't fade out; they simply stopped, as if the walker was still standing silently.

"Are you sure we're alone here?" I asked. No reply from Janet, just as one would expect from someone who is meditating.

I hesitated. When I visit haunted locales, I try to find a mundane reason to explain supposedly paranormal phenomena. But the opening of the locked door put me in a difficult position. The only rational explanation was that a burglar was in the house. Would a ghost be better, I wondered?

"Stay here," I said to the still silent Janet. She hadn't budged when I heard the door open, nor at the sound of the footsteps.

Slowly and quietly I walked upstairs. During the several seconds it took me to climb up, there were no sounds from upstairs even as the stairs creaked under me. I carried my camera, ready to take a picture if I saw a ghost; if I found an intruder, the camera would make a handy weapon.

234

Following my barely remembered infantry urban-warfare training from the army, I edged my way down the hall in a slight crouch, hugging the walls. I still didn't hear any sounds from the main room, which I peered into as I edged around the corner. Nobody was there, so I went through the rest of the restaurant to make sure the whole building was empty.

Returning to the main room, I tried the French doors and found them locked. I also looked out across the deck, which ran the entire length of the building. No one was there either. I opened the door, went outside, and looked over the edge of the deck and saw a line of posts anchoring it to the steep hillside. There was no way anyone could have climbed up those posts without a rope or climbing equipment. And how could someone have gotten through the French doors without a key? I trusted Janet enough to know she would never play tricks on me, so where did that leave us?

THE WET FOOTPRINTS

I opened the doors and prepared to walk back inside when something I saw stopped me in my tracks: a series of four wet footprints going from the entrance and across the hardwood floor—just four imprints that stopped in the center of the main room.

I bent over to examine the footprints more closely. They had dried some-

what, but I guessed that they were larger than my shoes. They didn't have a tennis-shoe tread like mine but looked more like the prints of flat-soled rubber boots—clear in places, with a kind of crisscross pattern.

I went downstairs and found Janet lighting her smudge stick. I asked her to stop long enough to show me her shoes. She was wearing leather boots, but since Janet was only about five feet tall, her boots were probably size four. I took her upstairs and showed her my evidence.

She laughed.

Janet explained that when she drew in her energy, the sailor felt the change and came inside to investigate. She pointed to the corner of the room and told me, "He's right there, trying to hide from me." I looked, but as usual didn't see anything. So close, but still no apparition! I did take pictures, but nothing came out in the negatives.

Janet went back to the basement and proceeded to methodically clear the house. The sailor refused to pass on to the next phase of his existence, but Janet believed she banished him from the building.

Maybe he's standing in the parking lot?

GAINESRIDGE DINNER CLUB
by Alan Brown

BUILT IN 1827, the GainesRidge Dinner Club restaurant in Camden, Alabama, was originally called the Hearn Place. Its first owner, Ebenezer Hearn, was a soldier in the War of 1812 and a Methodist circuit rider. Betty Kennedy, the owner of the restaurant, says that Hearn is known as "the Father of Methodism" in Alabama because he founded more Methodist churches than any other person in the state did.

Ms. Kennedy's great-grandfather purchased the house in 1898, and it has been in her family ever since. "My great-grandfather's last name was Fail. When we opened for business in 1985, nobody thought we'd stay open for more than six months, so we really couldn't call it the Fail Place with everyone thinking it was going to! While my mother owned the place, my father put a lot of work into it."

236   Some ghost experts might speculate that the spirits inside the old house were awakened when her father began remodeling. "The house has changed in appearance from when we first moved out here," says Ms. Kennedy. "My

father was an engineer, and he changed the front totally. Originally, there was a little stoop of a porch in the front. It was just an old farmhouse with a one-story porch. Somebody gave him some columns, so he felt he had to put them up. If anything was left over from a work site, he brought it out here and added it to the house.

"The kitchen we use is the original kitchen. At one time, it was detached from the house. My father jacked it up and put logs under it and rolled it over and joined it to the house. A lot of old houses were like that. They had a breezeway connecting the kitchen because of fire and heat."

BAFFLING INCIDENTS

The ghostly activity at the GainesRidge Dinner Club started after the restaurant had been open for three or four years.

"One night, I was getting the restaurant ready for a party the next day. And one of my cooks, whom I had known for about fifteen years, was helping me out. As we were working in the kitchen, I realized I needed a cook pot from upstairs. So I went up to fetch it from a room that's a good ways from the kitchen.

"While I was upstairs, the cook screamed out, 'Miss Betty! Miss Betty! Come quick! Oh, Lordy Jesus!' It just scared me to death because I thought she'd cut herself or that something had caught fire. She screamed so loudly that I dropped the pot and went flying down the stairs. I opened the door and burst into the kitchen.

"I said, 'Maggie Belle! What in the world is the matter?' She looked up at me and just calmly kept chopping onions. She said, 'Miss Betty, I didn't call you.'"

"The voice wasn't way off," continued Ms. Kennedy. "It was as if it came from the foot of the stairs. My great-grandmother's name was Betty, and because she lived here briefly I don't know whether whoever was calling out was calling to her or to me."

A different ghostly sound was heard by Ms. Kennedy's daughter one evening when the restaurant was almost filled to capacity. "I was in the kitchen," Ms. Kennedy says, "when my daughter came in and said, 'You've got to come out here. Somebody's fallen in the ladies restroom and we can't get the door open!'

"I walked over to the restrooms to find a knot of customers standing at the door. 'We heard her fall and her head hit the door,' one of them said, 'and so

237

we thought she was jammed up against the door.' I finally just shoved the door open, and there was nobody there. Also, nothing had fallen."

Ms. Kennedy says that a ghost occasionally revealed itself through a different sense—that of smell. "My sister and I have smelled pipe smoke up in the front room, even though no one was smoking a pipe at the time. I haven't smelled the pipe smoke in a long, long time, but we did when we first opened. Sometimes when we would go up there, it would be very strong."

ECHOES OF A TRAGEDY?

A family tragedy dating back to the nineteenth century could be responsible for some of the ghostly manifestation in the GainesRidge Dinner Club. "One of my great-aunts weighed 350 pounds, and she had thirteen children," Kennedy says. "Back then, particularly in the wintertime, parents slept with their babies for several months to keep them warm. One night, she accidentally smothered one of her babies. I think she rolled on the baby or placed her arm on him." Sometimes late in the evening, waitresses and kitchen help at the restaurant have heard the incessant crying of a baby coming from one of the upstairs rooms—but the source of the cries has never been determined.

Other reports of ghostly activity in the GainesRidge Dinner Club have come to Betty Kennedy's attention over the years. Her son told her that he once saw a white shape pass through the windows in a second-floor room and then walk down the stairs.

The GainesRidge Dinner Club has capitalized on its reputation, and from Kennedy's point of view the ghosts are almost as big an attraction as the food. "When people read the ghost story on the back of the menu, they're always really interested," she says. "I call it my 'ghost truth' because it's what has really happened to me. We serve a lot of groups here, and they all want to hear about the ghosts. I do embellish the stories a bit, though, when I tell them to children."

GAINESRIDGE DINNER CLUB
933 Highway 10 East, Camden AL 36726

THE SPIRITS OF C STREET

by Skyaire Alfvegren

NESTLED AT THE BASE of the Sierra Nevada Mountains, Virginia City, Nevada, is America's largest federally designated historic district. The site of the famed Comstock Lode—the world's largest silver strike—it was once known as "the richest place on earth." At today's rates, more than five billion dollars worth of silver (and a smattering of gold) was extracted from its mines, helping the North win the Civil War and making Nevada a state. A fire destroyed the heart of the city in October 1875, but in the grand spirit of the West, the town was rebuilt, bigger and better, until the mines played out not long after. As a result, Virginia City looks much as it did more than a hundred years ago.

At the height of the silver boom in the mid-1870s, nearly half of Nevada's population lived in Virginia City and nearby Gold Hill. The approximately 25,000 miners, entrepreneurs, and prostitutes there "had alcohol, money, and weapons," as one bartender put it, and C Street was the place where they could 239

abuse all of it. As one local put it, "We had fifty-two saloons and no town drunk . . . they took turns. We still do that."

Mines operated twenty-four hours a day within spitting distance of the saloons of C Street. Hundreds of men died both in the mines and in drunken street brawls, helping make Virginia City a very lively town.

Today, tourists stroll the wooden boardwalks of C Street in daylight. But after dark, shadowy specters still speak to the violence and excitement of long ago. They materialize on the deserted board-walks, perhaps heading, as they did in life, to one of C Street's many watering holes. The oft-heard bartender's verbalism "you don't have to go home, but you can't stay here!" means nothing to these ghostly patrons who've hung around places like the Delta Saloon and the Washoe Club for more than a century.

THE DELTA SALOON

As you drive into Virginia City, billboards invite you to "see the famous Suicide Table." Even without the hauntings, the fabled table in the Delta Saloon is a morbid attraction with a bloody history.

Black Jake owned the Delta Saloon, but that didn't stop him from shooting himself in the head when he lost a huge amount of money playing faro, the game of choice of nineteenth-century gambling halls. He was "bucking the tiger" a bit too roughly when he lost it all and shortly thereafter stained the green felt of the table with his blood. Two other of the saloon's owners killed themselves at the same table, one of them when a miner walked away with $80,000, a team of horses, and an interest in a gold mine.

If the suicides weren't enough to dissuade superstitious gamblers from playing at the table, the ghost of Black Jake began to show up and sit in on games. When unseen hands kept interfering with gambling, the table was finally retired to the back room. Years later, it was dusted off and put on display.

Other ghosts also haunt the Delta, including a woman in a long white dress who walks the staircase leading to the upper floor. Called Delta Dawn, she has been known to interfere when various employees have tried to organize weddings upstairs.

DELTA SALOON
18 South C Street, Virginia City NV 89440

THE OLD WASHOE CLUB

One of the most haunted places in Virginia City is the Old Washoe Club. The three-story brick building once housed the famed Millionaires Club, where nineteenth-century silver kings played all-night poker games on the second floor. The bar was downstairs, and extremely friendly ladies were the prime attraction on floor three.

Of singular interest is a spiral staircase in the center of the club. It had no center supports and was built without the use of nails. When the Millionaires Club opened, the bottom landing of the stairs was close to the front door. In later years, the staircase was moved to the center of the building so that wives who peered into the club to check on their husbands wouldn't see them descending from the third floor.

The unique staircase still gets plenty of use—at least from Lena and a little blond girl, the most famous of the ghosts who supposedly haunt the building.

Poor Lena. Lena, a redhead with a temper, is not only frequently seen on the staircase but also makes the chandeliers sway. The former owners of the Washoe Club used to leave a drink for her at the end of the bar when they closed up for the night. And Lena certainly could've used a stiff one, given her sad story.

In life, Lena worked at the Millionaires Club and all was well. But when her miner husband died suddenly, she was left with little money to live on. Fearing poverty, she changed jobs at the club and became a prostitute—a profession that would ultimately send her to her grave. One story says that the manager got into a fight with her and pushed her down the spiral staircase, breaking her neck and killing her. Another says her throat was slit as she bathed in a tub on the third floor.

Spirits of the Vault. In the back of the building, a cold storage room known as the Vault was meant for beer, oysters, and other perishables. However, during the winter when the ground was too frozen to dig graves, the room was used for the temporary storage of human corpses. The bodies were sometimes stacked ten high. An exorcism was once conducted to cleanse the Vault of spirits of the dead, but it failed. When the cameraman on a TV crew filming the exorcism looked into a glass box in the room, the word "stop" appeared on the dusty surface.

The Little Girl. Another ghost who haunts the building is a little girl who was killed outside the club. It is historical fact that a girl was run over by a carriage on the street outside, and legend has it that she was pulled inside and took her last breath in the bar. Dressed in white and usually carrying a bouquet of blue flowers, the blond child is usually seen on the staircase; at other times she wanders the second floor crying for her mother. Some people have reported seeing the girl in other parts of town.

The Thin Man. If you go to the Washoe Club at around 9:00 p.m. and sit at the bar, you might find a very tall, thin miner tapping you on the shoulder. (Some people say it feels more like a jab in the ribs than a friendly tap.) The man also likes to hang out in the restrooms—most often in the men's room but sometimes in the ladies room as well.

But back to those taps from the beyond. If you feel them, you're probably sitting on the tall miner's favorite barstool. So slide over, if you don't mind. He's been coming to this bar longer than you have.

OLD WASHOE CLUB
112 South C Street, Virginia City NV 89440

SPIRITS IN UNIFORM

by Katie Heenan

A FEW OCTOBERS AGO, I was sitting at my friend's bar in Al's Airport Inn, on Bear Tavern Road just outside of Ewing Township, New Jersey. The "Al" of the name is Al Jones, who has been dead for many years. Some other bar patrons had tried to frighten me with stories of ghosts seen late at night on the second floor, which is closed off to the public. But I always passed those tales off as drunken talk.

That night in October, it was different. Business was starting to pick up in the bar, and I was in my usual corner seat. Among the new arrivals were two confused-looking women, who took seats next to me and ordered drinks. I asked them if they were all right. The older woman said that as they walked from their car to the bar, they thought a costume party must be going on because they saw two men dressed as Revolutionary War soldiers walking in.

I told them that, yes, there was a costume party, but it wasn't until Halloween night. I suggested that they come again then, when costumed patrons would be out in full force.

They were further into their drinks when one of them asked, "How come nobody uses the front door?" I told them that in fact there isn't a front door at Al's; there once was, but it was closed off long ago. The only entrance is at the back, where the two women had come in.

They insisted that the two soldiers they'd seen had come in through the front door of the bar. I silently told myself they were probably just a little tipsy.

SEEING IS BELIEVING

Later that night, while helping clean up, I heard noises on the old front porch, which is now enclosed. But when I investigated, nobody was there. As I walked back into the bar area a little spooked, I was startled by what turned out to be my own image coming up in the Sam Adams mirror at the far end of the bar. It freaked me out, but what I

IS AL HERE, TOO?

WHY WOULD Revolutionary War soldiers haunt Al's Airport Inn? It's simple: After Washington and his forces crossed the Delaware into New Jersey on December 26, 1776, they marched south to fight and win the First Battle of Trenton—and they likely went through the area that today includes Al's Airport Inn. A storm raged that day, and some of Washington's troops froze to death en route. It's possible that some soldiers may still walk where they fought and died.

The current owners of the inn, Joe and Caroline Bondi, don't doubt that someone has seen soldiers going through the former front door of the tavern. They say they've seen shadowy ghosts of soldiers moving from one room to another in their nearby home, so it seems the entire area is subject to a haunting or two at the very least.

Caroline also says that the spirit of Al Jones, who many years before had turned the house into an inn, might haunt the place. One of Caroline's sons once told bar patrons he was going to call up Al's spirit on the second floor of the building. The patrons followed him upstairs and when he called for Al, sure enough, Al began to materialize in front of the entire group. The patrons immediately turned tail and rushed down the stairs, leaving Caroline's son behind.

saw was certainly no ghost or soldier.

As I got into my car to head home, I turned to look at the enclosed porch, where the women claimed to see the soldiers going into the bar. I saw nothing. Then, when I looked back toward the road to start my drive home, I saw two men walk past my car.

They were dressed in Revolutionary War uniforms and were walking up Bear Tavern Road toward Ewing. I was scared, but I kept watching them head up the road for what seemed forever. A car finally drove by mine and they disappeared in its headlights.

I believe the men appeared just to let me know that they had stopped by Al's Airport Inn for a drink that night. Needless to say the story has become one of our favorite ghost stories to share at the bar.

AL'S AIRPORT INN
636 Bear Tavern Road, Trenton NJ 08628

MISCHIEF AT THE COUNTRY TAVERN
by Fiona Broome

GHOST HUNTERS joke that every historic restaurant and inn in New England is haunted, and they may be right. I can vouch for the existence of a ghost at the Country Tavern in Nashua, New Hampshire.

Blond, mischievous Elizabeth Ford is a beloved spirit who haunts the Country Tavern restaurant. They've even named a gourmet dinner after her: Chicken Elizabeth.

According to local legend, Elizabeth and her husband moved to colonial Nashua—then called Dunstable—in the mid-eighteenth century. Because of its poor soil, unreliable transportation, and continuing hostilities with Indian tribes from Canada, New Hampshire remained decidedly rural.

Nevertheless, Elizabeth and her husband, a ship captain, were delighted with their new farmhouse. That it was near a well-traveled coach route not only provided peace of mind for the Fords but also meant that Elizabeth would feel less isolated when her husband was at sea.

245

The newlyweds were very happy during the early years of their marriage, in spite of Captain Ford's reputation for a volatile temper and fits of jealousy. Elizabeth's sweet and playful nature usually prevented serious arguments, and for that her husband was grateful.

Their lives seemed almost idyllic until Captain Ford returned home after nine months at sea and found his wife pregnant. When the baby arrived a couple of weeks later, Ford was convinced that his wife had been unfaithful. In a fit of jealous rage, he killed both Elizabeth and the baby.

In one version of the story, he buried their bodies in the yard just outside the farmhouse. Over their graves he planted a tree—possibly to conceal them— and it remains just outside of what is now the Country Tavern. Others say that he dumped the bodies in a well on the property, or that the graves lie beneath the house itself. But it seems that no matter where they're buried, Elizabeth never left.

ONE HAPPY GHOST

According to local lore, Captain Ford hastily signed on with the next ship out of Portsmouth, and soon was killed during an argument over a card game. No one mourned his loss.

246   Elizabeth's ghost began appearing soon afterward. Sometimes, she was spotted in the yard. More often, people saw her gazing out a window.

The farmhouse had many owners over the years before it became the Country Tavern restaurant. Since then—1985 to be exact—the building has been lovingly restored and the grounds artistically landscaped, a transformation that has delighted Elizabeth Ford.

I have actually seen the young Mrs. Ford. She's about five foot five and very slender, weighing about a hundred pounds. When I last saw her, she was wearing a deep red colonial gown. Her pale blonde hair was worn unfashionably loose, spilling over her shoulders and down her back. She was also translucent. Many restaurant patrons, however, say that Elizabeth can look as real and solid as anyone else—anyone living, that is.

Elizabeth skips and dances barefoot around the upstairs dining area. Her pranks include rotating patrons' dishes while they're dining and sending cups and saucers flying across the room. At the same time, Elizabeth is careful never to hurt anyone; she's merely being playful.

Downstairs, Elizabeth visits the ladies room and sometimes tugs on the hair of visiting patrons. The ladies lounge was once part of the nursery, near the center of the farmhouse. It was also where Elizabeth felt safest, waiting for her husband to come home.

Interestingly, there has never been any evidence that Elizabeth's newborn is with her in the spirit world, and people often wonder where the child is. The consensus is that the baby probably crossed over.

Elizabeth's ghost certainly hasn't crossed. In fact, the young woman doesn't seem to realize that she's dead. In her own mind, she's still living in the time before her pregnancy, when she was happily married. That's why she's often seen upstairs, watching out the window for her husband's return from the sea.

Some people have seen Elizabeth looking sadly out the window toward the tree in the yard where she and the baby may have been buried. But these bouts of melancholy are brief, and soon Mrs. Ford's mood again becomes light and playful. In general, Elizabeth Ford is one very happy ghost.

FLICKERING LIGHTS

When I first encountered Elizabeth, I was upstairs in the restaurant, showing some "ghost photos" to a TV show host. We were preparing to film a segment about the Country Tavern.

A shadow seemed to pass over my photo album, as if someone had just walked by. I looked up and saw Elizabeth standing on tiptoes gazing over my right shoulder. She was looking down at my photos, seemingly fascinated by them.

247

I didn't want to startle the TV crew, so I kept quiet about Mrs. Ford's presence. However, just a few minutes later, she announced herself in her typically mischievous fashion. The cameras were filming as the TV host and I walked around the restaurant's upstairs dining area. I could see Elizabeth watching us from behind one of the crew, when she suddenly vanished.

Then, as we began to discuss Elizabeth during the show, the lights on the wall flickered—and each time we mentioned her name or referred to her, they flickered again.

Finally, the host asked anxiously, "That's just loose wiring, right?"

"We'd better find out," I replied. "If it is, the restaurant needs to know before a short circuit starts a fire."

I looked around for someone from the Country Tavern staff, but they were all downstairs. It was up to us to solve the mystery of the blinking lights.

Even when I think that something may be evidence of a haunting, I look for logical explanations. So I climbed up on a bench by the wall and thumped my hand near one of the fixtures to see if I could make the lights flicker again.

Nothing happened.

I repeated my efforts, this time pounding the wall with my fist.

Still nothing.

More pounding just inches from the light fixture—and still no flickers.

"Let me try," the host suggested, gathering her courage. She tapped the wall very lightly and—amid some nervous laughter—asked if Elizabeth was there. The lights blinked on and off as if on cue. The TV host turned pale under her makeup.

For the next several minutes, I pounded the walls trying to duplicate what had happened. No matter what I did, the lights wouldn't flicker.

"Elizabeth is just teasing you," I joked. And, with that, the lights turned quickly off and on again.

Only the wall lights had blinked off and on; the other restaurant lights remained constant. The power hadn't failed, even for a second. And the only light switches in the room were those in plain view. No one from the restaurant staff had left the kitchen, either.

In other words, there was no rational explanation for the flickering lights. I laughed because I was used to ghosts, but the TV host and crew weren't quite so amused.

"SEE YOU LATER, ELIZABETH"

We briskly completed the TV segment, and the crew packed their equipment. As we headed toward the stairs, I glanced back over my shoulder and said quietly, "See you later, Elizabeth."

The lights flickered again, and I thought I heard a high, girlish laugh not far from my ear. I certainly felt a gentle swish of air, as if someone in a long gown had just dashed past me.

From what I've heard, Elizabeth Ford is still a regular visitor at the Country Tavern. The restaurant is best known for its fabulous meals and fresh seafood dinners. But it's also famous as the home of one of the sweetest ghosts in New England.

Watch for Elizabeth Ford next time you're in Nashua, enjoying the food at the Country Tavern. Just don't be surprised if an empty cup soars gracefully across the room, or the lights flicker when you mention her name.

COUNTRY TAVERN
452 Amherst Street, Nashua NH 03063

DEAD PRESIDENTS PUB & RESTAURANT
by Scott A. Johnson

A LATE NIGHT in a Little Italy bar in Wilmington, Delaware. The last of the thirsty patrons have gone home and the waitresses have counted their tips and left before the sun rises over the city. A lone bartender locks the doors and finishes wiping down the bar and tables, turning stools, and mopping the floors.

He then hears a sound coming from the liquor-storage closet downstairs— faint laughter. Perhaps there's still someone in the bar, he thinks. He walks toward the stairs and calls out, only to hear the laughter growing steadily louder. All of a sudden he feels cold, and the laughing presence seems to pass right through and past him, leaving him gasping for breath. He turns, intending to run out into the street, but he's stopped by glasses flying off the shelves toward him. He screams, and as suddenly as it began the attack stops.

Some historic buildings have seen their share of strangeness in their life spans, no matter what purpose they currently serve—but the walls don't forget. Such is the case with Wilmington's curiously named Dead Presidents Pub and Restaurant.

Little is known about the history of the two-hundred-year-old building that now houses the establishment. Still, there is evidence that it was once several separate buildings and households that were joined together as the years went by.

A PRANKSTER NAMED MULLERY
Though details are sketchy, it seems that Dead Presidents wasn't the first bar to set up shop in the building. An earlier bar had a regular patron who went by the name of Lemonade Mullery. A practical joker, Mullery liked to toss things at waitresses and play pranks on other patrons. While such behavior might have gotten anyone else escorted to the alley, those who frequented the bar held Mullery in high regard. But fate had other things in store for the prankster. After a lengthy drinking bout in the bar, he went down the stairs to the bathroom. Lore has it that he slipped on a puddle of urine and broke his neck when he fell.

In 1997, brothers Michael and Stephen Lucey opened the Dead Presidents Pub and Restaurant in the old building—with interesting times to follow. The truth of the story of Lemonade Mullery is open to debate, but there can be no

249

denying that something still lurks in the bar. Those who work there identify that "something" as Mullery, figuring it has to be him.

Waitresses and waiters often report the sound of screaming coming from the stairs leading to the area where Mullery supposedly died. More frightening is the occasional muffled giggle that originates from the same area, since the giggles reportedly erupt into peals of laughter as the listener's fear increases.

Mullery's nastiest trick is to throw things at the staff. Dishes, glasses, dominoes, and ashtrays are among the objects that have reportedly sailed through the air at the hand of an invisible assailant.

The staff is very open about speaking of their resident specter. Still, the basement area causes shivers to run down some employees' spines. Who knows whether a stifled giggle will follow them down the stairs as they fetch another case of alcohol?

The prankster phantom usually is most noticeable after the restaurant has closed—and he is apparently active year-round. If your curiosity gets the best of you and you want to "see" him for yourself, it might be smart to check the restaurant's calendar and participate in one of their annual events. That way, you can join in the festivities held afterward. Just don't be surprised if the laughter you hear isn't coming from the other patrons but from the stairwell across the room.

250

DEAD PRESIDENTS PUB AND RESTAURANT
618 North Union Street, Wilmington DE 19805

THE GOLD CANYON STEAKHOUSE
by Janice Oberding

THE SMALL BUT RAPIDLY EXPANDING town of Dayton, Nevada, has two claims to fame. The first has to do with Hollywood and movies. No one in these parts is likely to forget that many of Marilyn Monroe's and Clark Gable's scenes from their last film, *The Misfits*, were shot in and around Dayton. The second is somewhat more precarious. Dayton has dubbed itself Nevada's oldest city, but the nearby tiny town of Genoa makes the same claim. While historians argue the merits of each town's claim, residents go about the business of enjoying the Nevada lifestyle.

When folks who live in the Dayton–Genoa–Carson City area think of a fine steak dinner with all the trimmings, it's the Gold Canyon Steakhouse that comes to mind. Housed in a building well over a hundred years old, the steakhouse offers a uniquely Nevadan ambience: mirrors and brass, moose heads, rusting farm implements, and paintings of a youthful Mark Twain and of bawdy courtesans who ruled the hearts and pocketbooks of long-dead silver barons.

When Bonnie Stryker bought the building several years ago, she had no idea that a couple of ghosts might come along in the bargain. What she did know was that the building had once been a boardinghouse, and its location on Main Street was the perfect spot for her restaurant. So Bonnie remodeled, redecorated, and opened the steakhouse. Business was brisk as word spread of Bonnie's fine steaks and soups. Soon, rumors of supernatural activity were also spreading.

251

A Mustachioed Phantom

Employees were the first to notice that strange things were happening in the restaurant. "I know for a fact this place is haunted," said a former employee. "The first time I suspected it was the first time I closed up.

"It was after midnight," the employee continued. "The place was empty and I was alone. I walked through to the back room and the kitchen making sure all the lights were turned off. I had this feeling like someone was following me. I felt kind of silly looking around and making sure no one was there, but I couldn't shake the feeling. I didn't say anything to anyone the next day because, well, with most of the lights turned off the place does seem eerie. Maybe I let all the shadows and the old stuff on the walls get to me.

"A week later I closed up again. I still didn't like being in the steakhouse after everyone else left, so I tried to get things done as fast as I could. I was just about ready to leave when I heard someone walk right up to me and stop. I knew it had to be a ghost; I was so scared I didn't even turn around. There was a blast of cold air on my neck and something gently tapped me on the back of the head.

"I couldn't help it. I started to cry. Then I heard like a whoosh—and whatever it was, was gone. Now, that wasn't my imagination!"

Another woman told of seeing a mustachioed man one evening. "He

looked like he was really mad. It was a Friday night and we were incredibly busy, so I thought I'd better take a minute and explain that I'd take his order as soon as I could. I smiled and said, 'I'm sorry to keep you waiting, sir.' He glared at me and dissolved, just like they show ghosts doing in the movies. I was so scared I dropped my tray. I worked there another six months, but I never saw him again after that night."

One person who claimed no belief in the supernatural admitted to watching a heavy lantern slowly swing to and fro at the empty bar. "It wasn't an earthquake. I still don't know what moved that light."

While some employees laugh at the thought of ghostly residents in the

building, others are serious about their experiences.

"I've seen him," a former bartender claimed. "He looks like an old time gunslinger to me—all dressed in black and with a thick black mustache. He was pacing back and forth, back and forth outside the kitchen door. So I came out from behind the bar and said, 'Hey mister. What are you looking for?' He turned to me with this expression like he was sad or lost or something and then walked into the kitchen. You've got to remember that there's only one door that goes in and out of the kitchen. Wherever he went, he didn't come out the door. Yeah, he's a ghost."

GUNFIGHT ON THE DOORSTEP

Bonnie didn't know what to make of the stories her employees were telling, and she was very philosophical about the matter. Maybe there were ghosts in the steakhouse, she thought, and maybe there weren't. Then she, too, began to experience what cannot be easily explained: that certain feeling that something unworldly is very close by.

A local historian says that many years ago, a gunfight took place right outside the door of the old boardinghouse. Unfortunately, the sharpshooting gunslinger didn't have much time to enjoy his victory; he was lynched nearby even before his victim's body had cooled.

Not only that, but in Dayton's early days the old building that houses the steakhouse was the scene of several deaths. Is it possible that one or more of the deceased, including the gunslinger and his victim, came back to haunt the place?

A former employee sums it up. "The ghosts are here 24/7, and lots of people come in and joke and laugh about them. But when the last customer has gone, the lights are dimmed, and you're all alone, the laughing stops. That's when you know the ghosts are real."

253

GOLD CANYON STEAKHOUSE
160 Main Street, Dayton NV 89403

SCHOOL GHOULS

Ghosts can be very fierce and instructive.
—Flannery O'Connor

COLLEGES AND, to a lesser degree, grade schools seem to breed ghost stories. And the ghosts tend to reflect the student population: They're often the spirits of former students who have died tragically, their lives cut short on the path to higher knowledge and adult responsibilities. But why do these stories get more attention at this point in life? Are they just a sort of verbal roller coaster, scaring you at an age when you still think you're immortal? Are they designed to create boundaries, a way for upperclassmen to put younger students in their place? Or do they circulate in the spirit of experimentation that comes from shaking off parental bonds and moving one step closer to adulthood—and, in time, death?

As students learn more, belief in ghostly things seems to increase. That's according to a 2005 study about college students' paranormal beliefs that was published in *The Skeptical Inquirer*. The results indicate that "as people attain higher college-education levels, the likelihood of believing in paranormal dimensions increases."

So get ready to crack this book as we test your beliefs with some lessons from the dead. Learn why it's not a good idea to cut through Bunce Hall late at night. Go exploring with a deceased former college president as he seeks his missing portrait at an Alabama college. Study how fancy-hatted ghosts show up at colleges in New Hampshire and New Jersey. Ponder how the victim of a hazing prank haunts both his frat house and the railroad tracks where he died.

Are you taking notes? Death, you know, sometimes throws a pop quiz at you . . .

A GHOST WHO CARES

by Fiona Broome

IN THE SUNLIGHT, Colby-Sawyer College sparkles atop a hill in quaint New London, New Hampshire. Just two hours north of Boston, the small town looks perfectly normal to casual visitors.

The college is also one of New Hampshire's most haunted places. I know. I attended the school when it was Colby Junior College, a private college for young women.

Only a few single men lived in New London, and there were even fewer men on campus. We relied on dates from Dartmouth College in Hanover, the nearest town of any size. Meeting Dartmouth men wasn't easy unless we had a weekend mixer or this guy or that "just happened" to drop by, so we kept a close watch on ivy-laced Colgate Hall, the building where visitors to campus checked in.

In my dorm room, I placed my desk chair so that I had a clear view of Colgate Hall's door. I could dash from my Page Hall dormitory room to Colgate in less than two minutes, putting my shoes on as I ran. I'd practiced it many times.

In September 1969, Homecoming parties were fast approaching, and I was still dateless. Any single male on campus was fair game. That's why I sprang to action when I spotted an unfamiliar man at the door of Colgate Hall. It was about 1:00 in the afternoon, and just chilly enough that the visitor's flowing coat and wide-brimmed hat seemed unremarkable, if a little theatrical.

I assumed he was an actor. Because Colby staged well-respected theatrical

257

productions, our college often had colorful visitors. Many were actors from professional theaters, recruited to fill male roles in an otherwise all-girl cast. Some were also short-term instructors in subjects such as mime.

I grabbed my shoes and a notebook, hoping not to appear too obvious as I walked briskly across the grassy quad. My plan was to slow my pace as I approached Colgate. I'd saunter past the stranger as if I "just happened" to be on my way to Colgate Hall, getting a closer look all the while.

THE SLOW FADE
When I reached the quad, the warmly dressed visitor was leaning over the railing by the door to Colgate. I still couldn't see his face; the brim of his hat covered his features as he kept looking down.

I paused to put on my shoes. When I looked back up, he was gone.

I wandered over to Colgate Hall anyway, hoping to find him inside the building. After twenty minutes of cruising the building's corridors, I gave up. I didn't think anything of it; he'd probably stepped into an office or even left campus.

About a week and a half later, I saw him again. He wore the same hat, but I think he wore a suit instead of the flowing coat. This time, I approached him from the library—today the Campus Center—close to Colgate Hall. I could see him clearly in the fading afternoon light.

I glanced both ways before crossing the slim drive that separated the library from the quad, and then stepped onto the grass. When I returned my gaze to Colgate Hall, he was still there. Then the man literally faded from sight. It was as if I were watching him slowly evaporate.

His disintegration probably took no more than one or two seconds, but it was more than a little startling. I shook my head and actually rubbed my eyes. "I must need glasses," I told myself.

After that, he remained "the one that got away" in my memories. Until a few years ago, I never considered that he might be a ghost. Then, researching New Hampshire's ghosts, I found a book that described Colby-Sawyer's ghost of the man in the hat. I was tremendously surprised, and glad finally to learn why he had vanished.

AN INVENTORY OF GHOSTS
While visiting Colby-Sawyer, I heard about many other spirits. Almost every dorm has a ghost story: Burpee Hall has a field hockey player. Gilbert Ross, an

eighteenth-century male witch, haunts McKean. Page and Shepard halls each have "something" in the basement, and Austin has a spirit on the third floor. Colby Hall has a phantom cat. Best Hall is alternately too quiet and then echoing with unexplained noises, and breezes enter the dorm at places where no windows are open.

Something much darker haunts the old Colby Academy building. According to local legend, professors avoided the historic site after a few unpleasant encounters with a ghost. In 1999, Colby-Sawyer donated the building to the town of New London for use as a town hall.

Some say that when the college's archives were moved from the old Academy to the Colby-Sawyer library, at least one ghost moved with them. This ghost may be the boy who is heard in the loft area, or it could be the history enthusiast who rearranges the books overnight.

None of these ghosts are malicious, and some of them are amusing. Even better, most of them are quirky enough to appear in full daylight. Perhaps they're as comfortable at Colby-Sawyer as its students, and have just as much right to linger there.

COLBY–SAWYER COLLEGE
541 Main Street, New London NH 03257

EASTERN ILLINOIS UNIVERSITY
by Troy Taylor

ONE OF THE MOST FAMOUS school spirits in Illinois is undoubtedly the phantom who haunts a women's dormitory at Eastern Illinois University in Charleston: Pemberton Hall, filled with tradition and tales of ghosts.

Pem, as its residents call it, was the first college building in Illinois to provide housing for women on campus. It may also be the state's first college dorm to be haunted, considering the hundreds of strange events that have supposedly taken place there for almost a century.

The tales began after something terrible happened to a resident of Pemberton Hall on a bitterly cold night in January 1916. A young woman who had been unable to sleep decided to go to the fourth-floor music room and play the piano. It was very late, and she hoped playing soft music would help her to relax.

The story goes that a janitor who worked on campus somehow managed to enter the women's hall that night and discovered the girl alone in the music room. Her back was turned to the open doorway, and she was lost in her thoughts as she played. Before she realized what was happening, the man grabbed her and pummeled her with his fists. He then tore away her nightgown and raped and beat her, leaving her for dead before vanishing into the cold winter's night.

Still breathing, the young woman managed to drag herself to the stairs. After crawling down the steps, she pulled her battered body along the hallways, feebly scratching on doors and trying to awaken someone to help her. Finally, she made it to a counselor's door and managed to wake her. When the counselor opened her door, she found the victim in a pool of blood, her body bruised, bleeding, and now lifeless.

A COUNSELOR'S UNENDING PAIN

As the years have passed, residents of Pemberton Hall have heard echoes of this tragic event time and time again: dragging sounds heard near the stairs that lead to the upper floor and the sound of scratching on doors and walls. Most disconcerting are the bloody footprints that have appeared in the corridor, only to vanish moments later. Many believe the ghost of the murdered young woman has returned. But if she has, she doesn't roam this building alone.

The counselor who discovered the murdered girl was named Mary Hawkins. A young woman herself, she was barely older than the students she had been hired to assist. She was very attractive, with long blond hair and a bright disposition that made her a favorite among the residents of Pemberton Hall.

After the murder, Mary was devastated. Students told of seeing her pacing the hallways all night, tormented by horrible visions and guilt. Unable to cope with her depression and the accompanying nightmares, Mary was institutionalized. She later committed suicide.

Shortly after her death, residents started to report strange occurrences in Pemberton Hall—events attributed to Mary's ghost. And they do so to this day. Perhaps Mary's spirit is unable to rest after losing one of the women in her care, and she still roams the hall to protect the residents from harm. Her ghost is said to glide through the rooms locking and unlocking doors, turning off radios and televisions, and tending to other matters.

Alumna Amy Van Lear lived in Pemberton Hall for several years, and has since recounted many occurrences that students attribute to Mary. While Amy never came face to face with Mary, she did have a few disconcerting experiences. One involved the lights on the fourth floor of the building, where the music room was located and where the attack on the young woman took place. Even though the floor is now locked and off-limits to residents, Amy and a number of other former students have reported seeing windows open and close and the lights turn on and off, all without any logical explanation.

A former resident tells of a string of strange incidents that happened when she lived in the dorm in the fall of 1952. She says the girls were being awakened at all hours by banging on the doors and from knocks that seemed to be coming from inside the walls. No cause was ever determined, but most students just assumed Mary was trying to make her presence known.

REARRANGED FURNITURE, LOCKED DOORS

Throughout the 1960s and 1970s, residents reported hearing the sounds of whispers in Pemberton, especially on the fourth floor, and seeing apparitions on the stairwell. These figures appeared very briefly and then vanished.

A student who lived in the building in 1976 recalled the problems that the resident advisors had with the furniture in one of the lounges:

An RA walked into the room one morning and discovered the furniture had been moved around. She went to find someone to help her put it back in place; but when she and another RA returned, they found everything had been restored to order. Even stranger, the same thing continued to happen, with the furniture sometimes found overturned. The RAs learned to leave the lounge the way they found it, knowing the furniture would somehow be put back where it belonged. Could Mary, with her hall-monitor impulses, have had a hand in it?

Former resident Patty O'Neill told of an encounter she had with Mary in the spring of 1981. After studying late in one of the lounges one night, she went back to her room to sleep. Her roommate was already in bed, so to keep from waking her, she just pulled the door closed instead of locking it. (The old door was slightly wider than the frame, and the only way to lock it was to slam it firmly in place.)

Patty climbed into bed and drifted off. A short time later, she suddenly awakened and realized that the room was freezing cold. As she reached for her blankets, she was shocked to see a woman in a long white gown standing at the end of her bed. The woman remained there for several seconds before turning and walking toward the door.

"She opened the door and started to leave. Then, with one hand on the

PURLOINED CLOTHING

ACCORDING TO HELEN, a former Eastern Illinois student who lived in Pemberton, paranormal activity was especially active in the late 1980s. "I had a lot of weird experiences, from the door to our room refusing to stay locked to things that disappeared all the time." Helen then told of something even stranger.

"My roommate and I, along with several other girls, had clothing stolen from our rooms, all of which were locked at the time. We'd find the clothes later, scattered up and down the halls, hanging on doorknobs and fire extinguishers—all over the place.

"Almost all of the items that vanished were bras, nightgowns, and underwear—especially thongs. One of my friends thought Mary was trying to send us a message, saying that maybe she didn't approve of what would have been unsuitable clothing in her time."

knob, she turned and looked back at me for several seconds," said Patty. "She then left, closing the door behind her."

Apparently Patty's room wasn't the only one visited that night. As the apparition departed the room, she had locked the door. Strangely, a number of other students who distinctly recalled leaving their doors open found them locked the next morning. It was as if someone had been checking on them and was worried about their safety.

In recent years, most of the reports of weird happenings have centered on Pemberton Hall's fourth floor. Even though no one ever goes up there, residents have heard footsteps pacing overhead and the strains of faint piano music filtering down. Darkened and closed off, the floor remains empty save for old furniture and the dust of decades. Oh, and a piano is stored in the old music room. Is this where the music comes from? If so, one has to wonder whether the player is of our world or the next.

EASTERN ILLINOIS UNIVERSITY
600 Lincoln Avenue, Charleston IL 61920

THE FRAT BOY GHOST

by James A. Willis

KENYON COLLEGE was founded in the late 1820s, its campus built on a hilltop that overlooks the Kokosing River Valley in Ohio. It gained a reputation as a well-respected school of higher learning, and as a result many fraternities chose to establish chapters there. After Delta Kappa Epsilon arrived on campus, a single night's events would lead to one of the strangest mysteries in the school's history.

In the early years of the twentieth century, a student named Stuart Pierson decided to follow in the footsteps of his father and pledge DKE. Like all pledges, he was to be hazed before being sworn in as an active member.

On October 28, 1905, a few fraternity brothers led Pierson from his room on the fourth floor of the DKE house and across the campus to begin the hazing. Part of the hazing called for Pierson to walk onto a train trestle crossing the Kokosing River and to lie down on the tracks; he was to remain there until his brothers returned. The prank was designed not only to scare Pierson but also to determine how well he trusted his brothers. After Pierson stretched his body over the tracks, the brothers left, saying they'd be back for him in a while.

Of course, no trains were scheduled to run on that particular set of tracks that evening—or so the brothers of Delta Kappa Epsilon believed. When they went back to retrieve Pierson, they were hit with a horrible sight. A train had in fact passed through and had struck and killed the young pledge.

It was believed Pierson didn't get out of the way because he either fell asleep or expected the train to stop as part of an elaborate hoax. Pierson's watch stopped at the time of death: 9:41 p.m.

STUART'S RETURN

Pierson's death quickly brought controversy and scandal to the small college community. Rumors began circulating that the fraternity brothers had actually tied Pierson to the tracks, making his escape impossible—a story that has never been substantiated. Things got even stranger when Pierson's father, himself a member of DKE, refused to press charges against the fraternity or the college. With that, the tragic incident should have faded into memory.

265

But Stuart Pierson's ghost had other ideas.

After the accident, the train trestle where Pierson was killed was removed and replaced by a bridge, which now serves as part of a bicycle path. That hasn't stopped Pierson's ghost from wandering the spot where he met his demise. Every year, especially on the anniversary of his death, locals wander down to the area in an attempt to make contact with Pierson's spirit. Some have reported seeing his ghost walking along the bridge or—even creepier—lying in the middle of the bridge, just as he did on the tracks on the last night of his life.

Even those who don't come upon Pierson's ghost on the bridge might still catch sight of him by standing outside the DKE house; passersby have seen the ghost gazing out at them from the window of the fourth-floor room the young man once occupied. Even the brothers living in the fraternity house have reported hearing his ghost moving about on the top floor late at night. In fact, residents on the lower floor have gotten so used to the sound of hollow footsteps walking across the ceiling above that they now simply smile and say, "Stuey's making his rounds."

KENYON COLLEGE
Gambier OH 43022

THE DOMINICAN COLLEGE PACER
by Robert Zampella

DOMINICAN COLLEGE, in Orangeburg, New York, is a small private college that caters mostly to commuter students, but it also has a dorm for students who live on campus. My sister, a graduate of Dominican, told me about the strange things that happened one night in the dorm. This is her story.

"My friend Gary, who also lived in the dorm, would ask me to stay with him overnight when we were involved together in some school activity. He had a single room and I slept on the floor in a sleeping bag, my eyes level with the floor and the outside hallway.

"One night at around 3:00 a.m., I opened my eyes and noticed somebody walking back and forth in the hallway, right outside Gary's door. I saw the feet but didn't hear any sound. I guessed it was someone going to the bathroom, but the mysterious pacer kept going back and forth. After about an hour and a half, it all just seemed too weird.

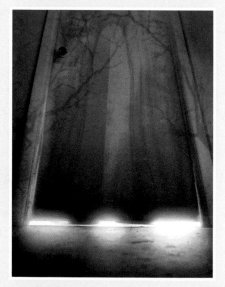

"I reached up, tapped Gary on his leg, and told him what I was seeing. He ignored me, and I could tell he probably thought what I said was ridiculous.

After about ten more minutes of pacing back and forth, the person finally stopped in front of Gary's door. I was stricken with fear as I jumped up and shook Gary awake. When I told him what was happening, he agreed to check it out. As he got up, I slipped back into my sleeping bag, leaving only my eyes exposed so I could see what was going on.

The feet were still visible as Gary walked toward the door. I begged him not to open it—a plea that fell on deaf ears. The instant he opened the door, the feet disappeared! I jumped up, ran into the hallway, looked in both directions, and saw. . . well, nothing. Gary thought I was nuts, but today I'm as convinced of what I saw as I was on that scary night."

NORTH DALLAS HIGH SCHOOL

by Jason Thomas

NORTH DALLAS, in the Oak Lawn area of Dallas, was one of the city's first high schools. And part of its history involves ghosts. More than one spirit reportedly roams its hallways after dark—a little girl in a blue dress who drowned in the old school pool over thirty years ago, a soldier who died in one of the wars, and an assortment of other presences who remain unidentified.

Several years ago, I experienced a ghost while serving as an assistant baseball coach at the school. The head coach and I were in the team's locker room late in the afternoon, preparing for the upcoming season. It was about three days shy of Christmas, and we were the only two people in the building.

The lights were off in the rest of the building, and if we ventured into the main building from the locker room, the alarm would be set off, bringing the Dallas police to the school within minutes. In addition to the alarm system, the locker-room door was secured with a padlock. Nobody but us was going to get into that room that day.

267

We were moving equipment around and discussing plans for the baseball season when the "secure" locker-room door creaked open. And it was a way-over-the-top creak, the kind you hear in a scary movie. But no one was there. For the life of me, I don't know how a padlocked door could've been opened.

A few minutes after that, the head coach decided we should go out to the parking lot. His wife was driving up to meet us for dinner, and we figured it would be nice if we were waiting out back when she got there.

As we passed the shower room, we heard a very faint yet rapid tapping on something metal—a peculiar sound we'd never heard there before. Because this sort of stuff fascinates me, I walked into the shower room to investigate. When I got to the center of the room, I was hit with the worst smell I've ever smelled in my life. I turned around to discuss it with the head coach, but he was already hastily making his exit.

THE BLUE LIGHT

Driven out by the terrible stench, I followed the coach outside. Before long, his wife came and we headed off to dinner. As we left the school grounds, we saw a blue light shining through the window of a second-floor classroom at the back of the building. We immediately dismissed it as a computer monitor left on by someone before Christmas break rolled around. At the restaurant, we spent a while laughing off the whole experience and explaining it away before our conversation turned to baseball.

On our return to the school, we saw something that left us shocked and confused. The blue light we'd seen earlier at the back of the school had moved. It was now floating in the third-floor stairwell on the building's west side. To our knowledge, there was no light bulb, computer, or even an electrical outlet in the third-floor stairwell. I went back and confirmed this to be the case the next day. We had a logical explanation for the blue light we'd seen earlier, but there was no way that a computer or anything else could've been plugged in on that third-floor landing.

Did the blue light we saw have anything to do with the little girl in the blue dress? I still wonder, even though we'll never know.

NORTH DALLAS HIGH SCHOOL
3120 North Haskell Avenue, Dallas TX 75204

SOUTHERN VERMONT COLLEGE
by Scott A. Johnson

EVERY SCHOOL HAS ITS LEGENDS, and most have their share of ghosts. But few are as steeped in tragedy, intrigue, and mystery as Southern Vermont College, in Bennington. Though the names of the key players are revered and their histories well known, the ends of their lives left questions—and in some cases, hard feelings—behind. Despite, or perhaps because of, the passage of years, the stories persist and grow, constantly giving students something new to talk about. And the stories at Southern Vermont begin with a very rich man named Edward Everett.

Edward Everett's career began inauspiciously as a salesman of jars for his stepfather, the man who invented the Lightning jar—a canning jar designed to be easier and quicker to open than the Mason jar. He turned his years of experience into innovation and money, becoming the first man to discover oil and gas in Ohio. Everett's wealth was estimated at nearly $50 million, which made him one of the wealthiest men in the world.

MR. HOBART'S SON
by Jeff Heimbuch

WHEN I WAS A FRESHMAN at William Paterson University in Wayne, New Jersey, my roommate and I heard a lot of stories about ghosts on campus. We were the type who had to check out things of that nature, so we did a little research and found out that Hobart Manor, the office of the president of the school, was supposed to be haunted. Hobart Manor was originally the residence of Garret Hobart, the twenty-fourth Vice President of the United States. He lived there with his wife, daughters, and son. More significantly, a few of the Hobarts died there.

One night we set out for Hobart Manor. Because it was around midnight and everyone was gone, we were sure we wouldn't be surprised by anyone who might still be working.

The manor has a patio to the left of the building, and a set of stairs next to the patio leads to a second patio directly below. After looking around the building for a bit—which wasn't easy, since it was built on a hill and there's a steep drop on some of the sides—we decided to go to the lower of the two patios.

Once there, we looked in the windows of the building but couldn't see anything; it was pitch-black inside. My friend decided to look somewhere else, so he went around a corner to find another window.

Now alone, I looked back through the window. To my shock, I could clearly see a man standing just inside, looking straight back at me. He had on a top hat and what looked like a long coat. He also seemed to be smiling slightly, but in an incredibly creepy way. His eyes looked like they were drilling a hole into my skull.

Whatever I was looking at scared the hell out of me, and I yelled out in surprise. I then called for my friend to come see what I was seeing. I tried not to take my eyes off the man for fear he would disappear. As it turned out, my friend was able to catch a quick glimpse of him just before he vanished, but that was enough. Freaked out, we left.

The next day, I looked online for reports of ghost sightings and found some that told me that other people had seen the exact same thing I had. Top hat. Long coat. Weird eyes. What I'd seen was believed to be the ghost of Mr. Hobart's son.

That was the only time I ever saw anything creepy at Hobart Manor, but once was enough!

In 1910, Everett purchased a five-hundred-acre parcel of land southwest of Bennington, Vermont, and with his wife Amy built what was to be their dream house. Construction began in 1911 and continued for three years, with materials imported from Italy, England, and even Cuba. The couple had three daughters and lived happily. Then tragedy struck: Amy died, reputedly by drowning in the upper pond near the mansion.

Everett married again, this time to a woman thirty years his junior. Her name was Grace, and Everett's daughters took an immediate dislike to their father's new wife. After Grace bore Everett two more daughters, the older girls' hatred intensified, leading to considerable family friction.

In 1929, Everett died, leaving behind a huge fortune. Hostilities between the children of Amy and their stepmother, Grace, led to a bitter struggle for the inheritance—a battle soon rendered moot by the stock market crash of October 1929, which quickly drained Everett's accounts. Grace Everett continued to live in the house for nearly thirty years, then sold it to the Order of the Holy Cross for use as a seminary in 1952.

270

For twenty years, the estate was used as a home for those seeking spiritual enlightenment and piety. Then in 1974, the property was traded with St. Joseph College, which blossomed into Southern Vermont College.

A QUARTET OF GHOSTS

The ghost stories at Southern Vermont, told by students and employees alike, center around the main house and grounds, giving the stately old Everett mansion a slightly darker cast once night falls. Many of the spirits who haunt the campus have yet to be identified, but four apparitions date from the site's early days.

The Black-Hooded Monk. The most common sighting harkens back to the days of the seminary. Though this specter's face is never seen, he is recognized by his black hood. The so-called Black-Hooded Monk is accepted by the students and whispered about to those who haven't seen him. Yet.

Edward and Grace Everett. Also seen in the mansion are a man and a woman identified as Edward Everett and his second wife, Grace. While the reasons behind their presence are unknown, certain assumptions can be made. Perhaps Grace roams the hallways of her previous home because she loved the place so much. Edward may wander the halls in despair over the family unrest surrounding his lost fortune. Whatever the reasons, they persist in making themselves known, albeit infrequently.

Amy Everett. Though the story of her death by drowning in the upper pond has never been verified, several people have supposedly seen Amy Everett near her watery grave. She is sometimes described as a woman in white, other times as a shadow in the moonlight. Some accounts place her alone at the site, while others see a ghostly child as well. No one knows whether  Amy died accidentally or as the result of foul play, but if numerous reports of sightings are to be believed she still walks her beloved estate.

271

Supporting Players

Inside the mansion, the third floor seems to be the center of activity. Phenomena in the Abbey room are common, with some claiming the room to be virtually alive with energy. The room, which now serves as a classroom, was once part of the servants' quarters in which a maid supposedly hanged herself. Other reports speak of smoke or fog in the hallways, as well as lights that go on and off in locked rooms, doors that unlock themselves, and windows found open after previous security sweeps.

The old carriage house, now housing classrooms, is also the scene of curious activity. It's been reported that doors and windows lock themselves from the inside and that computers power themselves off and on at will.

The ghosts who reside on the beautiful hilltop campus of Southern Vermont College hold to no schedule. The best way to see them is to enroll in a class or two. Barring that, campus tours can be arranged. Just take care to pay the proper respect. You never know who, or what, might be escorting you.

SOUTHERN VERMONT COLLEGE
982 Mansion Drive, Bennington Vermont 05201

BEWARE OF BUNCE HALL

by Nancy Condardo

I ATTENDED GLASSBORO STATE COLLEGE (now Rowan University) in the 1970s, and believe me, Bunce Hall is seriously haunted. It's the oldest building on campus, and at that time it housed the music department and the theater. My friends and I were music majors, and we decided to have a séance one night on the second floor of the building—our best chance, we felt, to experience some serious spookiness.

It was about 10:30 before we made our way up to the second floor of Bunce. Night classes were finished and our only concern was avoiding the night watchman. We chose a classroom near the middle of the second floor because it had a nice big oak table and enough chairs for all of us.

We started our séance by lighting a candle we had placed in the center of the table. We then joined hands and concentrated on calling forth any spirits that might be around.

We didn't have to wait long.

The first thing we heard was a series of sharp raps coming from around the room. "Maybe it's old plumbing," we agreed quietly, breaking the circle to see if the sounds continued. We waited quietly for about fifteen minutes, but nothing happened. We checked around the room and even tried rapping on the radiator to see if we could reproduce the sounds. We couldn't, so we resumed our séance.

The noises started up again immediately. Even more amazing was what was happening to the table: It began to shake, and the shakes grew stronger and stronger until the table rose from the floor! We were terrified, of course—afraid of what would happen if we didn't break the circle and afraid of what would happen if we did. We finally let go of each other's hands, and the table fell to the floor with a bang. We turned on the light and tried to lift the table with our knees to see if maybe one of us had been responsible for what happened. But the oak table was big and quite heavy, and none of us could move it—much less, secretly.

It was then that we noticed markings on the blackboard, which had been clean when we entered the room. They seemed to be words, but the odd, downward-sloping script was unreadable.

At that point, we'd had enough and left. The whole experience spooked us, to say the least, but we swore we would go back and try again.

A TERRIFYING CHASE

BACK IN THE WINTER of 1990, a Glassboro State student who had a night class often avoided the cold as he walked from his dorm to the classroom by detouring through the downstairs corridor of Bunce Hall. He would enter through the outer door, then the fire door. On a night he'll never forget, he was a few steps into the hall when the fire door behind him violently slammed closed twice. Here, he tells what happened next.

"Puzzled, I walked on. Then I heard footsteps behind me, even though there was no one there. I took off running for the other end of the hall, and the footsteps picked up the pace. Even more strange, the light shining through each of the classroom doors faded out as I passed by.

"As I neared the end of the long hallway, the footsteps of my spectral pursuer seemed almost on top of me as I slammed into the fire doors at full steam and raced to the exit door. I hit the sidewalk outside so fast that I almost fell on my face.

"At the same instant, I was shocked when the door behind me suddenly slammed shut faster than anyone human could've closed it. Not only that, but the window on the door fogged up and then iced over. I got the feeling that whatever had been chasing me was trapped behind the door and was furious I had gotten away. I decided I'd brave the cold from that night on."

273

CAUGHT ON TAPE

Our second séance resulted not only in the mysterious rapping and the levitations of the table but in something else: tapping on the blackboard. When we turned on the lights, this time we could read the words. In that strange, sloping script, we read, "Russel Knight 212."

Afterward, we did a little research and found there had indeed been a student named Russel Knight at Glassboro: a big man on campus in the late 1920s. He was president of his class, and even got married in Bunce Hall. We suspected that the wedding probably took place in a central classroom on the second floor that had a fireplace and French doors. There was no room 212 in the building anymore, but we thought that perhaps the college had built walls to make more classrooms and renumbered the rooms as a result. I'm not sure if that was the case, but it would make sense—especially considering what happened next.

The music department was housed in the basement of Bunce Hall and had set up student practice rooms there, including a corner classroom with a grand piano. After practicing one night, four of us met there.

I was a voice major, and though I play the piano pretty well, I was terrible at improvising. Yet when I sat down and put my hands on the keyboard, I started to improvise with surprising ease. My friends took advantage of this newfound ability and began to make up silly songs, which I accompanied. I remember being able to slide easily from one key to another. Susan, a flute major, had a tape recorder and some new tapes, and she suggested that we record the session.

After a few minutes of taping, we wanted to hear what we had. What we heard was noise overlaid on our music—a moaning voice, and a rhythmic pulsing sound. Annoyed, we thought the tape was defective. To test it, we left the recorder on "play" to see if the whole tape had the strange sounds. When we played it back, it was clean, so we figured the noises were just a fluke.

We recorded a few more songs, and when we listened to the tape, we again heard the moaning and rhythmic pulsing. This time, however, the voice was understandable. It said, "I must find, I must find," then rhythmically, "two-twelve, two-twelve, two-twelve . . ."

274

Now we were really spooked. We checked the other rooms to see if anyone else was around, though I don't know how they could have gotten the sounds on the tape without our knowing.

Scared but fascinated, we decided to keep taping. I just played the piano while the others listened. There was no other sound in the room, but on playback we heard the piano playing, the voice moaning, "I must find," and the rhythmic, "two-twelve, two-twelve, two-twelve." Suddenly, another voice appeared on the tape, clearer and higher pitched. Its words? "Circle of death."

We tore out of the room so fast that all I can remember is suddenly being outside. We had left the tape recorder behind, and it took all the courage we could muster to go back in and retrieve it.

We played the tape later at the dorm, marveling at what we had. When we heard the voice say, "Circle of death," it sent shivers down our spines. I'm sure Susan still has the tape, but the last time I heard it was in the late '70s. We never did figure out what "circle of death" means, and I'm not sure I ever want to.

ROWAN UNIVERSITY
201 Mullica Hill Road, Glassboro NJ 08028

SPIRITUS EMERITUS
by Alan Brown

THE UNIVERSITY OF WEST ALABAMA is in Sumter County, one of the most rural counties in all of Alabama. Founded in 1835 in the small town of Livingston, the university started out as Livingston Female Academy. By the 1920s, the small college had undergone a name change—to State Teachers College at Livingston—and an ambitious building campaign began. In 1928, the college was authorized to construct a two-story building with twenty-five rooms, five classrooms, three laboratories, one lecture hall, several offices, and an eight-hundred-seat auditorium.

Completed in 1931, the building was named after David Bibb Graves, the fortieth and forty-second governor of Alabama. In 1962, the Natural Sciences and Mathematics wing was added, making Bibb Graves Hall the largest building on campus. Fittingly, the office of the president was located on the first floor of this imposing structure. It seems that he has company: Since the late 1980s, sightings by students and faculty indicate that one of the university's past presidents isn't ready to leave.

WHO GOES THERE?
The first paranormal activity in Bibb Graves Hall was noticed in the Natural Sciences and Mathematics wing. In 1989, former student Becky Graham had some unsettling experiences in one of the laboratories on the first floor. "My youngest child was three months old when I went back to school," she said. "One of the first classes I took was genetics, which required lab work—which in my case meant working alone in the lab after I'd put the baby to bed. There were times when I was there until midnight.

"Some nights I would hear the elevator door open, and I'd think it was just the security guard coming to patrol the floor. But if I went out in the hallway, there was no one there. Of course, the elevator could've been malfunctioning. But if so, how come the empty elevator would stop only at night, never during the day?"

Unexplained occurrences persisted after Becky became a biology instructor at the University of West Alabama: "I would be sitting at my desk late at night and hear footsteps coming down the hall. One time I figured it was one of the graduate assistants coming up to do some work. The footsteps stopped

275

at the copier in the back part of the building; but when I went and looked, there was nobody there."

Becky's older daughter also heard the footsteps. "When my daughter was enrolled here, she'd be in my office doing her homework. One day she told me, 'Mama, there are some strange noises [in the building]. I could swear I heard footsteps.' I then told her the same thing had happened to me."

In 1998, a 23-year-old graduate student and former football player nick-named Cadillac Jack had an even stranger encounter in Bibb Graves Hall. Dr. John McCall, chairman of Biological and Environmental Sciences, recalled the incident.

"Jack was working late at night. He was on the phone, and he heard what he described as a ghoulish laugh outside in the hall. He said it was in the stair-well area in the center of the building and sounded like someone going up the stairs. I asked him if it could have been one of the security guards, and he said, no, his immediate check of the area showed that no one else was there.

"So Jack returned to his office to resume his phone call," McCall continued. "As he sat down, he heard the laugh again—this time, much closer and louder. He said at this point he'd had enough, and he left the building."

Later that same year, Becky received a phone call from Jack just as she was about to go to bed. "When I talked to him on the phone, Jack said he was get-ting gooseflesh just from remembering what had happened to him at Bibb Graves Hall. He said this was a very real experience. He called me because he had forgotten to perform one of his tasks. He said, 'Ms. Graham, I'm not going back in that building by myself.' He asked if I would go with him, and I said, 'No, I won't, because I've already experienced things there myself at night.'" Jack was so nervous about entering the building alone that he talked his girl-friend into returning with him.

PAGING DR. GREENHILL

The ghost of Bibb Graves Hall has never been positive-ly identified, but long-time librarian Neil Snider believes the disturbances might be caused by the uneasy spirit of a former president, Dr. Noble Franklin Greenhill. Dr. Greenhill was president of the college from 1936 to 1944, when he resigned after not being able to keep student enrollment levels up during World War II. Still, he made a favorable impression

A MESSAGE FROM DR. GREENHILL?

EVIDENCE SUGGESTS that the spirit of UWA former president Noble Franklin Greenhill haunts not only the corridors of Bibb Graves Hall but his former office as well. Here, writer Alan Brown explains why.

"On the evening of April 23, 2005, I conducted a ghost tour of the town of Livingston as part of the Sucarnochee Folk and Heritage Festival. The tour ended on the front steps of Bibb Graves Hall, where I pointed out that the office now occupied by teacher certification officer Nancy Taylor used to be President Greenhill's office.

"That Monday, I received the following e-mail message from Ms. Taylor, who had participated in the tour along with her daughter.

"'I think you got the ghosts stirring in Bibb Graves after the tour Saturday night. When I got in my office this morning, I noticed that some books on the shelf had fallen over—they have never done this before—and the book facing up is titled *Ghost Fox!* Coincidence??' One can only wonder."

277

when, during his tenure, in 1943 he enlisted in the army and was commissioned as a major in the Specialist Corps.

"The student body and the alumni wanted a portrait of Dr. Greenhill," said Dr. Snider, "so they asked local artist Virginia White Barnes to do it." The portrait was hung in the waiting room of the president's office in Bibb Graves Hall, but several years later it mysteriously disappeared.

"When I was chairman of the presidential portrait committee," said Dr. Snider, "I called Dr. Greenhill's grandson, and he told me that he knew the portrait was still there in the late 1960s. It is my theory that the ghost in Bibb Graves Hall is Dr. Greenhill, looking for his portrait."

THE UNIVERSITY OF WEST ALABAMA
U.S. Highway 11, Livingston AL 35470

BAYLOR UNIVERSITY
by Tim Stevens

THE ARMSTRONG BROWNING LIBRARY at Baylor University, in Waco, Texas, is a premier attraction. As much a museum as a library, it houses one of the world's most complete collections of the original works and personal possessions of the poets Robert and Elizabeth Barrett Browning, as well as art based on their poetry.

Waco, with its Wild West reputation, seems an unlikely place for the collection. It was Dr. A. J. Armstrong, head of Baylor's English Department in the 1950s, who initiated a project to collect as many works of the famed Victorian poets as possible. The Armstrong Browning Library is the result.

From the outside, the library resembles a large block of concrete in various shades of gray. Yet on entering the library, visitors find rich polished-wood walls aglow with golden light streaming through the panes of colorful stained-glass windows. The windows depict scenes from the life and poetry of the Brownings.

Each room's collection is assembled with great care and attention to detail. The desks, chairs, paintings, and other possessions on display create an evocative picture of the poets' world in an atmosphere that can only be described as reverent.

In this place where voices from the past seem to whisper from the walls, some interesting things happen at night. More than one person has claimed to see the ghost of Elizabeth walking the halls, forever attached to her worldly things. But in the Gift Gallery—a gift shop near the library's entrance—a different spirit may dwell.

WHO LOCKED THE GATE?

When it comes to the life and times of the Brownings and the particulars of the Armstrong Browning Library, Kathryn Brogdon, the library's facilities director, has an encyclopedic knowledge of both. Like others in the Baylor community, she has heard stories of specters and unexplained phenomena on campus—stories she dismisses as bunk. Given her skepticism, it's interesting that she once experienced something in the library that has yet to be explained and mystifies her to this day.

Though the library is warm and inviting, Kathryn noticed a spot near the

Gift Gallery that was sometimes inexplicably cold— something even she found disconcerting in a building where people had supposedly encountered ghosts.

After staying late one night to move files between floors, Kathryn was closing the library and stopped by the gift shop to lock the pull-down gate. To her dismay, she discovered her keys were missing. When a thorough search for the keys turned up nothing, she left for home after deciding the shop would be safe until morning. Still, she worried all night and returned to work earlier than usual the next day.

As she entered the library, Kathryn was surprised to find the gate to the shop pulled down and locked. All the more baffling was that on the previous night, any employees who could have locked the gate had left before she had. The exceptions were the security guards who make regular rounds at the facility, but her e-mail inquiries to them revealed the patrolling guards hadn't locked the door.

To ensure she was covering all the bases, Kathryn checked the logs for the library's electronic card-reader locks to see whether she might have missed someone who entered the building after hours; the locks require a PIN or an alarm will sound. The logs showed that only the guards had passed through the area. Even for a skeptic like Kathryn, this was all far too strange.

The story might have ended there if news of the curious incident hadn't traveled around campus and been printed in the campus newspaper. The story gained wider currency after it was reported by the Waco *Tribune-Herald*.

Soon afterward, Kathryn received a phone call from a *Tribune-Herald* reader who claimed to know the name of her ghost. Kathryn had been reluctant to consider anything supernatural as the cause, and now she feared receiving countless calls from well-intentioned people offering explanations or speculation. This caller, however, had information so intriguing that it caught her attention: He told Kathryn he knew of incidents that regularly occurred near the library's gift shop.

PREACHER JOHNSON: R.I.P.

In 1951, when the library was under construction, finishing touches were applied to the roof. When workers were taken to the top, they were hoisted up by a lift that used cables obtained from a nearby aluminum plant after they had become too old and weak to be used for the plant's heaviest work. Ignoring the warnings of many, the library construction company kept using the cables until the last day of the job.

Construction worker Preacher Johnson got his nickname because he was a part-time minister. He was making the last planned trip to the top when the cables broke and he fell three floors to the ground, breaking both legs and suffering fatal injuries.

After the accident, a lawyer contacted Preacher Johnson's family and offered to represent them in a lawsuit against the builders. The family agreed, and in time they won the suit and were awarded a large sum of money. Sadly, the lawyer disappeared with it all.

Kathryn's caller suggested that the circumstances of the tragic death and the heartless con job perpetrated on the family left Preacher Johnson's spirit in emotional turmoil—enough, perhaps, to explain why his spirit might still roam the library.

ARMSTRONG BROWNING LIBRARY
One Bear Place, Waco TX 76798

PHANTOM THEATERGOERS

by Christopher Balzano

HAUNTED THEATERS are nothing new to the world of the paranormal. Every major city seems to have at least one, but Emerson College's Cutler Majestic Theatre stands out among its spooky counterparts. It is the second-oldest theater in Boston's historic theater district, and Emerson uses it for student performances, traveling shows, and other productions. A few of the theater patrons, however, apparently date from the days when the Majestic was the toast of the town. And they don't buy tickets.

Walking into the theater is almost like walking back in time—one reason it's such a perfect setting for ghost stories. Add to that the students of Emerson College—

Boston, Mass. Majestic Theatre.

one part melodramatic, one part open-minded, and in some cases interested in the paranormal—and you have a recipe for weird tales.

The architect of the Majestic Theatre, which was completed in 1903, brought several styles of design together in an attempt to make the hall unique. Most striking was the way the light in the building shimmered, the effect of thousands of lights reflecting off a king's ransom's–worth of stained glass.

Over the years, the theater was used as an opera house, a vaudeville venue, and, in the 1950s, as a movie house. The neighborhood went downhill shortly after and came to be known as the Combat Zone because of its high crime rate. As the neighborhood went, so went the Majestic, and neglect hid the treasure that had once been a major draw. As the neighborhood gradually returned to its former self, so did the Majestic reclaim its former glory. Emerson's restoration of the theater began in 2002, and this grand venue for the arts reopened in 2003.

INTERFERENCE FROM BEYOND

Among the many ghosts said to haunt the Majestic Theatre is a little girl sometimes seen during rehearsals and technical setups. She skips through the balcony and is occasionally accompanied by a smaller boy who urges her to sit down. Others have seen a boy backstage who hides props and plays tricks on the actors. Students have seen actors on the stage who don't belong there, as well as an elderly janitor who disappears when called to. The laughter of what seems to be a woman echoes throughout the stage and lobby, especially in springtime.

One legend known to Emerson students holds that if the spirits don't like a show being performed, they shut down the sound board. Power remains for sound and everything else, but the shut-down board deprives the actors of cues and disrupts the performance.

Every theater major at Emerson is required do tech work at the Majestic, and most have experienced something supernatural. While there are myriad ghost tales set backstage and in the dressing room, the most haunted parts of the theater seem to be the third balcony and the sound area.

The third balcony was closed for a long period because the seating was too steep and it was deemed a fire hazard. The seats stay down only with force, but actors and stagehands often see the seats down when they're empty—of a living, breathing human being, at least. In fact, it's a tradition to say, "Excuse me," if you pass a downed seat, because you're blocking a ghost's view. One student was running lights for a rehearsal, and when she swung the light back to the balcony, she saw more seats down than up. When she went to investigate, she found clean areas in the centers

of the dusty seats—evidence that phantom patrons had been (or still were?) sitting there.

Another student was refocusing the lights late one night. He and the director were the only people in the theater. When at one point he looked up and saw the director sitting in the balcony, he jokingly taunted him, saying he should come down and get back to work. Suddenly the director called from behind him, and when the student looked back up to the balcony, the figure he'd just addressed had vanished.

A more disturbing story comes from two friends who were working on a show together. Steve and Donna, both wearing headsets, were on different sides of the balcony. The headsets were open to all the tech people, including the director and people on the boards. Steve's voice came over the microphone, "Donna, don't move. There's someone behind you."

Terrified, Donna asked who was there, but got no answer. She wanted to leave, but the rest of the tech people told her to stay, until finally she closed her eyes and held her breath. It was then that chair seats began slamming up and down in the rows between the two friends—and the mysterious disturbance continued until the end of the performance.

INVISIBLE SEATMATES?

The former manager of the Majestic agrees that spirits haunt the theater, saying that one in particular "helped" by turning off lights and locking doors at the end of the night when he himself had forgotten to do so. As he participated in the renovation of the landmark, the manager felt a bond to the building's old energies.

After closing briefly as renovations were completed, the theater celebrated its reopening in 2003, allowing the living to enjoy the show from the third balcony for the first time in decades. Today, the official position of both the college and the new manager is that the theater houses no ghosts, but rather echoes with the rich tradition of storytelling among Emerson's artistic students. Time will tell, however, if the old patrons claimed by some to watch the performances mind having their views blocked.

> **CUTLER MAJESTIC THEATRE AT EMERSON COLLEGE**
> 219 Tremont Street, Boston MA 02116

INSTITUTIONAL APPARITIONS

PRISONS ARE PLACES where the living experience emotional extremes, whether by their own hand or by fate. Inmates are subject to anger, regret, occasionally inhumane conditions (especially in solitary) and on-site executions that create the perfect environment in which a life term might be extended into the afterlife. It should therefore come as no surprise that spirits of the dead are sometimes encountered on the premises, regardless of whether the ghost in question died on-site or lingers because of a particularly horrid experience.

Then there are hospitals, mental asylums, and nursing homes. By their very nature, these institutions see death as a regular and expected occurrence. Barbaric experimental treatments and the misery of being misunderstood are among the reasons certain patients may return to the world of the living.

Most of the institutions in which the stories in this chapter are set were converted into something else—an apartment house, perhaps, or a school. Real estate is simply too valuable to leave such places to squatters and curious explorers. But that doesn't mean any spirits necessarily deserted the buildings. In California, Al Capone's banjo still echoes through the corridors of Alcatraz, and at the former Camarillo State Mental Hospital a patient apparently prefers picking on female employees over going into the light. In New Jersey, the ghost of a female resident of what was once a nursing home gets a little too intimate with the living. In an old Arizona penitentiary, the unexplained activity in a much-feared dark cell may in fact be that of a little girl.

In the meantime, the trend to convert imposing abandoned institutional buildings into apartments and condos continues apace. Of course, most new tenants are rarely aware that their mortgage or rental payments also might be going toward housing a former occupant or two—occupants who may or not choose to make their presence known. Sweet dreams!

GHOSTS OF ALCATRAZ

by Troy Taylor

SAN FRANCISCO BAY'S barren Alcatraz Island, long nicknamed the Rock, was originally a fort and then served as a military prison from 1859 to 1934. With the arrival of social upheaval and rampant crime in the 1920s and '30s, the federal government chose Alcatraz as the perfect site for an escape-proof prison that would strike fear into the hearts of criminals, thanks to the isolated location and the swift currents surrounding the island.

From the time Alcatraz became a federal prison in 1934 under the stern and watchful eye of Warden James A. Johnston until it closed in 1963, its steel doors clanged shut on more than 1,000 hardened convicts, criminals, and would-be escape artists.

From the start, the most incorrigible inmates from across the country were sent to the Rock. Each train that arrived in San Francisco to dispense prisoners seemed to have a "celebrity" of sorts on board. Among the first inmates were Al Capone, perhaps the most famous gangster of all; Doc Barker, the last surviving member of the Ma Barker Gang; George "Machine Gun" Kelly, the privileged son of a wealthy Memphis family who became one of the Prohibition period's

most notorious gangsters; Floyd Hamilton, a gang member and driver for Bonnie and Clyde; Alvin "Creepy" Karpis, a Canadian-born former Public Enemy No. 1 who was arrested by J. Edgar Hoover himself; and Robert Stroud, the amateur ornithologist who would later become known as the Birdman of Alcatraz.

Noteworthy or not, the inmates found that Alcatraz was a place where they had but five rights—food, clothing, a private cell, a shower once a week, and access to a doctor. Their methodical daily routine never varied.

While the cells the prisoners lived in were barren at best, they must have seemed like luxury hotel rooms compared to the punishment cells. In these, men were stripped of all but their basic right to food—and even then, they barely survived.

287

Confinement in the single Strip Cell was punishment for the most severe violations. In the Hole, the name for cells in the bottom tier of the main cellblock, the punishment usually included psychological torture, and sometimes physical torture as well. In D Block, inmates in cells above the Hole couldn't escape the screams of those imprisoned there. Prisoners who emerged from the Hole would often be senseless or sick and bound for the prison's hospital ward. Others never came out alive.

Even worse were the dungeons. A staircase in front of A Block led down to a large steel door, behind which were catacomb-like corridors and stone archways leading to the sealed-off gunports from the days when Alcatraz was a fort. In the dungeons off the corridor, the prisoners were chained to the walls, their screams unheard in the rest of the main cellblock. Food and sanitation in the dungeons were minimal, dignity nonexistent.

Early Ghostly Activity

A number of guards who worked in Alcatraz between 1946 and 1963 experienced the strange and the unexplained. From the grounds of the prison to the caverns beneath the buildings, they heard people sobbing and moaning,

289

smelled strange odors, discovered cold spots, and saw what they described as ghosts. Even families who lived on the island and the occasional guest claimed to have seen the ghostly forms of prisoners or phantom soldiers. The sound of what seemed to be gunshots made the guards think prisoners had escaped and obtained weapons.

A deserted laundry room would sometimes fill with the smell of smoke, though nothing was burning. The guards would be sent running from the room, only to return momentarily and find the air clear. Like the other mysterious happenings at Alcatraz, the phantom fires were never explained.

Even Warden Johnston, who had no time for those who believed in ghosts, once heard the unmistakable sound of a person sobbing in the dungeon as he led a group of guests on a tour. The sound was followed by an ice-cold wind felt by the entire group. Johnston could never arrive at an explanation for this weird occurrence.

During the twenty-nine years Alcatraz operated as a prison, there were at least fourteen escape attempts. Almost all the prisoners who tried to flee were either killed or recaptured, and only one is known to have made it ashore. The most traumatic and violent attempt, later dubbed the Battle of Alcatraz, took place over two days in May 1946.

What started as a well-planned breakout from the "escape-proof" prison

THE WELDED DOOR

VISITORS TO ALCATRAZ follow the same path once walked by the criminals who came to do time, passing through the warden's office and the visiting room and eventually entering the main cell house. Once inside the double steel doors, visitors can see that just past C Block, opposite the visiting room, is a metal door that looks as if it was once welded shut. Although tour guides don't usually mention it, behind that door is the utility corridor where the three attempted escapees were killed in the 1946 Battle of Alcatraz.

It was behind this very door that thirty years later a night watchman heard strange clanging sounds. He opened the door and peered down the dark corridor, shining his flashlight on the maze of pipes and conduits. Though he saw and heard nothing, the noises resumed when he closed the door. On reopening the door, he still didn't see anything that could explain the sounds. Could the eerie noises be the reason the door was welded shut?

290   turned into a disaster when the six inmates involved saw their plan fall apart. Realizing they couldn't succeed, they decided to fight it out. Before it was over, they had taken a number of guards hostage, killed three of them, and wounded several others; two of the guards were murdered in cold blood in cells 402 and 403 (later renamed C102 and C104). The failed escapees fared no better. Three of them climbed into a utility corridor to avoid the constant gunfire, only to die after being hit by bullets or shrapnel.

An escape attempt in 1962 was later documented by Hollywood in the film *Escape from Alcatraz.* Released in 1979, the movie was a big hit at the box office, but the prison had closed long before. Too expensive to renovate and properly secure, what could be called the world's most famous prison shut its doors for good in March 1963.

MYSTERIES OF CELL 14D

In 1972, the federal government put Alcatraz Island under the purview of the National Park Service, and after opening to the public, it became one of the park service's most popular sites. While in the daylight hours the old prison teems with tour guides and visitors, at night it is filled with mystery. Many believe that the energy of those who served time on the Rock remains, making the Alcatraz complex one immense haunted house.

Night watchmen patrolling the main cell house, divided into A, B, C, and

D blocks, say they've heard the sounds of what seems to be running coming from the upper tiers. Thinking an intruder has gained entry, the watchmen investigated the sounds but always found nothing.

One Park Service employee reported that on a rainy afternoon the sparse number of tourists allowed her some time off from guiding tours. She went for a walk in front of A Block and was just past the door leading down to the dungeons when she heard a loud scream from the bottom of the stairs. She ran away without looking to see if anyone was there.

Asked why she didn't report the incident, she replied, "The day before, everyone was ridiculing another worker who reported hearing men's voices coming from the hospital ward, and when he went to check the ward, it was empty. So I didn't dare mention what I heard."

Several guides and rangers felt something strange in one of the cells in the Hole: Cell 14D. "There's a feeling of sudden intensity that comes on when you spend more than a few minutes around that cell," one of them said.

Another guide described Cell 14D as "always cold. Sometimes it gets warm out here—so hot that you have to take your jacket off. The temperature inside the cell house can be in the seventies, and 14D is still cold."

The tour guides weren't the only ones to have strange experiences there. Several former guards at the prison have told of terrifying incidents that took place near the Hole, and in Cell 14D in particular.

During one guard's stint in the middle 1940s, an inmate was locked in 14D for some since forgotten infraction. According to the officer, the man began screaming within seconds of being locked in. He claimed that a creature with "glowing eyes" was locked in with him. Yet no one took the convict's cries of being "attacked" very seriously, probably·because tales of a ghostly presence wandering the nearby corridor were a continual inducement to practical jokes among the guards. The man's screaming continued into the night, until finally there was silence. The following day, guards inspected the cell and found the convict dead. A horrible expression was frozen onto his face, and there were hand marks around his throat. An autopsy revealed that the strangulation couldn't have been self-inflicted. Some believed that the man might have been choked by one of the guards, who had been fed up with all the screaming, but no one ever confessed to the crime.

On the day following the tragedy, several guards who were performing a head count noticed that there were too many men in the lineup. Then, at the end of the line, they saw the face of the convict who had recently been strangled in the Hole. As they all looked on in stunned silence, the figure abruptly vanished.

BANJO STRAINS

A park service employee who worked at Alcatraz in the late 1970s had a weird experience in another of the main cellblock's chambers. He was down near the shower room when he heard something he couldn't explain.

"It was banjo music," he said. "The room was empty, but I definitely heard banjo music coming from there. Maybe back in the days when it was a fort or army stockade, there was some guy here who played that instrument."

What the employee didn't know was that during the most traumatic days of his life, Al Capone, rather than risk going out to the exercise yard with the other inmates, would sit in the shower room strumming on his banjo.

Perhaps this lonely and broken spirit still plucks at the strings of a spectral musical instrument that vanished decades ago. Even today, tour guides and rangers who walk the corridors of the prison alone occasionally claim to hear a tune echoing through the abandoned building. Could Al Capone be its source? Or could it be another of the countless ghosts who continue to haunt Alcatraz year after year?

ALCATRAZ
Via the Blue and Gold Fleet Ferry, Pier 41
Marine Terminal, Fisherman's Wharf, San Francisco CA 94133

THE OLD IDAHO STATE PENITENTIARY
by Marie Cuff and Julie Decker

NOT TOO LONG AGO, an anonymous person wrote to Idaho Spirit Seekers, our paranormal research team, claiming to have seen the apparitions of two prisoners working in the rose garden on the grounds of the old Idaho State Penitentiary in Boise. We weren't surprised, since the garden is in the area where the gallows once stood, and where six state executions were carried out.

Other people have reported ghostly experiences while visiting, working at, or passing by the old penitentiary, now a museum. They have seen dancing orbs in the courtyard late at night and lights on in cellblocks that have no electricity. They've smelled odd odors in a certain cell. They've heard men talking.

Like most prisons, the old penitentiary has a history of violence and sadness. Inmates frustrated with poor living conditions rose up in anger that sometimes resulted in violence, and riots led to the old pen's closure in 1973. Today you can still see the strength of the inmates who built it, of the men who spent their sentences carrying the limestone that would shape the very place where they would spend their days paying for their crimes.

WHAT WE FOUND

An Idaho Spirit Seekers team investigated the old pen in October 2005. While in the rose garden, team member Dan said that he was getting a headache and that it got worse the longer he stood there. Another team member, Kelly, took a series of pictures of Dan in which two orbs appeared. One orb was very large—and the worse Dan's headache got, the brighter the orb became in each picture.

Just as suddenly as Dan's headache came on, it was gone; a final picture of Dan showed that the orb had gone away as well. Could the orb have signaled the presence of an inmate who was sent to his death at the gallows, letting us know he was still around?

Our team stayed at the penitentiary that night so we could investigate further. The windows in the massive old buildings were dark, since only one of the cellblocks had working electricity. The streetlights inside the courtyard provided hardly any additional light, and we could imagine what it must have been like to lie in a cell with only the light from the moon coming in from a tiny window—if, that is, you were lucky enough to have a window.

After investigating a number of the buildings, we were beginning to wonder if we would experience anything else paranormal. Then we entered Cell House 3, which was built in 1899. As soon as we all crossed over the threshold, we heard what sounded like someone working on one of the pipes with a wrench. It was a very clear and distinct sound, and the entire team heard it. We continued to check Cell House 3, but no explanation for the cause of the sound was ever found. No one was working in the building that night, and there was no operative plumbing in the building.

THE UNSEEN HAND

We moved up the cell-house stairs to a part of the prison that no one, including long-time employees, had been to in many years. Graffiti was scrawled on the walls, and scorch marks from a fire were evidence of the 1973 riots.

About halfway down the very dark, very narrow walkway in front of the cells, team member Marie noticed a picture of three men in prison garb on the back wall of a cell. She tried to stick her arm through the narrow bars to get pictures, but it proved too difficult. She and team member Kelly then continued down the walkway

295

When they arrived at the second cell from the end, Marie noticed that there was a similar picture on the back wall of this cell. This time it was of two men, but they wore the same prison garb as the men in the other photo. Marie once again leaned in close to the cell to see if she could get a picture.

Suddenly she felt someone reach out and run fingers through her hair. The cell was locked and empty—at least, of anyone who could be seen with the naked eye. It was a gentle touch, but just the same it was unsettling. As they left the tier, Marie and Kelly felt as though they were being watched.

Cell House 3 may have seen the last of prisoners who live and breathe, but at least two of our team members feel that the spirits of some of them never left.

OLD IDAHO PENITENTIARY
2445 Old Penitentiary Road, Boise ID 83712

CALIFORNIA DREAMING?
by Scott A. Johnson

CALIFORNIA has more than its share of ghostly residents, and, true to the West Coast way of life, many of them are stars from times past. While stories of the spirits of Marilyn Monroe and Howard Hughes are well known (these two legends have supposedly been glimpsed in dozens of locations), the state is home to places where the presence of spirits isn't merely a fabrication to boost the tourist trade. In fact, were these buildings left in their original condition, no sane tourist would set foot in them. And though such places usually get face-lifts, much like aging stars, their souls stick around. A case in point is Camarillo State Mental Hospital.

Built in 1936 in the small coastal town of Camarillo, a jumping-off point for the Channel Islands, the State Mental Hospital first opened its doors in an era when people with mental disorders were called crazies, lunatics, or criminally insane. The acreage around the facility was used as farmland, complete with a dairy. The patients—alcoholics, pedophiles, or those with mental illnesses, retardation, or violent tendencies—had no need to leave the grounds for any of their needs, nor were they allowed to.

By the 1950s, more than 7,000 people—some as young as eleven years old—were housed at the massive facility. Patients wore tan jumpsuits to distinguish them from the facility's staff and to make it easier to identify any patients who tried to escape. The rowdiest were routinely kept under control with powerful drugs; those who were still uncontrollable were subjected to electro-shock therapy.

Another routine treatment was to immerse the patients in hot water, then wrap them in ice-cold towels immediately after they were pulled out. Still others were strapped to their beds until they'd exhausted themselves. Investigations of the hospital revealed brutality on the part of the guards and incidents of inmates abusing and even killing one another. Given Camarillo's "house of horrors" atmosphere, it should come as no surprise that people who either worked or lived there have told some compelling stories of hauntings.

BRIEF ENCOUNTERS

A female janitor got a shock one evening when cleaning the women's restroom. As she bent to pick something up off the floor, she noticed a pair of legs, which she described as obviously belonging to a man, under the door of a stall. When she called out to the person, there was no answer. She pushed the door open, only to find the stall empty. She refused to enter the restroom again.

Another employee, a nurse named Debbie, had a strange encounter while sneaking a cigarette during a rainy day. Not wanting to go outside in the rain, she opened the doors to the courtyard and lit up. No sooner had she taken her first puff than, as she put it, someone grabbed her roughly by the shoulders and shook her hard. When she turned to see who it was, there was no one there.

On another occasion, a sixty-five-year-old nurse claimed to have been grabbed by the hair and pulled backward out of a chair by an unseen assailant, though there were no witnesses to the incident. One of the nurse's coworkers, a ten-year veteran of Camarillo named Sheryl Downey, thought the story eerie, but it wasn't until her own encounter with the supernatural that she began to

believe a former male patient was picking on women.

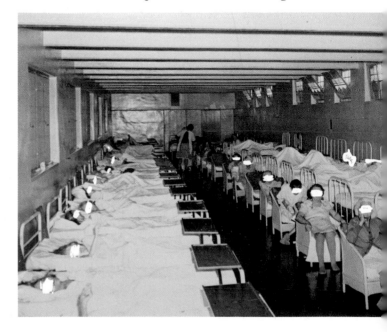

She says that during one of the busiest times of day, just after breakfast, she spotted a man she'd never seen before outfitted in the uniform worn by patients in the old days of the asylum. He was walking into the women's restroom. When she called out to stop him, he continued as if he hadn't heard her.

Sheryl called her coworker to roust the man out, but the room turned out to be empty. There were no other exits or windows, so the man couldn't have left without anyone seeing him.

As Sheryl puzzled over his sudden disappearance, her coworker screamed. The man was standing directly behind Sheryl, and then promptly vanished into thin air.

New Day, Old Ghosts

In the mid-1970s, things changed at Camarillo. The institution examined its policies and began working to actually heal the patients instead of locking them away. By the early 1990s, conditions had improved significantly. Patients were taught real skills and underwent less radical types of therapy. A petting zoo was even added to help the developmentally challenged children in residence.

Toward the end of the Reagan administration, the President instituted a new legislative mandate of deinstitutionalization. It heralded the end for Camarillo, as patients were moved to other facilities or released back onto the streets. Camarillo closed its doors in 1997, marking the end of an era.

Still, scars left by the old treatment methods remained. Future employees, as well as workers who would renovate the buildings, tell tales of phantom presences, moving objects, and several strangely coincidental deaths. Even movie crews, which have used the buildings for several set locations, have reported strange encounters.

Most people who enter the old hospital grounds are affected in one way or another. Headaches and nausea are common, as are dizziness and fatigue. Many who enter say they feel they're being watched or threatened. While such feelings can be put down to the imagination, it's the eyewitness accounts that provide a chilling view into the past of Camarillo State Hospital.

Many have heard the voices and laughter of children at the building once designated as the children's center, and at the former petting zoo as well. A beautiful woman in white, assumed to be a nurse, roams the hallways of the bell tower, only to vanish when confronted. There are also reports of an old woman who walks the grounds outside the bell tower and a man who sits at the bus stop. There's even a chattering ghost in the bell tower's ladies room.

While on a location shoot in May 2004, several members of a film crew reported tools missing–tools later found in unopened rooms. Set builders talked of windows slamming on their own, microwave ovens thrown to the floor, and strange knocking on walls. Cold spots were also common in the buildings. Several of the crew quit, saying the place was just too creepy.

There even appears to be something strange about the back road into the hospital, which has been the scene of several unexplained car accidents. Although the road wasn't heavily traveled, car crashes on it were frequent. Following an accident that killed a Camarillo nurse, an autopsy showed that the otherwise healthy woman had suffered a freak brain embolism.

CAMARILLO TODAY

Its connections to celebrities have amplified the reputation of the Camarillo State Mental Hospital. Jazz legend Charlie Parker stayed for seven months after a nervous breakdown in 1947, and soon after recorded his hit "Relaxing at Camarillo." The old hospital is also rumored by some to be the inspiration for The Eagles' 1976 hit "Hotel California."

The complex has taken on a new life since its 1997 closing. Renovations began in 2000, and two years later the buildings that were once considered the most notorious mental hospital in California opened their doors once again, this time as California State University–Channel Islands. The buildings look the same as before, on the outside. Inside, cells have been converted into classrooms and dorms. The restless souls, however, seem to remain.

Apparitions appear with little regard for time of year or day. However, the current school administrators and other governing bodies seem to want to forget about Camarillo's storied past. So your best chance of encountering a ghost on the campus is to enroll for a semester and keep your eyes open!

299

**CALIFORNIA STATE UNIVERSITY—
CHANNEL ISLANDS**
One University Drive, Camarillo CA 93012

Spirits in Solitary
by Ellen Robson

IN THE TOWN OF YUMA, in the far southwest area of Arizona, the former Yuma Territorial Prison is perched high atop a rocky hill. From 1876 through 1909, the prison housed more than 3,000 prisoners. Overcrowding essentially closed it, and in 1909 its inmates were shackled together and transported to the prison in Florence, far to the east. The facility thereafter housed Yuma Union High School until 1914, and in the 1920s hobos and bums took advantage of the empty cells for shelter. During the Depression, the building was used as a haven for homeless families.

Some of the prisoners' sentences, it seems, have extended into the afterlife. And a few of the other former occupants may haunt the premises as well. In what is now a museum, accounts of ghostly activity from staff members and visitors alike aren't uncommon—and they often have to do with one cell in particular.

The Feared Dark Cell

When an inmate broke the rules, he was confined in solitary in what became known as the Dark Cell, which measured ten by ten feet. The only daylight came from a small ventilation shaft in the ceiling. The inmate would be dressed in underwear only and be given one meal of bread and water each day. Sometimes he would also have his legs chained to two ringbolts.

After the sun went down, the inmate found himself in total darkness. He often shared the cell with scorpions and snakes, and whether these varmints slithered in from the outside or sadistic guards dropped them down the ventilation shaft as further torture, as prisoners claimed, will never be known. After serving their time in the Dark Cell, some prisoners were sent directly to the insane asylum in Phoenix.

Surprisingly, the most prominent ghost in the Dark Cell might be that of a small child. The ghostly phantom loves pinching, poking, and touching visitors with icy fingers, but only if they're wearing red clothing. A psychic touring the prison felt the spirit wasn't that of an angry adult, but rather of a little girl. Perhaps her family was one of the many who found themselves homeless and lived at the former prison until they could get back on their feet.

A staff writer for a regional magazine in Arizona, wanting to experience what the inmates went through, attempted to spend forty-eight hours in the Dark Cell. Shackled to the ringbolt and given only a jug of water and a loaf of bread, the writer fell short of her goal by eleven hours. She insisted that she wasn't alone in the cell, and it didn't help that a cover on the ventilation shaft blocked out all rays of light.

Eerie Happenings

The Dark Cell isn't the only area where ghostly activity occurs. Assistant Park Manager Jesse Torres was in the museum early one morning when he thought he heard a coworker calling out to him. "Did you get it?" he recalled her saying. "I went to the back office to see her," Torres says, "but found out she was in the Ramada building, which isn't even close to the museum. In fact, I was the only person in the museum."

Torres continues: "At the far end of the corridor is Cell 14, which was occu- 301 pied in the early 1900s by John Ryan. He was disliked not only by the guards but by the prisoners as well. When I pass his old cell sometimes, I find myself shivering because of the coldness. John was found guilty of a 'crime against nature,' which meant he committed rape or a sexually deviant act. Before his sentence was up, he committed suicide in his cell."

Other accounts tell of muffled conversations in vacant rooms, witnesses seeing things out of the corner of the eye, and a woman who sings in the visitors area early in the morning. Another harmless ghost, called Johnny, doesn't venture beyond the gift shop. There, he's content to flick coins in the cash register while leaving all the bills alone.

If you like being scared out of your wits, join the museum staff on the last Saturday of every October for a ghostly tour. You'll hear all about the killings and suicides that took place behind bars. You'll also learn firsthand from the tour guides about experiences they've had encountering former prisoners who haunt the dark corridors and dreary cells of the former Yuma Territorial Prison.

YUMA TERRITORIAL PRISON
1 Prison Hill Road, Yuma AZ 85364

THE HOMESTEAD NURSING HOME
by Markus Misery

IN THE EARLY DAYS of Freehold Township, New Jersey, then known as Monmouth Courthouse, a prominent family by the name of Ryan built a mansion on a plot of land surrounded by cornfields. As the town grew more crowded and neighbors replaced the corn, the Ryans decided to move on.

They sold their family home to a group of caregivers who converted it into the Homestead Nursing Home. To be blunt, folks went there to die, and the many bedrooms became hospice-style tenancies. The home was in operation for several years and later became an apartment complex.

My family moved into a second-floor apartment in the old mansion when I was in fifth grade. It didn't take long for the neighborhood kids to start talking about the residents who had never left—in particular, a Mrs. Kennedy. I didn't think much of it at first, but my curiosity was piqued by the building's oddities.

302

First were the room numbers. I didn't see them right away because they were covered with several layers of paint. You'd think that a previous tenant of our apartment would have removed them, but there they were: iron digits displayed on the door to each room. I thought they added charm, and had yet to see anything spooky in the building.

That changed when I discovered the basement. It had a hole in the floor just like the one in the movie *The Amityville Horror.* Also, there was an old iron furnace that was too heavy to move. One hidden crawl space led to another that led to a smaller, separate basement. I could only imagine what had previously been in that crawl space.

In the basement I found artifact of all kinds, including records of feed supply purchases; there were even dental records. Finally, in the small basement I noticed a Homestead Nursing Home sign still nailed to the heavy rafters on the ceiling. Until then, I hadn't known the former name of the place.

THE INTIMATE STRANGER
These oddities intrigued me, but I was still skeptical of any hauntings. In my younger years, the scariest thing that happened was feeling that I was being watched as I entered the basement. The circuit breakers regularly went out because of the decades-old electrical system, and my sister and I didn't relish

going down to the basement to trip them back on.

Things started to change in my twenties, when I came back from serving in the army. After a night of reading, I lay down to rest, when all of a sudden I felt as if I were being pinned down—as if someone were sitting on my chest and holding my arms at my side. I not only couldn't move but was unable to make a sound, much less call out for help. This went on for some time. Then just like that, it was over. Like a child, I hid under the bedcovers until I fell asleep.

From that point on, something very strange happened on more than one occasion: I felt someone lie down in bed next to me. Without getting graphic, whoever or whatever it was even tried to "get fresh." I often felt as if someone were staring at me right in front of my face, but I never opened my eyes. I guess I figured that if the entity was going to harm me, it would do so whether I saw it or not; and, if it wasn't, I'd just rather not see it.

My reaction apparently didn't please the entity, because the feeling of being watched was soon accompanied by what sounded like a wailing banshee: long, fierce, high-pitched screaming right in my ear. Even then I kept my eyes shut tight.

These nighttime occurrences continued without fail at least once a month. It became almost like a game. A few times, I opened my eyes, only to see nothing. Perhaps the entity was playing hide and seek?

WOMAN IN THE WINDOW
Soon, however, the entity—or presence, or whatever it was—would make itself known.

A friend of mine was being visited by a family member from California. Being the hospitable folk we were, a group of friends and I decided to show her around town. They were to pick me up, and when I heard the car pull up, I walked out to the large gravel driveway of the apartment house. That's when I noticed an old woman in a nightgown looking down at us from my upstairs window. She watched silently, her long, tangled white hair framing a grim face lined with wrinkles.

I asked my friends if they saw her. And in fact, they did. We looked on for a moment, and she turned away. As with the presence in the bedroom, sightings of this old woman became a regular occurrence.

When my wife first came to the house years later, she knew nothing of the legends or reputation of the place. Yet as we stood in the driveway, she looked up and asked who the old lady up there in the window was. "That's Mrs.

Kennedy," I replied. By this point, I knew that's who it had to be.

Other things happened that offered proof of the ghostly old woman's identity. For one, I met a woman who came to one of my family's summer yard sales. She introduced herself as the daughter of the elderly couple who lived across from us. Without hesitation, she asked me if I had ever seen Mrs. Kennedy, saying she had spied the apparition regularly as a child while playing in the neighborhood.

304

The years passed and my sister and I left home, after which my parents moved to a smaller apartment on the rear of the first floor. To this day, everyone who lives in our former upstairs apartment asks me what the hell is going on there. Several tenants have moved out after only a few weeks, apparently too afraid to stay. To this day, my sister won't go back, and won't talk about what happened to her there.

This whole business about Mrs. Kennedy may sound like goofy folklore, but I later learned by chance that she was a real person. One day at work, I was showing my collection of photos to the folks in the office. One workmate saw pictures of the house and said, "I know that place. I've been there." It turns out she had indeed been there as a child. Her mother had worked in the Homestead Nursing Home, and I'll give you one guess at the name of one of the women she tended to.

OLD WYOMING STATE PENITENTIARY
by Scott A. Johnson

IMAGINE YOURSELF confined to a room five feet by seven feet with only a bare cot and toilet. Down the hallway, terrified screams and sadistic laughter echo throughout the night, reminding you that you live in what may as well be described as one of Dante's lower circles of Hell. You'll be all right, you tell yourself, so long as you keep to your tasks and don't make eye contact with anyone who lives nearby.

Now imagine that same room shared with up to five other men—a prison cell in which every breath drawn might be the last and every setting sun heralds new terrors that come in the night.

A NEW BUT FEARFUL FACILITY

By 1873, the prison in Laramie, Wyoming, was bulging at the seams. Home to convicts from the surrounding areas, it could no longer accept new inmates, yet the stream of new arrivals never let up. The state government decided a new prison was needed, one that could accommodate the high number of miscreants who roamed Idaho at the time. Construction of what would be an enormous structure began in 1888. It took thirteen years, but on December 12, 1901, the Wyoming State Penitentiary in Rawlins opened its doors. The incarcerated were to be assigned meaningful duties that would not only put money in the coffers of both the prison and the state but would also plant in the prisoners the seed of a work ethic. Over the years, the prisoners manufactured brooms, shirts, and processed wool, when they weren't stamping out license plates. 305

Despite the state's good intentions, the new facility had tiny cells without running water or toilets, and their bare concrete walls bred more than a sense of punishment. They bred madness. Fights were common, as were stabbings and near riots. In just three years, the penitentiary saw several bloody battles between prisoners, one of which involved a prisoner attempting to cut another's heart out. The terrified guards, who sometimes felt themselves the real prisoners, often did nothing.

Such violence could only be tolerated for so long, prompting the construction of "the Hole" in 1906. Being confined to this windowless room was the punishment for anything from refusing to eat dinner to murder. The guilty were chained to a wall in the room and left in total darkness. During their stay, they were attended to only briefly and were fed miniscule amounts of bread and water.

It wasn't until 1914, years after the prison had already come dangerously close to its capacity, that the penitentiary cells were equipped with toilets, washbowls, and running water–cold only, however.

After several escape attempts by inmates, high concrete walls replaced the wooden stockades surrounding the prison buildings in 1915. The convicts were pressed into service to erect the walls and guard towers, partially to make them aware that escaping would be impossible.

ROUGH JUSTICE

Executions were commonplace, either by hanging or by gas, but it wasn't just the state that meted out capital punishment. Prison guards often enforced their own brand of justice or simply turned a blind eye to prisoner-devised hangings. In one case, the person hanged didn't die immediately, prompting his executioners to haul him up by the rope and toss him over the rail for a second time. This time the prisoner died, and the guards stayed mum.

By the late 1970s, tales of abuse and overcrowding reached the state. Stories involving the horrors of the Hole and other tortures, including thumb cuffs and the insidious Oregon Boot (a heavily weighted steel shoe), reached the proper ears, prompting an investigation. In 1981, the Wyoming State Penitentiary closed its doors for good, leaving decades of abuse and agony behind.

It is impossible to identify the restless souls that never left what's called the Old Pen; they're simply too numerous. What is clear, however, is that in many places whatever remains is angry and resentful–and not at all shy about showing its feelings.

Tour guides and tourists alike have reported seeing shadowy figures disappearing around corners and malicious presences throughout the structure. There are, however, a few places deemed hotbeds of activity. The showers,

TOUR IF YOU DARE

IN WHAT IS NOW a trend with old prisons, the Wyoming State Penitentiary has become something of a tourist attraction. Public functions are held on its grounds and inside, including a bazaar and a Haunted Halloween Tour. Those interested can follow the paths of the damned all the way to the gas chamber.

Guides are always willing to share their experiences in the building, and while some of the stories may sound unbelievable, there are always corroborating witnesses, be they employees or strangers. Tours geared toward paranormal enthusiasts are best taken during one of the evenings of Halloween. But that hardly means that All Hallows Eve is the only time to experience something unexplainable. As the guides themselves will tell you, there's always something happening, and you never know when something will catch you out of the corner of your eye.

where countless inmates were attacked, violated, or even killed, are the setting of many a story. Some tour guides won't even enter the area anymore. Also on the list of places to be avoided are the former Death Row and the gas chamber.

However, most agree that the worst hauntings occur in the black pit called the Hole. Whatever lurks there, according to those whose job it is to walk the halls, is angry and crazed, threatening anyone who enters. There are also specific cells in which voices are heard and presences felt. Also well known is Guard Tower No. 9, in which a guard committed suicide.

The buildings stand as they did, with cell walls still bearing the markings and artwork of those who occupied them. Death Row cells are adorned with photos of those prisoners who spent their last moments inside. The old prison cemetery is visible on the grounds, and many of the tombstones lie broken or stand propped against a fence.

In other words, the prison looks no less ominous for the lack of new prisoners. Time will tell whether the awful energy generated within its walls is here to stay.

WYOMING FRONTIER PRISON MUSEUM
500 West Walnut Street, Rawlins WY 82301

ACKNOWLEDGMENTS

MY THANKS to Mark Sceurman and Mark Moran for providing me with this scarily weird and immeasurably educational opportunity, for taking the risk in seeing where I'd go with it, and for giving guidance where needed. And to Ryan Doan for illustrating this book so well. It's inspiring to see such great imaginations at work.

I would also like to thank the writers I met in the process of compiling *Weird Hauntings,* regardless of whether their stories are printed here or not. It was a pleasure working with you, and in your own ways, you have taught me much about the writing life.

Thanks also to those who contributed information to give a historical one two punch to these stories, especially Ellie and Carol at the Ewing Township Historic Preservation Society and Joseph and Caroline Bondi of Al's Airport Inn.

The Barnes & Noble editorial team provided patience, expertise, and a peek inside the publishing industry for which I am grateful: Barbara Morgan, Fred Dubose, and Jane Neighbors.

I must also thank my personal cheering section of family and friends, who believe in and support my writing and editorial efforts, especially Mom, Dad, and Jim.

And finally, thanks to the ghosts, and the people who believe in them. Don't be strangers now, you hear?

–Joanne Austin

309

ACKNOWLEDGMENTS

FIRST AND FOREMOST, I must give my deep gratitude to Mark Moran and Mark Sceurman. You opened the door to my future, and for that I will forever be indebted. It is an absolute honor to share this adventure with you both.

To my parents for teaching me how to truly see people and, in that, the worth of everyone's story. For your unrelenting support and faith in my craft and path. You will always be the light guiding me home and leading me forward. Your love and faith in Lori and me is unparalleled.

To Margarita for giving me balance in my life and for showing me what true beauty is.

A special thanks to Richard Berenson for his uncanny sense of design. You took our words and drawings and made something beautiful out of them.

I would also like to thank Barbara Morgan and the entire staff at Barnes & Noble. It is wonderful to know that such serious talents can have such a great sense of humor. Your enthusiasm for my work is humbling.

To the entire staff of *Weird N.J.*—Rich, Sue, Abby—for making each day exciting and new. To my models and dear friends for helping me make my art, for allowing me to use your likeness never knowing if you will be glorified or victimized.

Finally, I would like to offer thanks to Joanne for your amazing efforts and talent in putting together this book and for making it a wonderful experience for me with each draft. You are such a pleasure to work with.

—Ryan Doan

DEDICATION

TO MY FATHER, my best friend and greatest ally.

To my mother, there is no creature or being in all of these books that is as unique as you. You are in all ways beautiful.

To Margarita for her constant love and support, for standing by me through both ends of the tide, for riding this wave with me wherever it goes, and for showing me that you don't have to be surrounded by the unknown to believe in and be fascinated by it.

To Papa for defining the word "hero" for me and for showing me that weirdness does not skip generations and that the greatest history is found in the minds and tongues of those who lived it.

To Grandma Liz for teaching me never to take myself too seriously and that if "you ever get hit with a bucket of @#&*@, be sure to close your eyes."

To the rest of my family and friends—thank you so much for your support.

—Ryan Doan

AUTHOR BIOGRAPHIES

RODNEY ANONYMOUS, often incorrectly identified as "The Father of the Steam Engine," writes a regular column for the *Philadelphia City Paper* and a highly irregular column for *Barracuda* magazine.

CHRISTOPHER BALZANO is the founder and administrator of the Web site Massachusetts Paranormal Crossroads. He has investigated the paranormal for ten years, and his writing has appeared in *Mysteries* magazine and *Haunted Times.* He has discussed ghosts and hauntings with the Boston *Globe,* Boston *Herald* and *Worcester* magazine, and has contributed to Jeff Belanger's *Encyclopedia of Haunted Places* and several other collections due out this fall.

312 **JEFF BELANGER** is a writer and journalist who launched Ghostvillage.com in 1999, where it has grown into the Web's largest supernatural community. He is the author of several books including *The World's Most Haunted Places, Communicating With the Dead,* and *Our Haunted Lives.* He's been a guest on radio and television programs and is a regular lecturer on the subject of the supernatural. He currently haunts Bellingham, Massachusetts, with his wife.

GREG BISHOP is one of the authors of *Weird California* and is the cofounder of the journal *The Excluded Middle* (www.excludedmiddle.com). He also wrote *Wake Up Down There!* and *Project Beta: The Story of Paul Bennewitz, National Security, and the Creation of a Modern UFO Myth.* His writing has appeared in the *L.A. Weekly, Fortean Times,* and others; and in several anthologies including *Conspiracy and Cyberculture.* He currently hosts the show *Radio Misterioso* at www.killradio.org.

FIONA BROOME is a psychic and a ghost researcher, investigating hauntings in the U.S., the U.K., and Ireland. She's writing a series of ghost-related books highlighting haunted places that anyone can visit. Broome's popular ghost Web site is www.HollowHill.com.

ALAN BROWN has been a professor of English at the University of West Alabama since 1986. He has written several books of ghost stories, including *The Face in the Window and other Alabama Ghostlore, Shadows and Cypress, Haunted Places in the American South,* and *Stories from the Haunted South.* His latest book, *Southern Ghost Hunters,* will be published in October 2006.

CHARLIE CARLSON is the author of fourteen books, including *Weird Florida.* He is a frequent guest on talk radio and has appeared in several television documentaries, including playing a professor on the SciFi Channel in *Curse of the Blair Witch.* He enjoys entertaining civic organizations across the Sunshine State with his own brand of wacky folklore. He resides on Florida's east coast.

RICK CARROLL is creator of *Hawaii's Best Spooky Tales, Volumes 1–7,* and *Madame Pele: True Encounters with Hawaii's Fire Goddess.* A former daily journalist with the San Francisco *Chronicle,* Carroll is the author of twenty books on Hawaii and the Pacific. He is now writing *In the Path of NightMarchers,* a memoir of spirit-haunted nights in old Ka'a'awa.

JOSEPH A. CITRO is an expert in New England weirdness. He is a frequent radio and TV guest and popular lecturer and writing teacher. His books, fiction and nonfiction, include *Cursed in New England, The Gore, Shadow Child, Passing Strange,* and *Weird New England.* His Web site is www.josephacitro.com.

JEFFERSON DAVIS has degrees in anthropology and archaeology, and has traveled to many faraway places in the world where he has encountered the paranormal and strange. But he always returns to the Pacific Northwest, where he has written five books on ghosts, including *A Haunted Tour Guide to the Pacific Northwest.* His Web site is www.ghostsandcritters.com.

CRAIG DOMINEY is the founder and producer of The Moonlit Road.com (www.themoonlitroad.com), an award-winning Web site and radio show featuring ghost stories and strange folktales from the American South, told by the region's best storytellers. Moonlit Road stories are regularly broadcast on XM Satellite Radio and numerous public radio stations around the world. Dominey lives and writes in Atlanta, Georgia.

CHRIS GETHARD served as the associate editor for *Weird N.J.* magazine for over four years. While there, he helped write and edit the book *Weird N.J.* and coauthored its follow-up, *Weird U.S.* Also an actor and comedian, he has contributed writing to shows on Comedy Central and has acted on a number of TV programs, including *Late Night with Conan O'Brien.* He is a performer and teacher at the Upright Citizens Brigade Theater in Manhattan.

LINDA GODFREY is an author, artist, former teacher, and award-winning journalist who works and lives in southeastern Wisconsin. She is the author of *Weird Michigan,* coauthor of *Weird Wisconsin,* and has also written two books on werewolves and a true crime saga, *The Poison Widow.* Her Web sites are beastofbrayroad.com, weirdmichigan.com, and cnb-scene.com.

ANDREW HENDERSON is one of the authors of *Weird Ohio.* He is a writer and researcher who has been exploring Ohio's weird places and history for years. He runs the popular Web site Forgotten Ohio, and his first book, *Forgotten Columbus,* was published in 2002. His work has been featured both locally and nationally—most notably in the *Washington Post.* Henderson lives in Columbus.

SCOTT A. JOHNSON is the author of novels *An American Haunting, Deadlands,* and *Cane River: A Ghost Story.* He also wrote the *Mayor's Guide* series of books about real haunted places in towns such as Augusta, Georgia, and Austin, Texas. He is the Literary and Paranormal Studies editor at The Horror Channel (www.horrorchannel.com), where he writes the column *Cold Spots.* His Web site is www.americanhorrorwriter.com.

MIKE MARINACCI is a lifelong California resident who combines a love of the state's history with a fascination for the bizarre and inexplicable. One of the authors of *Weird California,* he is currently working on another title about the outré side of Golden State culture. Marinacci lives in the San Francisco Bay Area.

JANICE OBERDING is the author of *Las Vegas Haunted* and five other books on the paranormal. Coproducer of the popular Las Vegas Paranormal Conference, Janice lectures at various venues and has appeared and consulted on numerous television shows on the paranormal. Her Web site is www.HauntedNevada.com.

ELLEN ROBSON is the author of *Haunted Highway: The Spirits of Route 66* and *Haunted Arizona: Ghosts of the Grand Canyon State.* She is currently working on her third book of haunted sites, which will cover the entire United States. Her Web site is www.spirits66.com. She lives in Tempe, Arizona, with her husband.

TIM STEVENS's interest in local legends and folklore led to the creation of his Web site about ghost stories and weird tales of Texas: www.chickenskin.net. That in turn led to contributing his work to *Weird Texas.* He lives near Austin with his wife, two kids, and an assortment of four-legged creatures.

315

TROY TAYLOR, author of *Weird Illinois,* has written more than forty books on ghosts, hauntings, and the unexplained in America. He is the founder of the American Ghost Society and the co-owner and manager of the Illinois Hauntings Tour Co. Born and raised in Illinois, he currently resides in the central part of the state in a decidedly nonhaunted house.

JAMES A. WILLIS has been chasing after ghosts and visiting crybaby bridges for over twenty years. He is also the founder and director of The Ghosts of Ohio, a paranormal research organization (www.ghostsofohio.org). Willis's previous brushes with weirdness include being a contributing author to *Weird U.S.* and coauthoring *Weird Ohio.* He currently resides in Columbus, Ohio.

PICTURE CREDITS

Front and back cover © Ryan Doan/ryandoan.com

Page 1 © Ryan Doan/ryandoan.com; 2–3 iStockphoto.com; 9, 11 © Ryan Doan/ryandoan.com; 12 © Gabe Palmer/CORBIS; 21, 23 iStockphoto.com; 24 © Ryan Doan/ryandoan.com; 29, 32 iStockphoto.com; 35, 40 © Ryan Doan/ryandoan.com; 43 © Time & Life Pictures/Carl Iwasaki; 44, 45, 47 © Todd Roll; 48 © GettyImages/Kim Westerskov; 51, 54, 57 © Ryan Doan/ryandoan.com; 60–61 iStockphoto.com; 62 © Justin T; 63, 66 © Ryan Doan/ryandoan.com; 67 © Joseph A. Citro; 71 © Ryan Doan/ryandoan.com; 72 © Philip Gould/CORBIS; 76 © Ryan Doan/ryandoan.com; 79 © James A. Willis; 80 © Ryan Doan/ryandoan.com; 82 © Jim Strongin; 86 © Ryan Doan/ryandoan.com; 90 © PEMCO – Webster & Stevens Collection; Museum of History and Industry, Seattle/CORBIS; 92 © Gary Braasch/CORBIS; 93 © Ryan Doan/ryandoan.com; 95 © Jim Strongin; montage Richard J. Berenson; 96 Library of Congress/Prints and Photographs Division; 98 iStockphoto.com; 99 © Ryan Doan/ryandoan.com; 101 © NASA or National Aeronautics and Space Administration; montage Richard J. Berenson; 104 © Ryan Doan/ryandoan.com; 111 © Bettmann/CORBIS; 115 © Orpheum Theatre; 117 © Ryan Doan/ryandoan.com; 120 courtesy Shelburne Museum; 123, 125 © Jeff Belanger; 127 © Lydia Rapoza; 128 © Ryan Doan/ryandoan.com; 132 © CORBIS; 133 © Bettmann/CORBIS; 134 courtesy John Benton, Floyd Collins Web Page, www.bluegrassgrotto.org; 135 © Bettmann/CORBIS; 140, 142, 144 © Ryan Doan/ryandoan.com; 147 © Photo Resource Hawaii/Alamy; 150 © Bettmann/CORBIS; 153 © Tamara Pellek; 154 © Casper Eldredge; 156, 159 © Ryan Doan/ryandoan.com; 160 © Chris Gethard; 163 © James A. Willis and Andrew Henderson; 165 © Andrew Henderson; 167 © Marie Cuff; 170 © Seth T. Klette; 172, 175 © Ryan Doan/ryandoan.com; 177 © Joanne Austin; 178 © Jeff Davis; 180, 181 © Nik Wheeler/CORBIS; 185 iStockphoto.com; 188 © James A. Willis; 189 © Bill Oberding; 191 iStockphoto.com; 192 Christopher Balzano; 195 iStockphoto.com; 196 © Kevin Fleming/CORBIS; 200 © Oklahoma City Ghost Club LLC; 201 iStockphoto.com; 205 © Ryan Doan/ryandoan.com; 207 top © Jeff Davis; 207 bottom © Ryan Doan/ryandoan.com; 209 iStockphoto.com; 210 © Mark Moran; 211 © Mark Moran; 214 © Ryan Doan/ryandoan.com; 217, 219 © Courtesy of Jeff Belanger/Ghostvillage.com; 223 © The Comtesse DeSpair; 227 © Fiona Broome; 233, 235 © Jeff Davis; 236 courtesy Gainsbridge Dinner Club; 240 Library of Congress/Prints and Photographs Division; 241 © Ghost Trackers Organization; 246, 252 © Ryan Doan/ryandoan.com; 254 iStockphoto.com; 257 © Fiona Broome; 262 ©

(continued)

PICTURE CREDITS (*continued*)

Ryan Doan/ryandoan.com; 264 Library of Congress/Prints and Photographs Division; 266, 271 © Ryan Doan/ryandoan.com; 280 © Tim Stevens; 282 courtesy Cutler Majestic Theatre at Emerson College; 284 © Ryan Doan/ryandoan.com; 289 www.alcaponemuseum.com, photo courtesy of Mr. Michael Esslinger; 291 © Ryan Doan/ryandoan.com; 293 © David R. Frazier Photolibrary, Inc/Alamy; 294 © image-broker/Alamy; 295 iStockphoto.com; 296 courtesy Alex Wellerstein, Harvard University; 297 © Bettmann/CORBIS; 298 © Greg Bishop; 300 © courtesy of Donald W. Larson/timeoutofmind.com; 304 © Ryan Doan/ryandoan.com; 306 © Michael S. Lewis/CORBIS.

EDITORIAL CREDITS

Page 69: Apparition on Snake Road, published on Ghostvillage.com.; 90: A Famous Market's Spirits originally appeared in *A Haunted Tour Guide to the Pacific Northwest*, Copyright 2001, Jefferson Davis, Norsemen Ventures, Vancouver, WA.; 141: The Camp Morgan Thing, published on Ghostvillage.com.; 143: The Ghost of Fiddler's Rock, Copyright 1997–2006, TheMoonlitRoad.com.; 145: Incident at Ili'ili'opae Heiau, adapted from *Hawaii's Best Spooky Tales 4*, Copyright 2000, Rick Carroll, Bess Press, Honolulu, HI.; 160: The Pinewoods Scratcher, published on Ghostvillage.com.; 181: The Bullock Hotel, published on HorrorChannel.com.; 184: The 17 Hundred 90 Inn, published on HorrorChannel.com.; 191: The Halloween Waiter, excerpted from *Hawaii's Best Spooky Tales 3*, Copyright 1999, Rick Carroll, Bess Press, Honolulu, HI.; 199: The Stone Lion Inn, published on HorrorChannel.com.; 217: Stone's Public House, published on HorrorChannel.com.249: Dead Presidents Pub and Restaurant, published on HorrorChannel.com.; 296: California Dreaming? published as Camarillo State Mental Hospital on HorrorChannel.com.; 305: Old Wyoming State Penitentiary, published on HorrorChannel.com.

Publisher:	Barbara J. Morgan
Managing Editor:	Emily Seese
Editor:	Fred DuBose
Copyeditor:	Jane F. Neighbors
Editorial Assistant:	Gina Graham
Production:	Della R. Mancuso
	Mancuso Associates, Inc.
	North Salem, NY